GW00630541

THE CLIFFORD CHANCE LECTURES

To Jean -
a friend in deed.

Basil

1 April '96

THE CLIFFORD CHANCE LECTURES

Volume I

Bridging the Channel

Edited and with an Introduction
By

BASIL S. MARKESINIS

With a Foreword
By

H.R.H. PRINCE CONSTANTŸN OF
ORANGE-NASSAU

OXFORD UNIVERSITY PRESS

1996

Oxford University Press, Walton Street, Oxford OX2 6DP

Oxford New York
Athens Auckland Bangkok Bombay
Calcutta Cape Town Dar es Salaam Delhi
Florence Hong Kong Istanbul Karachi
Kuala Lumpur Madras Madrid Melbourne
Mexico City Nairobi Paris Singapore
Taipei Tokyo Toronto
and associated companies in
Berlin Ibadan

Oxford is a trade mark of Oxford University Press

Published in the United States
by Oxford University Press Inc., New York

© Basil Markesinis 1996

All rights reserved. No part of this publication may be reproduced,
stored in a retrieval system, or transmitted, in any form or by any means,
without the prior permission in writing of Oxford University Press.
Within the UK, exceptions are allowed in respect of any fair dealing for the
purpose of research or private study, or criticism or review, as permitted
under the Copyright, Designs and Patents Act, 1988, or in the case of
reprographic reproduction in accordance with the terms of the licences
issued by the Copyright Licensing Agency. Enquiries concerning
reproduction outside these terms and in other countries should be
sent to the Rights Department, Oxford University Press,
at the address above

British Library Cataloguing in Publication Data
Data available

Library of Congress Cataloging in Publication Data
Data available

ISBN 0–19–826231–0

1 3 5 7 9 10 8 6 4 2

Typeset by Graphicraft Typesetters Ltd, Hong Kong
Printed in Great Britain
on acid-free paper by
Biddles Ltd., Guildford and King's Lynn

Foreword

Universities, like all institutions today, can no longer afford to be introspective. As the world opens up universities cannot lag behind. Cooperation between universities, enabling students and academics to travel and exchange ideas, as well as the internationalisation of the curriculum must have top priority.

In every field one finds trailblazers and followers. I am particularly glad to take part in celebrating the tenth anniversary of one of the most inspiring forces at Leyden University, the Institute of Anglo-American Law. In its first decade the Institute has grown consistently in size and popularity. Now firmly entrenched in the Leyden scene, it has opened up new areas of interest and created a whole range of possibilities for students from Leyden and other European universities. This feat, as we all know, is due above all to the tireless efforts of the Institute's director, Professor Basil Markesinis.

Professor Markesinis's drive and energy have manifested themselves in various ways—above all as a teacher. Those like myself who have had the privilege of hearing him lecture will agree that he represents the special type of professor who combines erudition and wit. Not only does he impart to his students an understanding of other legal systems, but his comparative law approach gives them a clearer insight into how legal problems are resolved at national level.

The present volume of lectures, delivered at the Institute by leading jurists, is a testimony to another of Professor Markesinis's qualities, namely his skill as a coordinator of talent and resources. The Institute's firmly established position in the Netherlands' oldest university, this book as evidence of a high and impeccable standard of learning, and the example of a great and inspiring teacher all augur well for a fruitful second decade for the Institute.

I fervently hope—and I am also confident—that the Institute will continue to be the stimulating centre of learning that introduced me and many other students to that other great legal tradition, Anglo-American common law.

H.R.H. Prince Constantÿn of Orange Nassau
October 1995.

Table of Contents

List of Contributors

David Anderson is Thompson and Knight Centennial Professor of Law at the University of Texas School of Law. He is the author of many books and articles and a practising attorney in the fields of media and entertainment law.

Sir Franklin Berman KCMG, Q.C. is the Chief Legal Adviser at the Foreign and Commonwealth Office in London.

The Rt. Hon. Sir Thomas Bingham has been the Master of the Rolls since 1992. He is the Visitor and an Honorary Fellow of Balliol College, Oxford.

Peter Birks, Q.C. (Hon.) D.C.L., LL.D. is the Regius Professor of Civil Law at the University of Oxford and Fellow of All Souls. He has been a Fellow of the British Academy since 1989.

Stephen Cretney, Q.C. (Hon.) D.C.L. has been Fellow of All Souls College, Oxford since 1993. Before his appointment to this post he was Professor of Law and Dean at the University of Bristol (1983–1993) and a Law Commissioner between 1978 and 1983. He was elected Fellow of the British Academy in 1985.

The Rt. Hon. the Lord Donaldson of Lymington was Master of the Rolls between 1982 and 1992. He is an Honorary Fellow of Trinity College, Cambridge.

The Rt. Hon. Sir Iain Glidewell has been a Justice in the Court of Appeal since 1985. He was Treasurer of Gray's Inn in 1994/95

Steve Goldstein started his career as Professor of Law at the University of Pennsylvania and then moved to the Hebrew University of Jerusalem where he was Dean of the Law Faculty. He is now the Edward S. Silver Professor of Civil Procedure.

Sam Issacharoff is Charles Tilford McCormick Professor of Law at the University of Texas School of Law and writes prolifically on matters of labour law, constitutional law, and civil procedure.

The Rt. Hon. the Lord Mackay of Clashfern was Lord Advocate of Scotland between 1979 and 1984 and has been Lord Chancellor since 1987. He holds honorary LL.D.'s from Dundee, Edinburgh, Strathclyde, Aberdeen, St. Andrews and Cambridge.

Basil S. Markesinis, D.Iur (Athen.), LL.D (Cantab.), D.C.L. (Oxon), D.Iur h.c. (Ghent), is Clifford Chance Professor of European Law at the University of Oxford and Professor of Anglo-American Law at the University of Leiden. He is a Member of the Academy of Athens and of the Royal Dutch, and Belgian Academies.

The Rt. Hon. Sir Martin Nourse has been a Justice at the Court of Appeal since 1985.

The Rt. Hon. the Lord Oliver of Aylmerton was a Lord of Appeal in Ordinary between 1986 and 1992. He holds an Honorary LL.D from Cambridge where he is also an Honorary Fellow of Trinity Hall.

The Leiden Institute of
Anglo-American Law

by *Professor Basil Markesinis*

I. THE CREATION OF THE INSTITUTE

I was appointed to the Chair of Anglo-American Private Law in the University of Leiden by Royal Decree dated 3rd June 1986. The initiative for my election came from Professor, later Judge, Tim Koopmans, Professor Dick Fokkema (now sadly retired because of a debilitating illness) and the indefatigable efforts of two Deans and now colleagues and friends, Professor Dr. P.H. Kooijmans and Professor Mr. H.G. Schermers. When offered the Chair I indicated to the above that I would accept it if I were also allowed to set up an Institute of Anglo-American Law, the only one of its kind on the Continent of Europe. They agreed and in the ten years that have gone by I have enjoyed the untiring support of the above colleagues as well as the advice and help of three Presidents of the University—Messrs. K. J. Cath, C. Oomen and Mr. L.E.H. Vredevoogd and the former University Secretary General and Registrar Mr. D. P. den Os. To them one must add Mrs. Yvonne In 't Veld de Bok, Administrator of the Law Faculty and currently the Institute's Treasurer, and Judge (formerly Professor) Jeroen Chorus, both of whom have provided constant encouragement, wise advice and invaluable assistance. The Institute's formal birth was recorded by notarial act drawn up on the 23rd June 1987 by my colleague A. J. H. Pleysier, who helped me greatly during the initial phases of the Institute's existence; and it was "officially" opened by H.R.H. the Prince of Wales on the 27th of October 1988. The visit of the Prince took place during the "William & Mary" celebrations and for many acquired a symbolic value in so far as it showed that in the field of law (and others) Anglo-Dutch relations not only have a successful past but also a promising future.[1]

---

[1] Scottish-Dutch relations have, if anything, been even closer in the past when law students from Scottish Universities were expected to spend part of their study in either Leiden or Utrecht. It was precisely because we were conscious of this link, and anxious to expand it south of the "border", that we deliberately chose to concentrate on Anglo-Dutch links and name the Institute "The Leiden Institute of Anglo-American law".

I think it would be fair to claim that in the ten years that have elapsed our efforts have born fruit. The number of students taking the Anglo-American option every year has grown from 3 or 4 in 1986/7 to over one hundred during the last few years. Nowadays, forty percent of these students are Erasmus students coming from as far apart as Sweden, Spain, France, and the new states which have emerged from the break up of the former Soviet Union. Thanks to the support of a number of benefactors—notably L.U.F., the Foreign and Commonwealth Office in London and the Shell Corporation—our book holding has grown significantly in recent years. Nevertheless, our needs remain considerable even if we can now proudly claim a small but functional library which holds most English Law Journals and all the various Law Reports in addition to all the major student text books.

2. THE SCHOLARSHIP PROGRAMME

This soon became the major part of my fund-raising drive and has consumed most of my time as Director of the Institute. The idea behind it was simple; and we believe it remains as valid now as it was when we started ten years ago. The purpose of a course on Anglo-American law in Leiden was, of course, primarily a "cultural" one: to make civilian lawyers conscious of the richness of an alternative system which had a radically different history and a different method of thinking but often reached results similar to those attained by the Common Law. That, however, was only the first step. Ideally, we wished to use this "initiation" to excite further interest in the Common Law which would encourage Dutch students to spend a further year (or more) in English universities working for a graduate degree. As will be explained in the next paragraph, this initiative was also crowned with success so, as of last year we have, with the invaluable assistance of Gray's Inn, taken the further initiative of providing "mini-pupillages" in London-based sets of chambers for those who successfully completed their graduate courses in English universities. My debt to my fellow Benchers at Gray's Inn is here gratefully recorded; and I hope in the years to come we shall be able to expand our exchange work to include other Inns as well as firms of Solicitors who have an interest in the Continent of Europe.

Once again the student exchange programme could not have been launched without funds, and our many friends were successful in helping us find them. The Dutch State, through the imagination and drive of

Professor Roel In 't Veld, currently at the University of Utrecht, was the first to put us "on course" with a magnificent donation which is still helping us in our mission. Successive grants from the Leverhulme Trust—whose former Director Sir Rex Richards I again thank in public—have in more recent years sustained us ever since and, most importantly, have enabled us to make this a "two-way" traffic with English students coming to Leiden for periods varying from one term to one year. Our last *major* donor was the VSB Bank which, two years ago, came up with a magnificent donation which is now enabling us to send Dutch students to London and Oxford to read for an LL.M degree and is allowing us to use other funds to bring law students to Leiden.

The success of the programme which is, essentially, privately funded, is demonstrated by the fact that in the first ten years of the Institute's life we have sent over 60 Dutch students to English universities (as well as a handful to Universities to the USA) and have supported financially some 30 English students to work in Leiden. These scholarships invariably covered tuition fees and travelling expenses as a minimum and, in many other instances, also covered part of the living expenses of the successful candidate. In practice this meant that they were worth anything between 10 and 20,000 DF which, given that these funds came (mainly) from the private sector, gives some measure of the success of our fund-raising efforts. Multiplied by ninety, this gives the reader some idea of the magnitude of our investment in transnational legal education. To put it differently, this has been a successful way of promoting comparative law in the real world and not merely encouraging its study in an ivory tower!

Before concluding this sub-section let me say something about the "competition" that precedes these awards. In my view, the success of our programme can also be seen in terms of how many *good* candidates apply every year for our limited number of scholarships. On average we have received four good applications for each scholarship awarded; and in many cases the standard was so high that those of us involved in the selection process had to agonize, quite literally for days, over the difficult matter of choosing one out of many good candidates.

3. THE CLIFFORD CHANCE LECTURES

From the early days the view was taken that the general lectures (for which I was responsible) ought to be supplemented by (a) seminars for smaller groups of students and (b) special lectures given on an annual basis by eminent British jurists.

The first aim was achieved thanks to a Leverhulme award which, three years ago, enabled my then Assistant Mr. Graham Wladimiroff (educated both in London and Leiden) to start giving seminars to smaller groups of students. This proved an immensely popular initiative since it gave our students the chance to explore in greater detail and in the company of a manageable number of fellow-students, topics which I had "touched upon" in the general lectures. It also gave them a "feel", albeit an inadequate one, of that unique Oxbridge institution—the tutorial. During the forthcoming academic year, the tradition will be continued by Mr. David William John Scorey, a recent graduate of the Oxford Law Faculty, whose appointment cements the association created recently between the Oxford and Leiden Law faculties.

These special lectures or, as they have become known, the "Distinguished Lecture Series" became possible thanks to a generous gift from the Amsterdam-based office of Clifford Chance and an initiative taken by its Senior Partner Mr. Joost van der Does de Willebois. This book reproduces without alterations the texts of the first twelve lectures[2] to mark the Institute's tenth anniversary. With hindsight, the "Distinguished Lecture Series" has also proved a success; but its launch was not without its problems.

Pitching the lectures at the right level was the first of our concerns. I am convinced that the readers of the book will admire, as I do, the success achieved by our eminent speakers. We told them that the audience was to be composed of students whose knowledge of English law would, by definition, be limited. Clearly, however, we could not ask senior judges and eminent jurists to give "introductory" lectures; nor would it be right to limit their choice of subject to what was actually taught in Leiden in a limited space of time. To this dilemma, another was soon added; the audience soon came to include not only students but also some of Holland's senior judges. Our speakers' decision to pitch their talks primarily for a student audience but also to offer their views on controversial topics, succeeded in satisfying this mixed audience. It was left to me afterwards to try and "integrate" the material of the varied talks into the main stream of lectures and attempt to spin off them comparative extensions. The overall result was to expose successive

---

[2] Unfortunately, lack of time prevented two of our distinguished speakers—Lord Brown-Wilkinson and Sir Arthur Watts—from delivering to us the manuscript version of their much appreciated lectures.

years of Dutch (and Continental European) students to some of the best British talent, different lecturing styles, and varying philosophies; and the variety of topics also enriched the staple menu of history, contract and tort on which I tended to concentrate. The reader of this book cannot thus get the full flavour of what has been achieved from these texts, alone; but even this restricted presentation will give him or her some idea of the challenges faced by anyone trying to teach English law in a Continental setting.

From the Leiden side we felt that somehow we must have struck the right balance since attendance at these lectures, which were held in the University's Great Auditorium, varied from 150 to 300 lawyers at a time. As stated, just as importantly, we have invariably attracted the interest of many Professors from the Leiden Law Faculty and a growing number of some of the country's most senior judges and practitioners. More importantly, we have had many who have asked to read these lectures and that is one (but not the only) reason why we have chosen to reproduce them here in book form. The other reason, of course, is the identity of the donors. For Clifford Chance, soon after their generous donation to the Leiden Institute, made an even more significant contribution to the Oxford-led *Europaeum*, underscoring in the most tangible of ways that they are a truly multi-national firm, dealing with major multi-national clients, and thus having a genuine concern in a broad training of a new generation of lawyers who might even end up by working for them in the future. A firm which pursues excellence so effectively in London, Paris, Brussels, Amsterdam, and Frankfurt—to mention but a few of its operating centres—has bridged the Channel; and this feat inspired the title of the book which, I hope, will be the first of many, to be published under the auspices of my two Centres—*the Oxford Centre for the Advanced Study of European and Comparative Law* and *the Leiden Institute of Anglo-American Law*.

Two concluding points about the lectures themselves.

First, among them we find three[3] American contributions which are not only learned and interesting but also mark our first tentative attempts (tentative due to lack of funds) to establish a presence in the area of American law which, after all, was deliberately included in the name of the Leiden Institute.

Secondly, it is for the readers to make up their minds about the lectures (though I hope they will read them in the context in which the

[3] If one includes in this category Professor Goldstein's learned contribution.

lectures were given and with the limitations imposed upon our learned speakers and to which I have already alluded). Suffice it for me simply to say that each, in its own way, presents a special, additional feature which careful readers will, no doubt, pick up for themselves. The Lord Chancellor's paper, for instance, was delivered at the height of the relevant debate in England and aroused as much interest in the Dutch Press as it did in England. Lord Oliver's speech had a prophetic tone since it foreshadowed the judgment (and the result) in *Murphy* v. *Brentwood District Council*[4] and poses the unexplored question,[5] namely to what extent does an extra-judicial paper by a senior judge give interesting clues as to how he may decide a case that comes before him at a late stage. Professor Birks' paper, to give but one last example, also caused much (admiring) reaction from a learned audience which is facing the same agonizing decisions that confront our legal profession this side of the Channel.

4. THE LEIDEN INTRODUCTORY COURSE

When I started lecturing in Cambridge in the early 1970's the late Harry Lawson, arguably my country's subtlest comparatist, advised me that a "good lecture consists of a studied measure of inaccuracy". Like many of his aphorisms this has haunted me ever since, not least because it has proved so correct. But how does one plan a course of forty hours that is meant to introduce a civilian lawyer to not one but two Common Law systems?

This last point was crucial to my planning of the syllabus; and, I think, it must be carefully considered by other Common lawyers who are asked to lecture on the Common Law to non-Common law audiences. For us, of course, the fact that the American and English Common Law are—to adapt Bernard Shaw's aphorism—two systems separated by a common legal tradition is obvious, though it is still rather rare to talk of structural differences (e.g. presence or absence of a written constitution, welfare state, or use of juries) in order to understand how they affect the operation of the substantial (private) law. But

---

[4] [1991] 1 A.C. 398.
[5] I have discussed this briefly in three lectures I gave at the University of Rome under the title "Five Days in the House of Lords; Some Comparative Reflections on *White* v. *Jones*" in *Saggi, Conferenze e Seminari* published by the Centro di studi e richerche di diritto comparato e staniero, no. 16 (1995).

this point, so eloquently made by Professor John Fleming,[6] is crucial when talking to modern civilians who are as apt to think that the Common Law is the same in England and America as Common lawyers are to think that there is such a thing as European or Napoleonic Law "across the Continent of Europe". The decision to attack this fallacy led me to concentrate on some of the areas of private or public law where the differences between the two Common Law variants were the greatest.

The Court structures in the two systems was thus an obvious example—not least since it gave me the chance to talk about European (e.g. German) variants to federal models. At the most speculative moments—and the maturity and dedication of my audience often allowed me such luxury—it made me (and my students) reflect whether American federalism can hold out some lessons—good, bad, indifferent—to whatever was going to happen to the European Union during the next decade or so. If this excursus tended to be longer than planned, it was because one sooner rather than later realised that once one starts talking of "models" one must consider at least all the major contenders; and that this was no reason why our students should be allowed to forget the lessons that come from Canada or Australia. It also gave us all ample opportunity to consider how federalism is seen as a source of concentration of power on one side of the Channel but as a possible way of diffusing power on the other side.

The example I gave is not, of course, unique. The jury system is another; and that, inevitably, led us to the effects it has had on different branches of private law such as the law of torts. Again, however, one was tempted—and I succumbed to this temptation—to turn these introductory lectures on the Common Law into exercises of "judicial" comparative law where my students were asked to contribute to the discussion of the issues under consideration by using their knowledge of their own case law. As someone who has agonized for at least two decades as to how to teach "foreign law" I think I can say that the Leiden courses were a source of great instruction for me, personally. Judging from the increase in the size of the class and the fact that my students invariably forgave me for going beyond the allocated time limits, I can only hope the experiment was attractive also to them. For someone like myself, who has decried the descriptive and conceptual presentation of the foreign material, the Leiden laboratory revealed both weaknesses and

[6] In his *The Amercian Tort Process* (1988).

strengths in my own way of teaching foreign law through cases, facts, and functionality. Needless to say, the method is still in its infancy!

History, too, figured prominently in the course since it is, of course, commonplace that historical accidents explain, as often as not, the different paths adopted here and there by the Common Law. But while stressing these differences I also remained aware of similarities of results and paradoxes that undermine our conceptions of each other's system. The decision of the Cour de cassation 16 June 1888[7] offers one of these starting points. For not only does it mark an important change in the development of the French law of contracts in favour of third parties; it also shows that in France the change came about by judicial decision whereas in England our (troublesome) 19th century rule was altered by our Married Women's Property Act of 1882. Here, of course, is the paradox; and it is strengthened by the fact that this "reform" (here as in many other instances) came about more or less at the same chronological period. And as if all this were not enough one can from there move to "styles" and note the rigid and limited consequences achieved by the English statute compared to the flexible result achieved by the French decision. Throw in, then, the American *Restatement (Second) on Contracts*, to show that English and American law are different, and you have the ingredients for an excellent comparative discussion.[8] This, of course, is only possible if one is dealing with a "mature" audience which is expected to have done some background reading. All this was, of course, made possible thanks to Zweigert and Kötz's *An Introduction to Comparative Law*, an outstanding text book which gives all the necessary background material and, in many cases, much more.

The same approach was chosen for the second part of the course which was devoted, alternatively, to contract and/or tort. A conceptual approach trying, for instance, to explain the notion of duty of care or that of consideration ran into enormous difficulties. These difficulties however were minimised (but not erased) when one opted for a functional approach and one chose to invite one's mixed audience to place before them 2 or 3 judgments from different jurisdictions and try and find what they had in common and where the differences were unbreachable.

---

[7] S. 1888.1.121; D.P. 1888.1.77.

[8] Which one finds in Professor Kötz's "Rights of Third Parties. Third Party Beneficiaries and Assignment" chapter 13, vol. VII of the *International Encyclopedia of Comparative Law*.

I have already mentioned the fact that the lectures given by our distinguished guests were primarily intended for a non-English audience. But the reflections of eminent jurists are always worth studying. For even behind introductory or "elementary" observations, one often finds thoughts for further reflection. Certainly, non-English lawyers can subject these texts, as I did with my classes, to further *comparative* analysis; invite their students to compare English law with theirs; and draw their own conclusions on a wide variety of topics. If they do, I am confident that they, too, will be as grateful to our speakers as our Dutch audiences have been for the last ten years.

The Anglo-Dutch legal co-operation is flourishing as never before; and all of us who were lucky enough to be part of the first decade of the Institute's life hope to be able to see the work grow even further during the one that follows.

Elunda Beach, Crete

15 August, 1995   B.S. Markesinis

I

Judicial Legislation

The Rt. Hon. the Lord Oliver of Aylmerton*

I. INTRODUCTION

English law, indeed, the whole English legal system—the organisation and administration of the courts—remain even to this day to some extent the slaves of their historical roots. Continental lawyers, more accustomed to a logical constitutional development and a codified system of law, do not find it altogether easy to understand what appears as a sort of legal amoeba in which the evolution of legal principle seems to occur, not as a result of conscious planning or centralised governmental direction, but amorphously and autogenously by a process of what can best be described as "judicial legislation".

Now that is a process which is deep-rooted in the English constitutional history and in the development of the common law and I would not attempt to cover it, even if I were competent to do so, in this contribution which has an introductory character. What I would like to do is to describe—necessarily in the broadest outline—a little of the English judicial method, the process of decision, against the background of the English constitution and its courts. That is not altogether easy to do because judges are not, in fact, much given to analysing their own thought processes. Their primary concern is with the decision of the case immediately before them and it sometimes comes as a surprise to them when they are subsequently told by academic commentators that they have, quite without knowing it and without intending to, evolved some new legal principle which has caused the law to lurch a few—sometimes even many—steps beyond boundaries of previously accepted norms. The process of analysis will, therefore, in the opinion of the

---

* This lecture was delivered at Leiden University on 29 April 1988 at the invitation of the Institute of Anglo-American Law. The text was first published in the Vol. 2, no. 1 of the *Leiden Journal of International Law*, pp. 3–18 (1989) and is reprinted here by kind permission of the Leiden Journal of International Law Foundation.

author, be easier and a little more interesting if it is illustrated by reference to a particular area of law: the tort of negligence.

First, however, let me set the scene explaining just a little about three essential background features, that is to say, first, the organisation of the English courts; secondly, the sources of law and the interface between them; and, thirdly, that most important principle which has dominated the whole of English legal thinking and methodology, the doctrine of precedent or to give it its Latin title *stare decisis*.

2. THE ORGANISATION OF ENGLISH COURTS

First of all then the English system of courts. This is peripheral to the primary theme but it may help a little in describing the process to say just a word about the factual background in which the process operates. There is a story of an American tourist in Ireland who stopped to ask an Irish peasant the way to Dublin. The reply was "Faith, if I wanted to go to Dublin I wouldn't be starting from here". And that is a pretty good description of English law. If you wanted to set up a legal system from scratch you would not start from here. In England it is a hodge-podge, partly the result of historical evolution, partly the result of statutory intervention or creation. The justification for it is not logical but pragmatic. It is cheap to run and it seems to work.

Starting from the bottom there are something over 900 magistrate's courts in England and Wales. Apart from a few stipendiary magistrates in London and the larger urban centres these are judicially staffed entirely by lay Justices of the Peace who give their services without remuneration. They are not legally qualified; they are advised—on matters of law and procedure only—by a legally qualified clerk; and, in addition to small domestic cases, they handle substantially all the petty crime in the country, that is to say about 90% of all crime. They are indeed a wonderful example of how England contrives to run its judicial system with a minimal charge to the Exchequer and without them the whole system would come to a grinding halt.

The next step takes us to the county courts—about 250 of them—for small civil work on the Crown Courts (of which there are about 85) for criminal work. Both are the creatures of statute and both are judicially staffed by full-time circuit judges, of whom there are about 350 to 400 and all of whom have had professional experience as either barristers or solicitors. Some crime and matrimonial work is also tried by part-time judges recruited from the legal profession. Serious crime is also tried by High Court judges sitting in the Crown Courts in London and provincial centres.

The next tier is the Supreme Court of Judicature which itself is divided into two tiers, the High Court and the Court of Appeal. The High Court which hears only civil causes, is organised in three divisions, Queen's Bench (handling anything from shipping to running down cases and including the important area of judicial review of administrative decisions); Chancery (which is concerned primarily with matters such as trusts, companies, testamentary and land disputes) and Family, which is self-explanatory. There are some 84 High Court Judges who sit singly and, in general, without a jury so that they decide both fact and law. The upper tier of the Supreme Court is the Court of Appeal, judicially staffed by 24 Lords Justices of Appeal and hearing both civil and criminal appeals. It sits in divisions of three or sometimes two.

Finally, at the apex of the pyramid is the final appellant court, the House of Lords, which is judicially staffed by the Lord Chancellor and 9 Lords of Appeal in Ordinary. It normally sits in two committees of five, each of which is, theoretically, a Committee of the whole house. That is a historical survival which pays lip service to Parliamentary sovereignty.

Well now, that is a distant bird's eye view of the courts' organisation and it is also an incomplete and not wholly accurate view because for instance it omits a number of administrative and quasi judicial specialists tribunals from which appeals lie to the Court of Appeal either direct or via the High Court. But for present purposes it will serve.

3. SOURCES OF LAW

The second feature that I want to say a brief word about is that which can best be designated as "sources of law". Nowadays we can offer effective purpose, ignore custom as a source of law and we can say with almost complete accuracy that there are two sources of law, Parliament and the judges. English law has no overall code by reference to which the whole law can be ascertained. Parliament makes the law by enacting statutes some of which, for instance the Sale of Goods Act, can be said to codify particular segments of the law, but there is no civil code as such, merely a large number of statutes regulating various activities and supplemented in many cases by a substratum of delegated legislation enshrined in statutory rules which have the force of statute. Beyond this there is an enormous mass of judge-made law enshrined in volumes and volumes of reported decisions of the superior courts, all operating on the theoretical basis that the law is permanent, immutable except by statute and simply "there" to be discovered. The judges, it is said, do not make the law—they simply expound it and declare it to be what it always was. Now I do not want to give the impression that these two sources of law are as it were separate and watertight compartments. The law embodied in rules arrived at by deduction from or extension of previous decided cases is always capable of being overruled by statute. If it is, then it is the statute that the judge must apply. But it is for the judge not merely to apply but also to interpret the statute and thus there is no clearly defined interface between the two sources because there tends to get built up, as a result of judicial interpretation of the statute, a body of case-law enshrining that interpretation and super-imposed upon statutory law. So that although the law derives from separate sources there is but one *corpus juris* constituted by an amalgam of the sources.

4. THE DOCTRINE OF PRECEDENT

That now brings us to the third and most important background feature—the doctrine of precedent. Because the English system of courts is hierarchical, every lower court is bound to follow the decision of the superior court on a point of law even though it may think that it is quite wrong. Thus although a High Court Judge may decline to follow the law as declared by another High Court Judge (although he does not usually do so), every circuit judge and every magistrate is bound to follow the decision of the High Court. One can readily see that there may be some uncertainty when a circuit judge is confronted with two conflicting decisions. There is no certain answer to this conundrum but the better view is probably that he is bound to follow the decision on a point of law of the Court of Appeal. The "decision" here means decision and not merely an expression of view. What binds other tribunals is the *ratio decidendi* of the case and not mere expressions of opinion on hypothetical facts which do not directly arise for decision—though, of course, those opinions will carry great persuasive force, a force which will vary with the calibre of the source from which they emanate. This hierarchical and compulsory observance of the law as it has been determined to be by a superior tribunal continues up the pyramid. Thus as the High Court is bound by the previous decisions of the Court of Appeal, however heretical those decisions may appear to be, so the Court of Appeal is bound to apply the law as it is distilled from and has been laid down by previous decision of the House of Lords. There is, however, this difference that, whereas the judge at first instance in the High Court may differ from another judge of equivalent status, the Court of Appeal is, in general, bound to follow its own previous decisions unless and until those decisions are nullified by inconsistent legislation or are reversed by the House of Lords. Finally at the level of the House of Lords the rule up to the 26th July 1966 was that, like the Court of Appeal, the House was bound by its own previous decisions. That had always been assumed as an absolute. A decision of the House of Lords was the ultimate unchallengeable declaration of what the law was and it could be altered only by an Act of Parliament. Hence the House was once, perhaps rather disrespectfully, described by Lord Justice McKinnon as "the voices of infallibility". What happened on the 26th July 1966 is a very good example of what may quite accurately be called judicial legislation and it raised a good many constitutional queries which have never really been satisfactorily answered. The judicial members of the House of Lords—who, after all, form only a Committee of the House as a legislative body—determined on their own motion, without consulting the House as a whole and certainly without consulting Parliament, to alter the established position. This was done simply by treating what had always previously been treated as axiomatic as merely a convention of practice and, declaring in pursuance of the court's power to regulate its own practice, that in future the House would consider itself free to depart from its own previous rulings. It is however, a power very sparingly exercised.

This is by way of being almost a footnote but it is just worth referring briefly to the case of *Miliangos* v. *George Frank (textiles) Ltd.*[1] decided in 1976, because it illustrates both the House of Lords' new freedom to depart from its own previous rulings—in other words, to alter the law without Act of Parliament—and also the House's attitude to the doctrine of binding precedent as regards the lower courts. The case concerned the question whether, in relation to an award of damages for breach of an international contract, judgment could be awarded

[1] [1976] A.C. 443.

in a foreign currency—a question of some importance in a climate of
fluctuating exchange rates. In the case of the *United Railways of Havana*[2] in 1961 the House had unequivocally declared that English law
permitted judgment in an English Court to be entered only in sterling
and in no other currency. Many eminent lawyers considered that rule
was outdated and in the case of *Schorsch Meier GmbH* v. *Henning*[3] in
1975 Lord Denning (very naughtily) persuaded one of his colleagues in
the Court of Appeal to concur with him in simply reversing the Havana
case, on the ground that the rule was out of date, and to enter judgment
in *Deutschmarks*. Following that decision the Miliangos case came
before Mr. Justice Bristow in the High Court[4] and he found himself in
the awkward position of having two conflicting decisions on the same
point—the earlier decision of the House of Lords in Havana and the
later case of Schorsch Meier in the Court of Appeal.[5] He loyally followed the House of Lords but was promptly overruled by the Court of
Appeal (presided over again by Lord Denning) which followed its
earlier decision in Schorsch Meier and entered judgment in Swiss Francs.
When the case went to the House of Lords,[6] that House reaffirmed that
the only court having power to depart from its decisions was the House
itself. On this occasion it did so in accordance with 1966 practice
direction and thus, in the event, upheld the decision of the Court of
Appeal. However, an interesting discussion of the operation of the
doctrine of precedent is to be found in the dissenting speech of Lord
Simon[7] which in this respect accurately sets out the position. First the
Court of Appeal was quite wrong to take the course that it did in
Schorsch Meier and to ignore a previous decision at the House of
Lords. Secondly, however, since that was the decision of the Court of
Appeal, even if it was wrong, it bound Mr. Justice Bristow and he was
wrong not to follow it in Miliangos. Thirdly, the Court of Appeal,
although wrong in Schorsch Meier, was right in the Miliangos case to
follow its own decision since it was bound by its own previous decisions. That then is the background against which the English judicial
methodology will be explained. With the law enshrined in judicial
decisions and which it itself has set and which represent the law, there is
scope for what can, quite properly, be described as "judicial legislation",
that is so to say, altering the law without the question of the wisdom
or desirability of the alteration ever being made the subject-matter of

---

[2] [1961] A.C. 1007.   [3] [1975].   [4] [1975] Q.B. 416.
[5] *Id.*   [6] [1976] A.C. 443.   [7] At 470 *et seq.*

Parliamentary debate. Nowhere is that more clearly illustrated than in relation to the tort of negligence.

5. LAW OF TORT OR DELICT

5.1. Introduction

The English law of tort or delict (to use the less insular expression) may be broadly described as that branch of the law which is concerned with the provision of remedies for civil wrongs not arising from contractual or consensual relationships. It is, again in broad terms, concerned with those duties which are imposed by the law otherwise than as a result of consensual assumption. And one of those duties is not to cause physical injury to other people or to their property. It has long been recognised that that duty embraces as much unintentional as intentional injury and it is summed up in what has now become almost a technical expression, "the duty of care". What remained unclear until 1932 was the ambit of the duty. The prevailing view up to that time was that it arose only where there was between the plaintiff and the defendant some direct relationship created, for instance, by physical proximity or by invitation to the work with or on defective equipment or a defective structure. The case of *Donoghue* v. *Stevenson*[8] decided by the House of Lords in 1932 opened up an entirely new horizon and it provided a general test of the duty of care which was to remain undisturbed for the next 30 years and, indeed, which is as valid today as it was in 1932 but which has now been greatly expanded in its ambit by a series of further decisions of the House of Lords.

5.2. *Donoghue* v. *Stevenson*

Donoghue v. *Stevenson* was the case of the snail in the ginger beer bottle that may never, in fact, have been there. The plaintiff claimed that while she was out with her boyfriend, he bought her, from a shop in Paisley, a bottle of ginger beer, part of which she drank. When the remainder was poured into her glass there emerged the remains of a decomposed snail, the sight of which, so she alleged, caused her serious nervous shock and the presence of which in the mixture she already had

---

[8] [1932] A.C. 562.

drunk, made her ill with gastro-enteritis. She sued the manufacturer. The case came before the House of Lords on a preliminary point, which was whether, even assuming facts to be as she alleged, there was any action to be tried, since it was not claimed that she had any contract either with the manufacturer or the shopkeeper. The argument was that a manufacturer of goods owed no duty to anyone with whom he was in no contractual relationship except where the article which he manufactured was either dangerous in itself or was dangerously defective to his knowledge. That was decisively rejected by the House of Lords and the principle was summed up in what has become a classic speech by Lord Atkin and, in particular, in this passage:[9]

Acts or omissions which any moral code would censure cannot in a practical world be treated so as to give a right to every person injured by them to demand relief. In this way rules of law arise which limit the range of complainants and the extent of their remedy. The rule that you are to love your neighbour becomes in law, you must not injure your neighbour, and the lawyer's question, who is my neighbour, receives a restrictive reply. You must take reasonable care to avoid acts or omissions which you can reasonably foresee would be likely to injure your neighbour. Who then in law is my neighbour? The answer seems to be—persons who are so closely and directly affected by my act that I ought reasonably to have them in contemplation as being so affected when I am directing my mind to the acts or omissions which are called in question.

Now here was a clear, definite and easily applicable principle capable of covering all circumstances. If you, as a reasonable man, can foresee that lack of ordinary care on your part in doing whatever you are doing will be likely to cause injury to another person or to his property, you are under a duty to take such care and will be liable for injury caused by each breach of that duty. Obviously there are cases in which it is not altogether easy from the facts to determine what the reasonable man could reasonably foresee, but the principle of law from 1932 onwards was clear and was firmly settled. One mildly amusing feature of the case is that it was decided on a preliminary point. The only actual decision made was that there was a case to be tried on the facts as they were then assumed to be. The trial never actually took place because the plaintiff in fact died before it could be determined whether the decomposed snail ever really had existed. So far as is known she did not die of snail poisoning. So the whole course of English law of negligence was altered by what may well have been a non-event. But

---

[9] *Id.*, at 580.

the interesting feature of the case in the present context is the way in which Lord Atkin reached his decision. He would have been the first to disclaim any intention to change the law and in the course of his speech was at pains to point out the dangers of propounding too wide a definition. The way in which he arrived at his decision was by a careful review of previous cases, the extraction from them of a number of propositions and an extrapolation from those propositions to the broad general proposition of the foundation of liability which is enshrined in the passage from the speech above. The case is an excellent example of the way in which English judges develop the law by extension from what has gone before, each decided principle being used as the stepping stone to a further step forward by way of what at least is claimed to be a logical progression. *Donoghue* v. *Stevenson* certainly resulted in the establishment of a joint broad general position, but it was not one which, at any rate in the intention of its author, was conceived as a massive step forward in the legal development, propounded because this was clearly what the law ought to be. Judges do not, or at least they do not avowedly, make law in that way. The process is essentially an incremental one, built up from case to case, the conclusion being reached by deduction from what has gone before. Lord Atkin was not inventing a principle. He was merely stating in terms which had not previously been universally perceived, the principle which he was able to deduce from the previously decided cases. We shall see, however, that whilst that is said to be the judicial method, and whilst that is always what judges claim to be doing, certainly in the more recent cases and in, to the mind of this author, the most controversial decision of recent times in this branch of the law, the courts have in fact indulged a taste for inventiveness, sometimes with disastrous results.

5.3. Qualifications and limitations

What has to be borne in mind about *Donoghue* v. *Stevenson*, however, is that it was decided in the context of a state of the law where the only form of injury which was in anybody's contemplation was physical injury to the person or property of the plaintiff. Of course, that might involve, and ordinarily would involve, pecuniary loss to the plaintiff in repairing himself or his property and in making good wages or profits lost as a result. But no-one, at that time, contemplated the possibility of a claim of negligence for pure direct economic loss with no anterior injury to person or property and certainly not economic loss to a third person resulting from the plaintiff's injury. Lord Atkin's principle has, therefore, to be looked at in that context. This sort of loss—the pecuniary loss which is not consequent upon other damage but is itself the primary injury (indeed the only injury)—cannot ordinarily arise directly as a result of the defendant's carelessness in doing whatever he is doing in any physical sense, except in circumstances where it involves some other actionable invasion of the plaintiff's rights. You can, for instance, inflict pecuniary damage on your neighbour by carelessly parking your car across his driveway and so prevent him from keeping a business appointment. But your liability then will not be because you have been negligent but because you have committed the sort of nuisance which itself creates a cause of action. Pure pecuniary loss, in the ordinary way, arises from some statements made to the defendant upon which he has relied to his detriment—a statement made either as a result of contract (as for instance the advice of a lawyer, or a stockbroker or an architect) or made with a view to inducing a particular course of conduct (for instance, subscribing for shares in the company). And the accepted and generally acknowledged view of the law at the time when Lord Atkin gave his classical definition of the duty of care was that there was no liability—apart from contractual or fiduciary relationship—for purely pecuniary damage caused by a negligent statement, though of course there might well be liability if a contract could be proved or if the statement could be proved to be fraudulent. This was the so called rule in *Derry* v. *Peek*[10]—a case where the plaintiff had suffered loss as a result of investing on the strength of a public prospectus for shares in a tramway company which contained some highly optimistic and untrue statements which were held to have been made negligently but not fraudulently. He failed in his action. The principle was sometimes expressed as "no liability in tort for a negligent statement", but that was never in fact universally true. The words "pure pecuniary damage" are emphasized because, of course, there are cases where physical damage can be and is caused by reliance upon negligent statements—for instance the doctor who carelessly misdiagnoses and injures his patient by prescribing the wrong treatment (though usually that, before the days of the National Health Service, would be a breach of his contractual duty); or the architect who tells the workmen standing under an archway that he can safely remove the keystone so that the whole edifice falls down and injures him.

[10] [1899] 14 A.C. 337.

University of Oxford

Centre for the Advanced Study of European and Comparative Law
Institut des Hautes Etudes Juridiques Européennes et Comparatives
Institut für Europarecht und Rechtsvergleichung

With compliments of the Director

B.S. Markesinis, d.Iur.(Athen), Ph.D., LL.D.(Cantab), D.C.L.(Oxon.),
D.Iur.h.c.(Ghent), Clifford Chance Professor of European Law

Tel. (01865) 28/6/2

Moreover, the rule in *Derry* v. *Peek* was in truth merely a facet of a broader rule that there was no liability in negligence to one who has suffered only pecuniary loss. Thus if A negligently injures B so that B cannot fulfil his contract with C, C has no remedy against A for the loss which he suffers as a result. So, as regards pure pecuniary damage, one has to approach Lord Atkin's principle initially with this limitation in mind. It was not expressed but it was certainly assumed.

Another limitation of quite a different character lay in the area of causation. Carelessness *per se* clearly would not suffice as a ground of liability. The duty is not a duty to be careful but a duty not to cause injury by carelessness. You can drive a car down the street at 60 m.p.h. and you may be in grave trouble with the traffic police; but you will not be liable to anyone unless you cause damage. It has always to be shown that the carelessness caused the injury complained of and there were difficult questions which arose where the injury sustained stemmed not directly from the carelessness of the defendant but from the act of some third person, the defendant's connection being only that he had been involved in the *mis-en-scène* in which the injury occurred. We shall see in a moment how Lord Atkin's principle—sometimes described as "the neighbour principle", sometimes as the "doctrine of proximity"—has been used as the base for the extension of the law of negligence both into the realm of pure pecuniary damage and into the area of damage actually occasioned by persons the other than the defendant himself.

6. CASE LAW AFTER *DONOGHUE* V. *STEVENSON*

English law is developed by the judges and that is true in the sense that it is the judges that expound and declare the law. But the real development is by the legal profession. A judge does not pronounce *in vacuo* and he does not set himself up of his own motion as a law reformer. He decides only the particular case before him and what really causes the law before him to develop is the argument advanced by the ingenuity of council appearing before him. Each step forward represents not so much an individual judge's ingenuity but a successful attempt by council to advance the law to a point where it covers his client's case. The years followed by *Donoghue* v. *Stevenson* witnessed a number of unsuccessful attempts to persuade the courts that the neighbourhood principle could be extended to cover the case of advice carelessly given and relied upon to the financial disadvantage of the recipient.

An attempt was made in 1939 to hold a surveyor liable for a negligent valuation report which had been relied on, not by his client, but by a third person. That failed. In the case of *Candler* v. *Crane Christmas*[11] in 1951 an attempt was made to hold some accounts liable for company accounts which had been negligently prepared and on the basis of which the plaintiff had made an investment. That again failed although Lord Denning would have held them liable. This, however, was one of the comparatively rare occasions on which he failed to carry his colleagues with him. The breakthrough came in 1964 with the case of *Hedley Byrne* v. *Heller and Partners.*[12] That was the case in which the appellants, who were advertising agents, had incurred considerable expense in placing advertisements for a client. Before doing so they had sought from the client's bankers an assurance of the stability and standing of the client—that had been given by the bankers but without any proper enquiry being made and the appellants lost a lot of money as a result of the client's subsequent insolvency. They then sued the bankers for negligence in issuing the reference on which they had relied. In fact the action failed because the bankers had covered themselves by an express disclaimer of responsibility but the House of Lords after careful consideration of the authorities, decisively rejected the submission that there could be no action in negligence for pecuniary loss caused by a careless misstatement if the circumstances were such that it was intended to be relied upon, that it was known that it would be relied upon and that therefore it could be foreseen that damage would be caused if it were acted upon. The principle was, however, carefully limited in this way. The duty of care was expressed to arise where the information relied on had been sought from the party possessed of special skills and where that party knew or ought to have known that reliance was being placed on his skill and judgement. This was a decision of immense importance in the development of the law of negligence for, in opening the door, albeit narrowly, to claims in tort for negligent statements, it opened the door also to claims in negligence of pure pecuniary damage and this led onto another decision of critical importance. Although the House of Lords was careful to limit the decision in the way in which it has been referred to, as so often happens, the limitations have tended to become more and more eroded as other cases on slightly different facts have been decided. Once again, the decision was reached by careful review of the existing authorities and a logical exposition of principle from

---

[11] [1951] 2 K.B. 164.   [12] [1964] A.C. 465.

them. But it was more than just one logical niche forward. It was a major step because the moment you open the door for this sort of claim—based as it has come to be on a general duty of care not to cause foreseeable damage of any sort to your fellow citizens—you run into immediate difficulties of definition. This was foreseen by those who decided the case and within the strict limitations which they sought to impose on their decision there is no particular reason why it should have been. The difficulties have arisen because of the extensions which have been made using *Hedley Byrne* v. *Heller and Partners* as a basis for a much more widely expressed duty of care. There is nothing particularly odd about a general duty to take care not to inflict physical damage to person or property—the simple *Donoghue* v. *Stevenson* principle. It is difficult indeed to imagine circumstances in which such damage could lawfully be inflicted intentionally and there is no logical reason why liability should not follow equally for doing it carelessly. But can you have a general duty not to inflict economic damage? Foreseeable pecuniary damage to someone is the inevitable consequence of the very concept of commercial competition. So how is the court to determine when the injured plaintiff is or is not to recover compensation? No intellectually satisfactory answer to this conundrum has yet been found. So the Hedley Byrne case was a landmark in the law but one which left a good deal of uncertainty about the way forward.

An equally important decision was reached some six years later in relation to liability for the acts of third parties. That was the case of *Dorset Yacht Company Ltd.* v. *Home Office*[13] in 1970. What happened there was that the authorities in charge of an institution for the training and correction of youthful delinquents sent a working party of boys under the charge of a number of responsible prison officers down to a small island in Poole Harbour on the South Coast of England. Owing to the officers' negligent supervision of their charges seven of the boys escaped from the island, stole a boat and they did considerable damage to the property of the Dorset Yacht Company who then sued the Home Secretary who was the Minister in charge of the government department responsible for the institution from which the boys came. The Home Secretary pleaded that they could not be held responsible for the acts of the boys who were not in any sense their agents or servants but who were simply young criminals on the run. That plea was rejected and the House of Lords, following *Donoghue* v. *Stevenson*, held that,

---

[13] [1970] A.C. 1004.

since it could reasonably be foreseen that if the officers were not watch-ful the boys might escape from the island and that, if they did escape, they would be likely to steal or damage a boat in the course of escap-ing, the Home Secretary was liable. Again this was advanced simply as an application of the neighbourhood principle. But it is a case which raises almost as many questions as it answers and there is still a wide area of debate about how far the neighbourhood principle can be pushed. Will it for instance involve liability in a prison governor for negligently allowing the escape of a dangerous prisoner who steals a car and who breaks into a house 100 miles away? Is that not equally foreseeable? And when, if ever, does the liability end? If it is foreseeable that a prisoner may cause damage in the course of his escape, is it not equally foreseeable that he will do the same thing the next day or the day after or a month hence if he is not recaptured?

Various answers were suggested in the course of the case but none is logically very satisfactory. What is important about this case how-ever is this, that the duty to take care not to inflict foreseeable injury has now been translated by extension into a duty to take care to prevent foreseeable injury and the question is: what are the limits of that duty? Building on this case, more recent attempts have been made to attach liability for criminal acts of other people to innocent citizens whose only fault has been that they happen to own property near to that of the injured person. The proposition upon which the profession has sought to build and to which, fortunately, the courts have at the moment shown themselves resistant, is that because the infliction of damage by the criminal act of a third party can be foreseen if an opportunity is pro-vided for it, it follows: (i) that to provide the opportunity is to cause the damage and; (ii) that there is a duty of care not to provide the oppor-tunity. How that notion has been allowed to get about will become evident when we get to the final important decision in the series be-cause it is merely the logical application of a general principle which has not been produced by the normal process of incremental decision (although it was expressed to be so) and so has been expressed too widely. Mention will be made of three cases, in two of which the undersigned was involved in the Court of Appeal. The first is *Lamb* v. *Camden Borough Council* [14] in 1981. There one of the council's work-men, who was doing roadwork outside the plaintiff's house, carelessly put his pneumatic drill through the water main and that started the most

---

[14] [1981] 1 Q.B. 625.

extraordinary chain of disaster. The water swept away the earth at the front of the house so that the foundations slipped and as a result substantial work of underpinning had to be undertaken. As a result of that, the house became temporarily uninhabitable and had to be vacated. Then, about a year later, when the house was still vacant, some youthful squatters spotted it and moved in. They occupied the house for some months before they could be evicted and they did an enormous amount of criminal damage to the interior and the fittings. The Council accepted liability for the damage to the foundations and for the loss of rent and the inconvenience of the owners whilst the underpinning was in progress but they jibbed at paying for the damage caused by the squatters who were, as they contended, merely criminals over whom they had no control. The Court held that they were not responsible.

The second case, again in the Court of Appeal, was *Perl* v. *Camden Borough Council*[15] in 1983. What happened there was that the Council owned a block of flats the front door of which was inadequate to keep trespassers out. Some burglars broke in, but instead of robbing the flats, they entered the basement flat, bored through the main wall and thus got into the shop next door from which they helped themselves to some valuable property. The shopkeeper sued the Council claiming that they owed him a duty to provide a proper front door for their premises and so prevent trespassers on their premises from committing further trespasses on his premises. Again that claim failed.

Finally, in the *Smith* v. *Littlewoods Organisation*[16] in 1987, the owners of a cinema had some work done by contractors. The premises were secured but were left unattended while the work was carried on. Some children got in and started a fire, as a result of which the cinema was destroyed. The fire spread, however, to adjoining premises and in particular to a church, the trustees of which (being sadly under-insured) sued the owners of the cinema. The case went to the House of Lords, where the claim failed. It is to be noted, however, that the House did not altogether deny the possibility of a duty of the owner of the premises to take adequate steps to prevent harm to his neighbours' premises if, for instance, he knows that his premises are likely to be used as the vehicle for causing harm to adjoining property.

That brings us to the most critically important decision in this field in recent years and one whose ripples are still being felt. That is the case of *Anns* v. *Merton London Borough Council*[17] in 1978. It is a case

---

[15] [1984] 1 Q.B. 342.   [16] [1987] 1 A.C. 241.   [17] [1978] A.C. 728.

which embraces a bit of all three of the cases which have been referred to. It pushes the neighbourhood principle of *Donoghue* v. *Stevenson* one step further. It was in fact a case of pure pecuniary loss, as in Hedley Byrne (although it was said not to be). And it is a case where the loss resulted from the act of a third party as in Dorset Yachts. The plaintiffs were the lessees of a block of flats. Only two of them were in fact original lessees, the remainder having bought their leases from original lessees or from purchasers from original lessees so that they had no relationship at all with the people who put the building up in the first place. Now under the Public Health Act of 1936, the Merton Borough Council had made bye-laws regulating the construction of buildings in their area—among other things the depth of their foundations—and they had on their staff building inspectors whose function it was to ensure that the bye-laws were complied with. When this particular block of flats was built in 1962 it was erected on foundations which were in fact quite inadequate and failed to comply with the Council's bye-laws, a circumstance which their inspector carelessly failed to notice before the foundations were covered in. In the 1970s cracks started to appear in the building and the plaintiffs were put to great expense in having repairs executed and the building underpinned. They sued the Council who pleaded that if they had any duty it was merely a public statutory duty and not a duty which they owed to the plaintiffs. That plea failed and the Council were held liable.

This represented an entirely new departure. It is another example of judicial legislation which, in the opinion of the author, goes beyond mere incremental decision making. The consequence of it had been far reaching and the repercussions of it are still being felt. What the House of Lords did in this case was to recognise, alongside the statutory public duty cast on the Council by the Public Health Act, a parallel private duty of care to persons who they could reasonably foresee might suffer loss if they were careless in the performance of their public duty. Here the Council had done nothing. Their fault was one of omission only. The plaintiffs had not relied on them. The injury was inflicted not by the Council, but by a builder for whom they had no responsibility. Their neglect lay solely in not ensuring that the public duty of enforcing compliance with their own bye-laws was properly carried out. Now that is all a very long way from *Donoghue* v. *Stevenson* and in finding private law duty of care the House had to resort not so much to previous authority as to what was described as "principle". "On principle", said Lord Wilberforce, "there must surely be a duty to exercise reasonable care". But what has provided the springboard for yet further extensions of the duty of care is the following statement of general principle taken from his speech:

Through the trilogy of cases in this house, *Donoghue* v. *Stevenson, Hedley Byrne & Co.* v. *Heller & Partners Ltd.* and *Dorset Yacht* v. *Home Office*, the position has now been reached that in order to establish that the duty of care arises in a particular situation it is not necessary to bring the facts of that situation within those of previous situations in which a duty of care has been held to exist. Rather the question has to be approached in two stages. First one has to ask whether, as between the alleged wrongdoer and the person who has suffered damage there is a sufficient relation of proximity or neighbourhood such that, in the reasonable contemplation of the former, carelessness on his part may be likely to cause damage to the latter in which a prima facie duty of care arises. Secondly, if the first question is answered affirmatively it is necessary to consider whether there are any considerations which ought to negative or to reduce or limit the scope of the duty or the class of person to whom it is owed or the damages to which a breach of it may give rise.

Now this, with respect, is judicial legislation with a vengeance. What, on the face of it, it does is to establish an initial and universal test of liability going well beyond *Donoghue* v. *Stevenson*—if you can reasonably foresee that carelessness on your part in doing something or failing to do something which you are bound by law to do may result in injury of any kind to any person and that injury is in fact sustained you will be liable unless the court, in effect as a matter of policy determines that there are some unspecified and undefined reasons for denying liability in any given case. So the case not only pushed the law further along the path but, by postulating an undefined and necessarily flexible standard by which the court could determine the issue of liability or no liability, it opened the door to yet further judicial legislation. It is, perhaps, not surprising that this had led to a spate of claims which have become more and more repugnant to common sense and that the courts have recently shown a tendency to retreat from the position to which their own logic has driven them. We have had a claim against a local authority in circumstances rather similar to those in Anns by the very person who is responsible for the erection of the defective building. We have had a claim by a purchaser of a house against an authority which had lent money to the previous owner to put up an addition to the home which was badly constructed, on the ground they ought not to have lent money without ensuring that the work was properly performed. And we have had a claim by an investor for the negligent performance of duty by a public regulatory agency in Hong Kong as a result of which, so it was claimed, a deposit-taking company was able to continue business. The plaintiff invested some money with it and the company lost it. The House in both the former cases and the Privy Council in the latter refused to carry the principle of Anns to this extent and, indeed, Lord Wilberforce himself, in a subsequent case, declared that the mere forseeability of damage is not sufficient. There must, in addition, be a further ingredient described as "proximity"—but the difficulty is that no-one has yet successfully defined what this ingredient is.

7. CONCLUSION

This is a very inadequate description of the point at which the law of negligence has arrived at the moment. To describe and analyse that, so far as it is capable of analysis at all, would require far more space. As a result of the Anns case the law is in a very fluid state which is probably true to say that there is now no satisfactory discernible general definition of what constitutes "proximity". The courts answer yes or no pragmatically according to the circumstances of individual cases. At present, however, there is no rationale behind these answers.

Perhaps the high-water mark of the attempts to enlarge the duty of care is the case of *Hill* v. *the Chief Constable of West Yorkshire*[18] which is an interesting example of how a perfectly bizarre result can be obtained by a process of logical arguments from premises which are too widely expressed. Peter Sutcliffe had a penchant for killing young women in a particularly nasty way. He committed a large number of crimes in the north of England, particularly in Yorkshire. Once it became clear that there was a pattern behind the killing and that they were the work of one man, an intensive man-hunt ensued. There were a lot of misleading clues but a number of indications pointed to Sutcliffe as the man responsible and he was in fact interviewed by the Police on a number of occasions.

Nevertheless, there was a failure on the part of the Police to collate the information and on each occasion he was released. His last victim was a Miss Hill. After that crime he was finally arrested and charged and is now serving a life sentence in prison. The mother of the last victim however sued the responsible police authority for damages for

---

[18] [1988] Q.B. 60.

negligence leading to the death of her daughter and the action came
before the court on the preliminary point whether, assuming the police
had been thoroughly careless in the way in which they carried out their
enquiries, they owed a duty to Miss Hill individually or to the plaintiff
as her executrix, to prevent Sutcliffe from committing further crimes.
The argument was a very simple one. The police owe a duty to the
public to do their best to prevent crime. Anns establishes a parallel
private duty not to perform a public duty without taking proper care. If
the public duty is not performed properly it can be foreseen that someone will be injured as a result, in this case Miss Hill. Therefore the
police owe Miss Hill a duty in private law to take reasonable care to
detect and apprehend the criminal and prevent him from injuring her.
Therefore the police are liable to pay compensation. In the courts below, the action failed on what may be called the second branch of the
Anns principle, that is to say, that there were considerations of public
policy which dictated that the action should not lie. A decision of the
House of Lords is awaited.[19]

In the context of what is discussed, however, it is an interesting
example of the point to which previous judicial decision has brought
us. The Courts are constantly urged to develop and extend the law yet
further.

This article is an attempt to describe what is by definition a continuing process and there is therefore no easily discernible logical conclusion. We live in a rapidly changing world and the law has to adapt to
conditions which alter with bewildering rapidity.

The method of judicial law-making which is attempted to describe
above has the twin advantages of flexibility and pragmatism and it also
has the advantages of speed. Lord Denning, who was never afraid of
doing a bit of judicial legislation in the Court of Appeal, once observed
there was little to be gained by waiting for parliament to alter the law.
It ought to be done now when its inadequacy to meet the case before
him had become perceptible. That is the plus side. But there is a minus
side also. First, the development of the law in this way can only be
achieved at the expense of certainty and the present state of the law
relating to the duty of care and negligence is an excellent example. The
courts are still looking for some certain definition of what element is
required additional to that of the reasonable foreseeability of harm.

---

[19] The decision of the Court of Appeal was affirmed by the House of Lords [1988]
2 W.L.R.

Secondly, it involves the alteration of the law, sometimes a quite radical alteration, as in the Anns case, without any extensive consideration of the practical and economic result such as would take place in the course of parliamentary scrutiny and debate. That can be important and the Anns case is a very good example, because it has had the practical effect, unforeseen at the time, of bringing about a significant increase in building costs. Local authorities became so alarmed at the prospect of being held liable, possibly many years hence, for defective buildings erected in their areas that they now insist on digging extravagantly deep foundations which very much increase the cost of building. Judges are not the elected representatives of the people and the methodology of English Judges which results in the development and alteration of the law without the benefit of parliamentary debate may not perhaps be altogether a satisfactory democratic process to a constitutional purist.

2

The Family in English Law: Some Recent Trends

by Professor Stephen Cretney, D.C.L. (Oxon) F.B.A.*

INTRODUCTION: SOME SOCIAL AND DEMOGRAPHIC INFLUENCES

The traditional view of English law has been well expressed by Sir Leslie Scarman: "the family" (he said) "is not a legal person, and it attracts to itself neither legal rights nor duties".[1]

Accordingly, for many years, the law focused mainly on the law of marriage (and divorce); it was concerned with the law of persons, rather than with the law of families.

The main reason for this narrow approach was that marriage created status, that is to say "the condition of belonging to a class in society to which the law ascribes peculiar rights and duties, capacities and incapacities".[2] For many years, students studying what we today call family law would have found their examination papers entitled "The Law of Matrimonial Causes". It can be argued that the concept of marriage is gradually evolving towards a more contractual basis, in which the terms and legal consequences of relationships are left to be settled by the parties rather than imposed upon them by law. But the fact that marriage does create a status in the traditional sense has recently been vividly illustrated by the case of re *Collins:*[3] a woman obtained leave to be allowed, exceptionally, to prosecute divorce proceedings within the first three years of marriage on the ground that the

---

* This text represents an expanded and up-dated version of a lecture given by Professor Cretney in the University of Leiden on March 6th 1989 at the invitation of the Institute of Anglo-American Law.

[1] Contrasting sharply with the approach of many systems of customary law.

[2] See Cretney, *Principles of Family Law* (4th ed. 1984), p. 4.

[3] *The Amphthill Peerage* [1977] A.C. 547, 577, Lord Simon of Glaisdale.

case was one of exceptional depravity by the husband or of exceptional hardship; and she was granted a decree *nisi* against him based on his behaviour.

However, at the date of her death this decree had not been made absolute. She was thus in law still married; and all her property passed by operation of law to the—apparently wholly unmeritorious—husband.[4]

The Chancing Nature of The English Family

A law which continued to be so dominated by marriage and its legal consequences may at one time have satisfied social needs; but a glance at recent demographic data demonstrates how unreasonable such a view would be today. In the decade ending in 1988, the number of single parent families rose by 20% from 840 thousand to 1 million. Of these, almost one quarter (230 thousand) were headed by a person who had never been married, 410 thousand were headed by a divorced person, and 190 thousand where headed by a separated spouse.[5,6] Moreover, it can no longer be assumed that a couple leading what might appear to the outsider to be a married life are in law married. It has been estimated that in 1986/7 there were about 900 thousand couples in Great Britain who were co-habiting but not married to one another, and over 400 thousand children were living in households headed by such a couple.[7] It is difficult to resist the conclusion that—for one reason or another—the institution of legal marriage has become irrelevant to a large proportion of the population; and a glance at the proportion of births which take place outside marriage (25% of all births in 1988) reinforces the view.

It is interesting to note that illegitimacy rates vary markedly between different ethnic groups: amongst those mothers born in Bangladesh, for example, the rate of illegitimate births is only 2%, whereas amongst

[4] [1990] 2 W.L.R. 161.

[5] The law permits applications by specified categories of dependants on the ground that the distribution of the estate does not provide reasonable financial provision for the dependant concerned: Inheritance (Provision for Family and Dependants) Act 1975.

[6] Such an application was made in this case by the two children born to the deceased. The result of their application provides another illustration of the continuing significance of legal status: one of her children had been legally adopted by a third party after the mother's death; and the result was that that child was no longer eligible to apply for provision as her son. In contrast, another child—albeit cared for by third parties—remained in law her child and thus remained eligible to apply.

[7] These data are extracted from the national Audit Office's survey of *DSS Support for Lone Families* (1990).

those born in the Caribbean it is as high as 25%;[8] and this fact illustrates another profound change in British society which must inevitably influence the development of family law. This is that Great Britain now has a substantial ethnic minority population[9] with markedly diverse social customs which are not always easy to reconcile with the traditional doctrines of English Law.

There is yet another pressure to which—although it is still not yet of great significance in purely statistical terms—the law is now having to respond. This is the rapid development of the science of human assisted reproduction, which has the consequence that (for example) the person who carries a child as an embryo may not be the person who actually bears the child to delivery; whilst those who have contributed the genetic material resulting in the child's conception may well have played no other role in gestation or birth and certainly did not intend to have any involvement in the child's upbringing. Even though these activities still seem somewhat remote from every-day experience, it is interesting to note the 1987 Government estimate[10] that artificial insemination by a donor (where the child's genetic father will not be his social father) was the means whereby some 1,700 children a year were born in the United Kingdom. When we note that only 8,000 children a year are legally adopted, law teachers at any rate must begin to question whether the heavy emphasis which they have traditionally placed on adoption and other formal methods of creating legal kinship structures can still be justified.

Effects on Legal Policy

In the result, it is obvious—indeed trite—that Family Law cannot today regard marriage and its legal consequences as being its primary concern; yet the question of what is, in law, "the family" remains a difficult one. In part, this is because the word "family" is a heavily emotive one and one which in recent years has become much used in party political dispute in Britain. For example, it has been asserted that the "integrity and independence of the family is the basic building block of a free and democratic society and the need to defend it should be clearly perceivable

[8] Figures on these matters are to be found in *Social Trends* 18 (1988), p. 47; and see generally Haskey and McKiernan (1989) 58 Population Trends 23.

[9] See *Social Trends* 18 (1988), table 1.13.

[10] It has been estimated that 4.5% of the population of Great Britain were from ethnic minority groups. For an excellent treatment of the legal implications of these factors, see S.M. Poulter: *English Law and Ethnic Minority Customs* (1986).

in the law;"[11] whilst the belief that the "family" should take responsibility for its own members is currently a prominent feature in English
political rhetoric.[12]

To some extent, these beliefs are reflected in the provisions of the
most recent legislation directly affecting the legal framework governing the family—the massive Children Act 1989, which codifies and
reforms the law relating to children—and this legislation is certainly
thought by some to be part and parcel of the Thatcher Government's
determination to roll back the boundaries of the welfare state. Thus
although it is true that the Act imposes a duty on local government[13]
authorities to safeguard and promote the welfare of children within
their area who are in need by providing an appropriate range and level
of services, it is also provided that the authority must so far as is
consistent with that duty promote the upbringing of such children "by
their families".[14]

How has English Family Law responded to these pressures? It is
hoped that the reader will find it helpful to have a brief conspectus[15] of
developments under the following headings:—

(i)   Marriage and its Legal Consequences.
(ii) Divorce and its Legal Consequences.
(iii) The role of the Court in Divorce, the limits of Private Ordering.
(iv) Children; Legal Parentage; Parental Authority.
(v)   The boundaries of State Intervention.

---

[11] Human Fertilisation and Embryology: a framework for legislation, Cm. 259, annex
A, para. 3.
[12] Lord Mackay of Clashfern, Joseph Jackson Memorial Lecture [1989] *New L.J.* 505,
508.
[13] A similar approach seems to have influenced some expressions of judicial opinion.
"The best person to bring up a child is the natural parent. It matters not whether the
parent is wise or foolish, rich or poor, educated or illiterate, provided the child's moral
and physical health are not endangered": *Re KD (A Minor)* [1988] A.C. 806, *per* Lord
Templeman, at p. 812.
[14] It should be explained that local government in Great Britain has been entrusted
with responsibility for many social services (including those concerned with child care);
but that relationships between local and central government are sometimes uneasy, not
least because they may reflect strongly opposed political philosophies.
[15] It may be that not all those who have seen in this particular allocation of responsibility a re-affirmation of traditional values will have noted that the statutory definition
of a "family" for this purpose is quite remarkably wide, since it extends to any person
with whom the child "has been living": Children Act 1989, section 17(10); and it would
therefore in fact be consistent with the discharge of the Local Authority's duties to
support the child's relationship either with a partner of his or her own choice or with
somebody with whom the child has no legal kinship ties whatever.

I. MARRIAGE AND ITS LEGAL CONSEQUENCES

Notwithstanding the demographic facts referred to above, the majority of families in England are still founded on marriage. However, marriage according to English law can no longer realistically be described as a voluntary union between one man and one woman for life[16]—a fact of which many of the participants in weddings must be well aware, since they will themselves have been previously married and divorced.

1.1. The Marriage Ceremony

The English law governing the formation of marriage is by any standards complex and could not be understood—much less justified—without a detailed exposition of its historical evolution, quite inappropriate in a paper such as this. Suffice it to say that the special and distinctive role of the Church of England—established by law—in providing facilities for marriage continues to be preserved; but that the legal system also makes provision in this context for a wide diversity of religious and secular practice. Indeed, there are no fewer than four distinct systems governing the celebration of marriage in England and Wales:[17]

1. Marriage according to the rites of the Church of England;
2. Marriage according to a religious rite other than that of the Church of England;
3. Quaker and Jewish marriages;
4. Civil Marriages.

This diversity is one of the features of English law which surprises visitors from most continental European states; but it should be noted that, although in recent years there has been a trend towards civil marriages, some 70% of the marriages in which both parties are marrying for the first time are solemnised in a religious ceremony.[18]

Moreover, although the Government has recently proposed reforms

---

[16] The most accessible academic texts are Bromley and Lowe, *Family Law* (6th ed., 1987), and Cretney and Masson, *Principles of Family Law* (5th ed., 1990).

[17] The description given by Lord Penzance in *Hyde* v. *Hyde* (1866) LR. 1 P. & D. 130.

[18] The reader should be warned that the United Kingdom has three distinct systems of law: (a) the law of England and Wales (with which this article is concerned); (b) the law of Northern Ireland (which is similar to English law); and (c) the law of Scotland (which is in many respect fundamentally different from English law).

relating to the formation of marriage, the proposed reforms will not do anything to introduce a single system even for the preliminaries to the marriage ceremony. It was thought that a "wider consensus" was needed on the issues involved[19] even in respect of the formal preliminaries to marriage—a view which may have been influenced by the powerful opposition of the Church of England to any change in the system whereby the calling of banns in the Church satisfies the legal notification requirements. In view of this cautious approach it can be seen that the prospect of England following the pattern common in continental Europe of universal civil marriage must be regarded as non-existent.

The proposed reforms may, however, directly affect those opting for a civil marriage; since some degree of choice in relation to the building in which marriages may be celebrated is to be permitted—for example the owners of stately homes or hotels may make such facilities available for wedding ceremonies, whilst video and photographic facilities may also be offered. It is thought that such facilities—to be provided by private enterprise, no doubt at a competitive market price—will enable secular weddings to be celebrated in surroundings more attractive than those currently provided by some local authorities (on whom responsibility currently lies).[20] In the result, although the consumer may be able to purchase a more attractive venue for the wedding, the lawyer will still face astonishing complexity. However, it may well be that this decision fairly reflects an assessment of market forces: the complexities of the statute book are of interest to few, whereas the celebrations incidental to weddings are of interest to many.

Indeed, one eminent English family lawyer has remarked (possibly somewhat cynically) that recent statistical trends indicate not so much that the institution of marriage remains popular in England, but that weddings are popular.[21]

1.2. Prohibited Degrees

In any event, even for the lawyer, formalities are often regarded as comparatively unimportant compared with the rules governing capacity to marry. But paradoxically the rules governing capacity—in principle, of far greater potential controversy than those governing the form of the

---

[19] See Haskey, (1983) J. Biosoc. Sci. 15, p. 253.
[20] See *Registration: Proposals for Change* (1990) Cm. 939.
[21] See note 13 above.

ceremony—have been very significantly changed in recent years, largely in response to the social pressures resulting from the increasing phenomenon of marriage breakdown.

English law had inherited the Canon law doctrine whereby marriage makes a man and woman one flesh: accordingly if it be wrong to marry one's sister, it must be equally wrong to marry one's wife's sister. It is true that the remorseless logical application of this doctrine had been somewhat mitigated over the years; but the English legislature[22] has refused to go so far as to abolish the rule that relationships by affinity are not to be obstacles to marriage. Instead English law has been amended—in an extremely complex way[23]—to take account of the fact that increased divorce and re-marriage has correspondingly increased the risk that intending spouses who had never been previously members of the same *de facto* family unit would nonetheless be debarred, by reason of an affined relationship, from the marriage they wished to contract. The new legislation was in fact prompted by a number of cases in which a man was debarred from marrying his own former wife's daughter notwithstanding the fact that he had never had any familial relationship with his intended bride during her childhood or youth.

Accordingly, the law has now been amended to permit a man to marry his step daughter, his daughter-in-law (and indeed his mother-in-law) provided that certain conditions are satisfied. These conditions are evidently intended to give effect to the policy that a man is not to be allowed to marry his step daughter if there has been a parent-child relationship between them, and that he is not to be allowed to marry his daughter-in-law in circumstances where it may be thought that his sexual overtures could have played a part in the breakdown of her marriage to his son.

It is noteworthy that these reforms in the law were significantly influenced by the Report of a Review Body established by the Archbishop of Canterbury;[24] and the influence of the Church of England as a catalyst permitting change remains great—perhaps even greater than its potential influence in obstructing change. In particular, the influence of the Church of England was a significant, and probably decisive,

---

[22] Mrs Ruth Deech (1990) 106 *L.Q.R.* 229, 234.

[23] Compare the boldness displayed in Australia: see H.A. Finlay (1976) 5 *Univ. of Tas. L. Rev.* 16.

[24] Marriage Act 1986: see Cretney and Masson (1990), pp. 41–2 for an attempt to provide a comprehensible summary.

factor in permitting the liberalisation of the divorce laws effected by the Divorce Reform Act 1969.[25]

1.3. The Legal Consequences of Marriage

The repeated emphasis placed above on the fact that it is marriage—and in English law only marriage—which creates a legal status between a man and a woman who intend to share their lives may not reflect the popular understanding of what the law does, or at least should, provide. Thus in *Rignall (Inspector of Taxes)* v. *Andrews*[26] a man claimed that he was entitled to the special tax allowance then available to married men. He did not in fact claim that he was legally married, but he asserted that since he had been living with a woman for eleven years she had become his "common law wife" and that accordingly he qualified for the allowance. Not surprisingly, the Court rejected this claim;[27] but the case is only one of a number in which claims have been pursued to the courts which were apparently based on the belief that living together in a relationship similar to that of a married couple had legal consequences similar to those flowing from marriage. All have failed.[28]

It remains a fundamental principle, therefore, that marriage confers legal rights and duties on the parties; but it can plausibly be argued that such rights and duties pale into insignificance when contrasted with the fact that on *divorce* a court can make far-reaching financial provision and property adjustment orders. Indeed, it could be said that the most important single legal effect of marriage in English law today is that marriage gives the parties the right subsequently to be divorced.

2. DIVORCE AND ITS LEGAL CONSEQUENCES

2.1. The Divorce Rate

As in most countries, the subject of divorce in England has been a profoundly emotive one. However, amongst the enormous quantity of dogmatic assertion, certain demographic facts are clear. The divorce rate in England and Wales is now one of the highest in Europe—and indeed at 13.2 divorces per thousand existing marriages per annum it

---

[25] No Just Cause (1984).   [26] See below.   [27] [1991] F.L.R. 332.
[28] See also *R/S* 6/89 which involved a claim to Social Security benefits; and *Mossop* v. *Mossop* [1988] 2 W.L.R. 1255.

appears to be the highest in any EEC country.[29] Contrary to the apparent expectations of the advocates of a reformed divorce law in 1969, the divorce rate has sharply increased since the introduction of a "liberalised" regime: in 1966, there were 3.2 divorces per 1,000 married persons; in 1971, there were 6; whilst in 1987 there were 12.7. The divorce rate has thus doubled since the introduction of the new divorce law, and quadrupled over the last 20 years.

2.2. The Ground for Divorce

It has for many years been part of the conventional wisdom that easier divorce does not necessarily indicate an increase in marital breakdown, and that any increase in such breakdown that there may have been is not to be attributed to the liberalisation of the divorce laws but rather to sociological developments. However, this conventional wisdom has recently come under attack. It has been pointed out[30] that an increase in the divorce rate inevitably results in increased familiarity with divorce and its effects as a potential remedy for marital problems and thus to an increased willingness to have recourse to divorce and to make legislative provision for its aftermath.[31]

Be that as it may, the objective of the 1969 legislation was to create a divorce law which would "buttress rather than . . . undermine the stability of marriage", and also to give a decent burial to dead marriages by enabling the empty legal shell of such marriages to be destroyed with the "maximum fairness and the minimum bitterness, distress and humiliation".[32] The legislation was based on the principle that a marriage should be dissolved if, but only if, it could be shown to have broken down irretrievably. But—with consequences which were probably not at the time foreseen—it was decided that the question of whether a marriage had indeed broken down was not a justiciable issue which

---

[29] Cohabitants have sometimes succeeded in establishing a claim to property. Such claims depend on proof of the parties' intention about the ownership of the property rather than on their intentions as to the use to which the property is to be put, much less on the nature of their relationship: see *Grant* v. *Edwards* [1968] Ch. 638; *Lloyds Bank plc* v. *Rossett* [1990] 2 W.L.R. 867. An attempt to explain the law is made in Cretney and Masson (1990), Chap. 11.

[30] *Social Trends* 18 (1988), table 2.17.

[31] Deech (1990) 106 L.Q.R. 229, 242.

[32] To much the same effect, it has also been said that "the availability of a possibility which was previously unthinkable or not thought about transforms the psychology of the subjects as well as the legal possibilities. Their expectations and tolerances alter": A. Allott, *The Limits of Law* (1980), p. 183.

could satisfactorily be resolved by a court; and that to permit divorce only after a full judicial inquest into the marriage and its breakdown would be unnecessarily humiliating and distressing to the parties and also impracticable in the absence of a vast increase in expenditure of money and human resources. Hence the 1969 legislation[33] embodied a compromise: irretrievable breakdown was to be the sole ground for divorce, but such breakdown should be presumed—and, in effect, irrebutably presumed—solely by inference from proof of certain speci-fied facts. Of the five specified "facts", three were in fact akin to the old matrimonial offences of adultery, cruelty or desertion; but the fact that the parties had lived apart for two years (if the respondent con-sented to divorce) or five years (without any consent requirement) were also included in the "facts" on proof of which a divorce would be granted.

2.3. Effects of the 1969 Reforms

As the statistics set out above indicate, this legislation has undoubtedly been successful in facilitating the legal dissolution of marriage which has in fact broken down. Moreover, there is a wealth of evidence[34] to the effect that lawyers will invariably advise a spouse that there is no way in which an application for divorce sought by one party to a marriage can, in the long term, be resisted. But it seems much more questionable whether the 1969 legislation has been effective in achiev-ing the reformers' other objectives. Indeed, the Law Commission has recently[35] asserted that the law falls far short of those objectives. The fault based "facts" are those most frequently relied on; and it is said that the retention of the fault element in three of the 'facts" which must be alleged to enable courts to make a finding of irretrievable breakdown causes hostility. It is also said that the law is so complex that it is neither understandable nor respected.

2.4. Further Reform?

The Law Commission has accordingly made proposals for further reform of the law. Divorce will still, in theory be based on the fact that

---

[33] Field of Choice, para. 15.

[34] The 1969 legislation has subsequently been consolidated in the Matrimonial Causes Act 1973.

[35] See notably G. Davis and M. Murch, *Grounds for Divorce* (1988).

the marriage has irretrievably broken down; but it would be available as of right after a "period of transition" in which the parties would be given the time and encouragement to "reflect" and make the necessary arrangements for their future. It remains to be seen whether these proposals will attract the necessary support: on one view, they are unlikely to increase general understanding of, or respect for the law of divorce and merely create an elaborate legal machinery in an attempt to disguise the fact that divorce—like marriage, in the traditional doctrine of Western Christianity—has become a private matter in which the state's interest is confined to protecting the weak (notably the children and others financially dependent on one or both spouses).

2.5. The Legal Consequences of Divorce—Money and Property
(i) Extent of court's powers

Whatever may happen to the law governing the availability of divorce, there seems little pressure for any major change in the law governing the wide powers of the Court to make financial orders on or after granting a decree of divorce.[36] The extent of these powers is remarkable. In effect, English law puts at the disposition of the Court virtually all the assets of the two spouses. The court may make income orders unlimited in amount, or orders—again unlimited in amount—for the transfer or settlement of property; and these powers are in practice freely exercised: periodical payment orders for as much as £70,000 per annum have been made[37] as (apparently) have orders requiring capital payments in excess of 2 million pounds.[38]

(ii) Principles for exercise of discretion

In deciding on the exercise of its discretion to make orders under these wide powers, the Court is given certain guide lines considered below;

[36] See *Facing the Future. A Discussion Paper on the Ground for Divorce* (Law Com. No. 170, 1988).

[37] Legislation has been enacted which attempts to reinforce the financial obligations of spouses and parents to their partners and children: Maintenance Enforcement Act 1991. This Act does not involve any significant direct change of substance in legislative policy; but the provisions of the Child Support Act 1991 envisage a transformation of the law and practice governing maintenance for children. Parental liability is to be assessed by reference to a formula applied by an Administrative Agency, which will also enforce the liability. The courts will no longer have power to make orders against a parent for the support of his or her child.

[38] *S* v. *S note* [1987] 1 W.L.R. 382, C.A.

but perhaps the most remarkable feature of the law is that English law (unlike almost all other systems of law, including the law of Scotland) largely ignores the provenance of the assets which it has power to redistribute. It is immaterial, for example, that the property in question was inherited or that the assets represent compensation awarded to one of the parties in respect of that party's pain and suffering or disability (resulting, for example from a road accident or an industrial injury); it is immaterial, even, that the asset was acquired after the termination of the marriage.[39]

Not surprisingly, the question of the principles which should govern the exercise of such extensive powers has been controversial; and here (as so often) history is revealing. When the divorce law was reformed in 1969 there was widely voiced concern for the economic plight of married women who might, it seemed, be economically penalised in consequence of a divorce granted to a guilty and perhaps irresponsible husband. The legislation was therefore drafted to require the court "so to exercise its powers as to place the parties in the financial position they would have occupied had the marriage not broken down"; and the result was that substantial orders might be made even in cases where the marriage had been only of a short duration, and where no economic prejudice to the applicant could be shown.[40]

Not surprisingly, some divorced husbands regarded themselves as having been unfairly treated. Again, some women who had married divorced men, apparently felt that it was they who were effectively being required to contribute out of their resources—for example, from their earnings—for the upkeep of the husband's first family. In fact it could be demonstrated that the courts never made orders which would require the husband to have recourse to assets to which he was not personally entitled; but emotionally—and indeed in terms of economic reality, since the effect of an order would almost inevitably be to deplete the overall spending power of the re-constituted family—the "second wife's" arguments seemed to have some substance.

---

[39] The highest figure in a case officially reported in the Law Reports is £1,300,000: *Gojkovic* v. *Gojkovic* [1990] 1 F.L.R. 140, C.A.

[40] See *Schuller* v. *Schuller* [1990] 2 F.L.R. 193 where the fact that the wife had inherited an apartment (under the will of a man for whom she had worked as a house-keeper after the end of her marriage) was held relevant in weighing up the spouses' relative needs for housing, and to have been properly taken into account in deciding that the husband's needs were greater than hers.

2.6. The 1984 Changes

In response to such pressure, the Law Commission again investigated the law;[41] and some changes were made.[42] In particular, statute no longer imposes on the court the duty so to exercise its powers as to place the parties in the financial position in which they would have been if the marriage had not broken down. Emphasis is given to the need to regard the welfare of children as the first consideration; and there are various provisions which require the court to give weight to the desirabity of achieving a so called "clean-break" between the parties after divorce. As Lord Scarman has observed[43] "the law now encourages spouses to avoid bitterness after family breakdown and to settle their money and property problems. An object of the modern law is to encourage each to put the past behind them and begin a new life which is not overshadowed by the relationship which has broken down".

2.7. Needs—Housing

It is difficult to obtain precise data about the operation in practice of these provisions governing the allocation of financial resources after divorce; but research at Bristol and elsewhere supports the impression derived from the reported jurisprudence that the courts are primarily concerned with the "needs" of the parties. This term is not confined to the safeguarding of a minimal subsistence level of support, but takes into account the legitimate expectations of the parties;[44] although it is true that in many cases, the satisfaction of the parties' needs is achieved by making orders which will preserve a home for occupation by the wife and the children of whom she has the care, whilst putting the husband (who is more often in a financial position to raise further mortgage facilities to finance the purchase of another home) in a position to do so—often by awarding him a sum sufficient to meet the initial payment towards the cost of the home.

---

[41] See *Brett* v. *Brett* [1969] 1 W.L.R. 437; and generally the discussion in Cretney and Masson (1990), pp. 381–4. For a fuller account of the evolution of policy, see the Law Commission's Report on "The Financial Consequences of Divorce: The Basic Policy" (Law Com. No (103).

[42] See *The Financial Consequences of Divorce: The Basic Policy* (1980), Law Com. (103), and the subsequent Report—Law Com. No. 112.

[43] See generally Cretney and Masson (1990), pp. 383–4, and the sources referred to in Chap. 19 of that work.

[44] In *Minton* v. *Minton* [1979] A.C. 593, 608.

2.8. The Settlement: A New Lease of Life?

Those interested in the distinctive features of the English legal system may wish to note that the attainment of this objective of providing housing for divorced middle-income families has been achieved very largely by adapting the institution of the "settlement" of land—at one time associated with securing the devolution of substantial landed estates or protecting the interests of middle-class families against a matrimonial property regime unduly favourable to husbands. Today, however, the courts routinely employ settlement provisions of some subtlety in the divorce context. For example, it is not uncommon for the former family home to be settled on terms that both parties retain their beneficial interests, but that the house not be sold until the wife's death or re-marriage; or it may be settled on terms that she retain the house only during the infancy of children.

2.9. The Clean Break

This identification of housing as being the main "need" in most divorce cases also brings into focus another salient feature of the exercise of the court's discretion, that is to say the use of the so-called "clean break" solution in many cases. The essence of the clean break is that the financial links between the parties are in effect wholly severed at the time of the divorce, so that the parties may "go their separate ways without the running irritant of financial interdependence or dispute".[45] Thus, in effect, the emphasis of divorce settlements is shifted from continuing income provision to once-for-all capital transfer. If there is substantial capital the wife will not receive any ongoing periodical payments; and even if periodical payments are awarded, there is some statutory encouragement to make the award only for a limited term— sufficient to enable the parties to re-adjust to the situation resulting from the ending of the marriage.

2.10. Maximizing Welfare Benefits

In the case of the affluent, the utility of the clean break is self-evident: a division of capital may well represent adequate or even ample provision

[45] As for example in the case of *Gojkovic* v. *Gojkovic* [1990] 1 F.L.R. 140 where the sum of 1.3 million pounds was awarded to the wife in satisfaction of her needs—in that case to preserve the hotel business from which she derived her income.

for the future. But the clean break is also used in cases in which it is the availability of welfare benefits which makes such a solution realistic. In particular, it has already been said that orders are frequently made under which the matrimonial home is transferred outright to the wife; but in such a case the wife may be ordered to pay a sum of capital to the husband estimated to be sufficient to enable him to pay the deposit on a home for his own occupation. The effect of such an order will often be that the wife receives substantially more than half the family's assets; and the court accordingly compensates the husband by relieving him of any obligation to make periodical payments. The wife will then depend on welfare benefits for her income; and her entitlement to state-provided income support—rigorously means-tested though it is—is not affected by the fact that she has a substantial capital asset in the former matrimonial home.[46]

Moreover, the sum of money which she pays to the husband in satisfaction of his interest in the property will often be raised by mortgage; and the income support authorities will (in effect) pay—in addition to the scale rate of income support—the interest (both on the loan incurred to purchase the property in the first place and on the further loan contracted to "buy out" the husband).

In this way, the ingenuity of those negotiating divorce settlements—both lawyers acting for the parties and the judges who make the orders—has been successful in achieving greatly enhanced resources for the parties, albeit at some considerable cost to the state. Indirect corroboration of the hypothesis that the "clean break" is being used in this way to maximise welfare benefit entitlement may also perhaps be found in the fact that between 1981 and 1988 the proportion of lone parent income support recipients who were receiving periodical maintenance payments fell from 50% to 23%—a phenomenon entirely consistent with the practice of allocating the former family home described above.[47]

2.11. Conclusion on Financial Consequences of Divorce

This account leads to two conclusions. First, the divorce jurisdiction furnishes a remarkable example of the readiness of English law in recent

---

[46] *Tandy* v. *Tandy* (1986) as cited in [1988] 2 F.L.R. 189, 199.

[47] This particular asset is disregarded in deciding whether the wife has the modest level of capital which normally disqualifies from receipt of income support.

years to confer extraordinarily wide discretion on the court. In the words of Lord Denning,[48] the court

takes the rights and obligations of the parties altogether and puts the pieces into a mixed bag. Such pieces are the right to occupy the matrimonial home or have a share in it, the obligation to maintain the wife and children, and so forth. The court then takes out the pieces and hands them to the two parties—some to one party and some to the other—so that each can provide for a future with the pieces allotted to him or to her. The court hands them out without paying any too nice a regard to their legal or equitable rights but simply according to what is the fairest provision for the future, for mother and father and the children.

Secondly, it provides a striking example of the ability of the legal profession ingeniously, to adapt not only the statutory provisions so as better to protect the interests of clients, but also to do so in a way which will maximise assistance available from the state.

3. THE ROLE OF THE COURT IN DIVORCE: THE LIMIT OF PRIVATE ORDERING

So far, the emphasis of this paper has been on the traditional view that it is for the state to define the legal consequences of marriage; and that the parties cannot modify or change the rights and duties arising from the status of marriage.[49] This policy was vigorously pursued in relation to divorce and its consequences. Divorce was a matter of such high importance as to require careful judicial scrutiny; it was widely thought that to allow divorce by consent would destroy the institution of marriage and the sanctity of family life. In particular, until the 1969 reforms, "collusion" was a bar to the grant of decree of divorce; and for that and other reasons (contrary to the general principle of English civil litigation) the court's role was in principle inquisitorial: the court was required to enquire into the allegations which had been made; and it

---

[48] It should be noted that there have been recent judicial indications (*Ashley* v. *Blackman* [1988] Fam. 85 and *Delaney* v. *Delaney* (1990) *The Times*, 4 June) that the courts are prepared to accept that a man should not be expected to provide permanent—or even long-term—support for his former family after the irretrievable breakdown of a relationship. This policy seems to be inconsistent with the view (vigorously advocated by Ministers) that spouses should accept financial responsibilities for their families; and it is not surprising that the Child Support Act 1991 and the Social Security Act 1990 seek to reassert the primacy of the spouse's continuing obligation to support the family.

[49] *Hanlon* v. *The Law Society* [1981] A.C. 124, 146.

was not simply to accept the evidence which the parties chose to adduce but to go further in order to get at the truth.[50]

The 1969 legislation brought these issues into question since, in some ways, the whole thrust of the new law was contrary to the long-accepted philosophy. As already mentioned, collusion ceased to be a bar: agreement, far from being a bar to the grant of a divorce, was to be encouraged, and the parties were, if at all possible, to seek to resolve the issues which had arisen between them. But that new principle was not specifically embodied in the statute (which, indeed, still preserves the duty of the court to investigate the facts); and the jurisprudence in the early days of the legislation emphatically denied that it could have been the intention of the legislature to permit divorce by agreement.[51] In the result there is a degree of internal contradiction in the law; and it is becoming apparent that today the divorce process now reflects the ambiguity of English law about the role of the state in relation to marriage, its dissolution, and the consequences.

This ambiguity is particularly apparent at two stages: first, on the decision whether a divorce should be granted; and secondly in relation to the resolution of financial and other issues.

3.1. Administrative Divorce?

The grant of a divorce has now assumed the appearance of an administrative, rather than a judicial, process: in the great majority of cases, the parties complete forms and a divorce is duly granted[52] without there being any formal court hearing of the issue at all.

In respect of the grant of a divorce, therefore, the issue seems to have become very much one of an administrative ratification of the parties' private decision; but in relation to the consequences of divorce matters are much less straightforward. So far as concerns the resolution of financial issues between the parties, it has (as we have already seen) been asserted[53] that the law now encourages spouses to avoid bitterness after family breakdown and to settle their money and property problems. To this end a great deal of effort has been devoted to the provision of facilities for conciliation between the parties (that is to say, the

---

[50] *Adams* v. *Palmer* (1863) 51 Maine 480, 483, per Appleton CJ.

[51] A high ranking official (the Queen's Proctor) was appointed to carry out duties including questions of whether there had been collusion.

[52] *Santos* v. *Santos* [1972] Fam. 247.

[53] Under the so-called "special procedure": see Cretney and Masson (1990) Chap. 6.

helping of parties to resolve their disputes—the cynic might say that even more effort has been expended by intellectual analysis of the issues which arise in this context). But the law still embodies the principle that spouses, to the extent that their means permit, should provide for themselves and their children, and that the state has an interest not only in ensuring that private obligations should not effectively be passed onto the tax-payer but also in ensuring that spouses should not act under pressure or in ignorance.

3.2. Financial Issues

In the case of the resolution of financial problems the outcome of these conflicting pressures is comparatively clear. On the one hand, it is not possible for parties to make a private agreement restricting their right to apply to a court for financial relief[54] but on the other hand if the court has been furnished with the information which is requisite to enable it to discharge its statutory obligations it may make an order by consent of the parties, without any hearing and without any formal investigation. It is true that the rules now contain provisions about the information which is to be given to the court by the parties; but the extent to which the court can do more than act as a "rubber-stamp" in considering the proposals which the parties make is not at all clear. It is certainly true that a high proportion of the orders regulating the financial consequences of divorce are made effectively by consent of the parties with only minimal supervision by the court; and, indeed, if it were not so, the legal system would long since have been swamped by the number of cases requiring adjudication. The courts have, of course, had to grapple with problems which have arisen when one of the parties has subsequently repented of his or her agreement; but in statistical terms such cases do not appear to be numerous. In any event, it does seem to be possible to state principles determining the basis upon which the court will interfere where it is alleged either that there has been a non disclosure or—in practice a much more difficult issue—whether the court should interfere if there has been a change of circumstances such that the one party would manifestly not have entered into the agreement had he or she been able to foresee what was to happen.[55]

---

[54] Lord Scarman, *Minton* v. *Minton* [1979] A.C. 593.
[55] Matrimonial Causes Act 1973, section 34(1).

3.3. Children

In contrast, the role of the courts has (until recently) been much more avowedly interventionist in relation to the making of post-divorce arrangements for the upbringing of children. It was recognised that the traditional procedures of the courts did not in practice enable them to look behind the evidence which the parties chose to put forward; and for that reason a procedure was developed[56] intended to ensure that the parents gave full consideration to the question of their children's future welfare, and that the courts could exercise an effective scrutiny in order to protect the welfare of children involved in divorce. Statute accordingly provided[57] that no final decree of divorce could be made unless and until the court had (after a hearing conducted by a judge) declared itself satisfied that the arrangements made for the welfare of children were satisfactory or (at least) the best that could be devised in the circumstances.

In practice, the hearing of these cases (at so called children's appointments) was often extremely unsatisfactory[58] in achieving these objectives; and—more conceptually—it has been pointed out that the court's duty in children's appointment was not really adjudicative and indeed that it smacked of paternalism. Accordingly, the Children Act 1989 effectively abolishes the children's appointment system. The court is simply to consider whether it should exercise its *powers to make orders* relating to the upbringing of those children (as distinct from expressing an abstract opinion on whether or not the arrangements made by the parents for the children's upbringing are satisfactory). The new legislation seems, in this way, to re-assert the principle that the role of the legal system is a limited one; and that adjudicative and welfare functions should not become confused.[59]

---

[56] A striking example of the problems which may arise is to be found in the case of *Barder* v. *Barder (Caluori intervening)* [1988] A.C. 20, where the husband agreed to an order involving outright transfer of the family home to the wife in order to provide a secure home for her and the two children of the marriage. Shortly afterwards, she killed the two children and committed suicide. Was the husband still bound by the agreement (which would in the circumstances have led to the house being transferred to the wife's mother)? The House of Lords held that where a change in the circumstances occurring shortly after the agreement destroyed its underlying fundamental assumption the agreement should not be enforced.

[57] Following recommendations made by the Royal Commission on Marriage and Divorce (Cmd. 9678) 1956.

[58] Matrimonial Causes Act 1973, s. 41.

[59] See Davis, MacLeod and Murch (1983) 46 *M.L.R.* 121.

3.4. Conclusion on Private Ordering

It will have become apparent that English law, on the extent to which
private ordering should be encouraged, still reflects an uncertainty of
policy. On the one hand, to confer the responsibility for decision-taking
on the individual adults concerned is perceived as having two distinct
kinds of advantage: it may minimise unnecessary and personally damaging hostility often arising in the course of divorce litigation; and
secondly—consistent with the philosophy of the Thatcher government[60]—it emphasises that the citizen should not look to the state and
its organs to relieve him or her of what are essentially personal responsibilities. On the other hand, the need to avoid adults putting their own
interests ahead of the welfare of their children, and the need (again,
consistent with the Thatcher government's repeatedly declared policy)
to ensure so far as possible that financial obligations are not transferred
to the state[61] would seem to require some considerable element of investigation into the terms, and restriction on the extent, of private bargains
in these sensitive areas.[62]

It seems likely that a strong element of compromise between these
irreconcilable objectives will continue to be found in English family
law, although it may be thought that in recent years there has been a
shift of emphasis in favour of private bargaining.

4. CHILDREN: CAPACITY AND AUTHORITY

Whatever may be the position about the consequences of the legal
status created by marriage, the law about the legal status of children
would seem at first to be unambiguous: in the terms of legal terminology a child lacks legal capacity. It is true he or she may (like a cat or
dog) enjoy the protection afforded by the criminal law; but the standard
text states the general rule comprehensively and starkly: an infant[63] is

---

[60] See S. M. Cretney "Defining the Limits of State Intervention: the Child and the
Courts: *in* D. Freestone (ed.), *Children and the Law, Essays in Honour of Professor H.K.
Bevan* (Hull, 1990).

[61] See Douglas "Family Law under the Thatcher Government" (1990) 17 *Journal of
Law & Society* 411.

[62] It cannot be said that the present practice effectively reflects this philosophy particularly in respect of arrangements often made about the family home: see p. 41, above.

[63] For a discussion of the impact of the Children Act 1989 in this context, see S.M.
Cretney, "Privatizing the Family. The case of the Children Act 1989" [1989] *Denning,
L.J.* 115; and see also A. Bainham, "The Privatisation of the Public Interest in Children"
(1990) 53 *M.L.R.* 206.

under a general incapacity to exercise the rights of citizenship or perform civil duties, or to hold public or private offices or perform the
duties incidental to them.[64] An infant may not in person assert his rights
in a court of law as plaintiff or applicant[65] nor may an infant defend,
counterclaim, or intervene in any proceedings except by a guardian.[66]

This general principle was carried into the law of domestic relations:
the child's parent—and until 1973 this meant the father to the exclusion
of the mother[67]—was, unless and until the court intervened, entitled to
exercise any of the bundle[68] of rights included within the concept of
legal custody. These rights included the right to have physical possession of the child, the right to the child's domestic services, and the right
to determine the surname by which the child should be known, the right
to control the child's education, to choose the child's religion, to inflict
moderate and reasonable corporal punishment and otherwise to discipline the child, to consent to medical treatment,[69] to withhold consent
from a proposed marriage, to administer the child's property, as well as
the right—already referred to—to act for the child in legal proceedings.[70]

In 1991 it can be said that these traditional doctrines have now been
almost (but not entirely) supplanted. First it had long been a principle
that the court would in deciding any issue relating to the custody or
upbringing of a child regard the child's welfare as the first and paramount consideration; and—at least after the emphatic assertion that this
principle applied even in disputes between an "unimpeachable" parent
and a third party with no genetic link with the child at all[71]—that the
only remaining relevance of the concept of parental authority was in
those cases in which the court had not been involved.[72]

---

[64] Terminology in this area is confused and reflects changing legislative fashions:
"infant" is the conventional term for a person under the legal age of majority, but the
Family Law Reform Act 1969 preferred to use the word "minor". Recently fashion has
veered towards use of the word "child": see Children Act 1989, s. 105(1).

[65] Halsbury's Laws of England, 4th Ed., Vol. 24, para. 492.

[66] *Ibid.*, para. 895:1.   [67] *Ibid.*, para. 896:3.

[68] Guardianship Act 1973 section 1(1).

[69] *Hewer* v. *Bryant* [1970] 1 Q.B. 357.

[70] Including (it then seemed) the right to give an effective consent to the sterilisation
of an eleven year old handicapped girl: *re D (A Minor) (Wardship: Sterilisation)* [1976]
Fam. 185. But see now *re B (A Minor) (Wardship: Sterilisation)* [1988] A.C. 199 where
the opinion is expressed—albeit by only one member of the House of Lords—that irreversible sterilisation of a female incapable of giving a valid consent herself should only
be carried out on the authority of a court order.

[71] See further S. M. Cretney, *Principles of Family Law* (4th ed. 1984), pp. 300–8.

[72] *J.* v. *C.* [1970] A.C. 668 (where the House of Lords applied the principle to deny
unimpeachable parents the right to remove a child from the care of those who had
brought him up for many years).

In cases in which outsiders had come to be concerned about an actual
or intended exercise of parental authority it would be comparatively
easy for the courts' jurisdiction to be invoked, because English civil
procedure permitted any person with a legitimate interest—an expression which was not defined, and was certainly not restrictively interpreted—to invoke legal proceedings by making a child a ward of court.
In the result, parental authority was rarely the determining factor if the
facts became known outside the immediate family circle, and the issue
was such as to make it appropriate to litigation. The position is well
illustrated by the remarkable case of *re D (A Minor) (Wardship: Sterilisation)*[73] where the mother of an eleven year old handicapped girl
had—it was then thought—authority to give consent to the child being
sterilised. Accordingly, if the operation[74] had been carried out neither
the daughter nor anyone else would have had any effective legal redress.[75] But the girl was made a ward of court by a concerned individual, and the court held that her welfare would not be served by such
an irreversible operation being carried out.

Second, a fundamental change in the whole concept of parental authority in English law has been effected by the decision of the House
of Lords in the case of *Gillick* v. *West Norfolk and Wisbech Area Health
Authority.*[76] A mother asked the court to declare unlawful and wrong
Government advice that young people could in some circumstances be
given contraceptive advice and treatment without the knowledge and
consent of the parent; and the mother asserted that the giving of such
advice adversely affected her right as the child's parent. The House of
Lords, holding by a bare majority that her application should have been
dismissed, made a radical reappraisal of the whole notion of parental
authority; but it has to be admitted that not all the implications of the
decision can confidently be predicted.

It is clear that the House of Lords rejected the view that a child
remained under parental control until he or she had attained a fixed or
specified age. Parental rights (so it was said) exist "only so long as they
are needed for the protection of the person and property of the child"[77]

---

[73] For a full explanation of the continuing significance of parental authority, see the
Law Commission's Report on *Illegitimacy* (1982) Law Com. No. 118, paras. 4.19–22
(reproduced in Cretney; *Principles of Family Law* (4th ed., 1984), pp. 294–5).

[74] [1976] Fam. 185.

[75] Which had been recommended by a consultant paediatrician and by a consultant
gynaecologist.

[76] But see now *re B (A Minor) (Wardship: Sterilisation)*, [1988] A.C. 199.

[77] [1986] A.C. 112.

and accordingly parental authority must yield to the child's right to make decisions whenever the child has attained a sufficient understanding and intelligence to be capable of forming a view on the matter requiring decision. The question whether a child does in fact have sufficient understanding and intelligence depends on the complexity of the issues involved and on the child's emotional and intellectual maturity.

In relation to contraception, the House of Lords asserted that a high level of maturity and understanding was to be required—so high, indeed, that it could be doubted whether many adults would be able to satisfy the requirements of intellectual understanding and emotional maturity which the Law Lords considered necessary to reach a decision on the moral, ethical and biological issues involved. Be that as it may, it can readily be seen that the approach adopted by the House of Lords may make it exceedingly difficult to state with confidence whether a child has in fact authority to carry out any particular transaction or whether the parent still has authority on the child's behalf; and it would seem to follow that in many cases the decision could only safely be made retrospectively by a court. Of course, it is equally clear that there will be many cases in which a child will have the intellectual and emotional maturity to reach simple decisions (for example, whether to ride a bicycle—even in traffic conditions which in England and Wales are always dangerous) whilst still lacking the capacity to take other decisions (for example, about the choice of education).

There are obvious difficulties in this approach. What, for example, is to be the position of a third party? Suppose that parents purport to forbid a child from accepting employment, or from living away from the parental home? It may in practice be that this aspect of the difficulty will not be great, since in many cases it will be impossible to show that the parent has suffered any quantifiable loss by reason of the third party acting inconsistently with the parent's position; and indeed the courts have recently held[78] that no interference with the parental right to take care of a child could lead to a cause of action in damages.

A second—and conceptually much greater—difficulty is that the decision creates anomalies in the law: different rules apply to issues

---

[78] *Per* Lord Scarman [1986] A.C. 112, 184. But note that in a decision reported as this paper goes to press—the suggestion has been that a parent may retain a right to over-ride a mature minor's refusal to submit to medical treatment: see *Re R (A Minor) (Wardship: Medical Treatment)* [1991] 4 All E.R. 177, CA *per* Lord Donaldson of Lymington, M.R. All members of the Court of Appeal accepted that the High Court could, in the exercise of its wardship jurisdiction, over-ride the refusal of a mature minor to accept treatment.

where legislation deals expressly with questions of capacity from those which apply to cases where answers have to be found in the uncodified common law. For example, as recently as 1987 Parliament enacted legislation[79] which denied a "minor" any general contractual capacity; whilst other statutes deny to an "infant" of seventeen the right (enjoyed by any capable adult) to dispose of property—however small in value— on death.[80] Even the procedural rules which prohibit a child from lit-igating directly remain unaltered: and there is more than something of a paradox in a body of law which, on the one hand, asserts in case-law that children have rights, whilst on the other retains a procedural code which effectively denies them the means whereby those rights may be asserted in a court of law.

The mis-match between the judicially-created child's right-based *Gillick* doctrine on the one hand and much of English statute law on the other is even more striking when the position is considered from a parent's perspective. For example, a parent is guilty of a criminal of-fence if his mature but school-age child fails to attend school regu-larly[81] but such a rule only makes sense if a parent has the legal right (irrespective of the child's wishes) to dictate how and where the child is to spend his time. As a result of *Gillick* a parent may commit a civil wrong if he denies the mature fifteen year old the right to absent him-self from school, yet the parent will commit a criminal offence if he fails to enforce the child's attendance. It might, perhaps, be thought that this is an anachronism, stemming from the fact that the truanting legislation is now almost half-a-century old and was enacted at a time when concepts of authority and obedience were still the basis of much of the community's activities.

But it is to be noted that even recent legislation[82] confers on the parent (and not the child) the legal right to opt out of the religious education which English law compels a school to provide, and that the same recent—and widely discussed—statute permits the parent (rather than the child) to dictate that a child be withdrawn from the religious education provided by the school in favour of some other form of religious education. It would thus appear that the *Gillick* decision has

---

[79] *F.* v. *Wirral Metropolitan Borough Council and another* [1991] 2 All E.R. 648, C.A.

[80] Minors' Contracts Act, 1987.

[81] Only in exceptional circumstances may an infant make a valid will: Wills Act 1837, section 7.

[82] Education Act 1944, section 36.

created a major conceptual problem; but, perhaps unsurprisingly, it is not one which the Government or its advisers have shown any anxiety to resolve.[83]

4.1. Disputes between Adults

In practical terms, however, the problem may not be so much as to whether it is the parent or child who has legal authority, but rather which of several adults, each with some claim to be the child's "parent", is endowed with the relevant legal authority. Where the child's mother and father disagree, for example, which of them is to be entitled to determine issues affecting the child's upbringing?

For many years, English law on this subject was (as already stated) disarmingly simple. The child's father was the legal parent and thus had the relevant authority.[84] Only in 1973 did legislation concede that both parents of a *legitimate* child were equally entitled to exercise parental authority over the child; and, in a rule in theory potentially inconvenient, it is provided that each parent may act without consultation unless the other has "signified disapproval". In the case of an *illegitimate* child, however, the mother has parental authority exclusively; and the child's father has no legal rights unless such rights are conferred upon him by court order. However, in a further shift towards accepting private agreement as the determining factor in family matters, the Children Act 1989 contains provisions whereby the father and mother will be able to agree on the allocation of parental authority between them. If the parents disagree, they may refer a specific issue to the court; and either of them may seek to have the care of the child exclusively. Finally, it should be noted that if a parent seeks a divorce, the law still embodies an assumption that parental agreement is insufficient; the court must consider whether to exercise any of the powers relating to the child's upbringing which it has under the Children Act 1989.

---

[83] Education Reform Act 1988, section 9(2).

[84] The Children Act 1989—whilst expressly empowering mature minors to refuse compulsory medical examination or assessment in certain circumstances—substantially ignores the conceptual problem discussed in the text. Indeed, "parental responsibility" is defined in pre-*Gillick* terms by reference to a parent's "rights, duties, powers, responsibilities and authority": Section 3. Again, although the Act allows a child to apply for leave to seek orders about its upbringing, it is not clear whether such an application has to be pursued through the agency of an adult "next friend".

4.2. Who is the Child's Parent?

This discussion assumes that parentage is a well-understood concept; and it is only recently that English law has had to take account of the scientific developments now commonly subsumed under the terminology of: "human assisted reproduction" in determining parentage.

In the past, the law was able to adopt unquestioningly the simple assumption that—save in the case of adoption—a child's parents[85] were his genetic parents. For many years, doubts about the correct identification of genetic parentage were usually resolved in law—if not in the minds of those concerned—by the application of certain *presumptions* about legal parentage. In particular, English law had (and indeed retains) a presumption of legitimacy—embodying inevitably a presumption of parentage—under which there is a rebuttable presumption that a child born to a married woman is the legitimate child of her husband.[86] Moreover, although English law does not have any counterpart to the comprehensive systems regulating civil status of the kinds familiar in many countries of continental Europe, the system of birth registration was allowed to create a presumption of parentage: in particular, the entry of a man's name[87] as the father of a child was prima facie evidence that the man named was the child's father.

In respect of motherhood, it seemed unnecessary even to ask questions: as recently as 1977, Lord Simon of Glaisdale could assert[88] that motherhood was "proved demonstrably by parturition".

Developments in technique of human assisted reproduction—and particularly the development of artificial insemination as a treatment for infertility—inevitably led to fresh consideration being given to the law on this subject. The first reform, made on the recommendation of the Law Commission[89] was intended as a short term and provisional way of dealing with the problems which had arisen in the significant number

---

[85] This proportion is strikingly illustrated by the case of *re Agar-Ellis* (1883) 24 Ch.D. 317 where the separated parents of a sixteen year old girl could not agree on her religious upbringing. The father was granted an injunction by the court restraining the wife from taking the girl to Roman Catholic services; and the court rejected a request made by the girl herself that she be allowed to spend her holiday with her mother in preference to being cared for by third parties and moved about from one lodging to another under the father's arrangements.

[86] See the assumptions in the Family Law Reform Act 1969 relating to blood testing, in the Law Commission's Working Paper 74 on *Illegitimacy*, Part X; and *re C (A Minor) (Wardship: surrogacy)* [1985] F.L.R. 846.

[87] *The Banbury Peerage* (1811) 1 Sim. & St. 153.

[88] Under the Births and Deaths Registration Act 1953, s. 34.

[89] *The Ampthill Peerage* [1977] A.C. 547, 577.

of conceptions—some 1,700 each year, it appears—resulting from artificial insemination by a donor.

The Family Law Reform Act 1987 provided[90] that where a child is born as a result of the artificial insemination by a donor of a woman who was at the time of the insemination a party to a marriage, then the child should be treated in law as the child of the parties to the marriage, and not as the child of any person other than the parties to the marriage unless it is *proved* that the other party to the marriage did not consent to the insemination.

This provision could scarcely be advanced as an example of perfect law making;[91] but the Committee on Human Assisted Reproduction,[92] after lengthy deliberation proposed that the principle adopted in the 1987 legislation should be generalised, with one exception. The exceptional case was that the Committee thought the carrying woman rather than the egg donor should be treated as the child's mother[93] and that similar provisions should apply to cases of embryo transfer. These recommendations form the basis of the Human Fertilisation and Embryology Act 1990, which also introduces a provision—somewhat inelegant, it must be admitted—to deal with the problem of attribution of parentage in cases of surrogate parenting.

4.3. The Human Fertilisation and Embryology Act 1990

The Human Fertilisation and Embryology Act 1990 introduced rules defining legal parentage; and the combined effect of the common law and the legislation can be summarised as follows:

---

[90] See report on *Illegitimacy*, Law Com. No. 118, part XII.

[91] Section 27.

[92] First of all, it was limited in scope: it was applicable only to the child born as a result of artificial insemination by a donor, and is irrelevant to other methods of assisted reproduction. Secondly, the provision was only applicable to a child born to a married couple — and this restriction might be thought somewhat paradoxical given that it was enacted in the context of legislation designed to minimise the distinctions between the legitimate and illegitimate. Thirdly, the provision only applied where a child was born as a result of *artificial* insemination: it had no application to the cases in which a woman has, with her husband's consent, been impregnated as a result of intercourse with a third party in order to bear a child to be brought up by herself and her husband. Finally, the provision produced apparently strange results in some cases of surrogate parenting. It is by no means uncommon for the surrogate mother's husband to agree to her being artificially inseminated, and in such a case the effect of the statutory provision is that the surrogate mother's husband has to be treated as the legal father of the child. This produces the surprising result that it is his agreement which is required if (for example) the commissioning parents seek to adopt the child in order to regularise the legal position.

[93] The Warnock Report [Cmnd. 9314, 1984].

(i) The woman who bears a child will, at the child's birth, always be regarded as the legal mother.[94]

(ii) In principle, the father of a child is the person who provides the sperm which leads to conception. However, this rule is subject to a number of exceptions:—

    (a) The husband of a woman who is artificially inseminated is treated as the father of the child, unless it is proved that he did not consent to the treatment.[95]

    (b) Where a woman has been artificially inseminated in the course of treatment provided for her and a man under the licensing procedure established by the 1990 Act, then that man is treated as the child's father.[96]

    It should also be mentioned that there are special rules applicable to the situation in which conception has resulted from the use of a man's sperm, or of an embryo created from it, after the man's death.[97]

In many cases, the application of exceptions (a) and (b) above will mean that a sperm donor is not treated as the child's father; but the Act, in an attempt to protect donors from possible legal responsibility as father of a child goes further. It is provided that a man who donates sperm for the purposes of "treatment services" provided under the 1990 Act—in effect, at an officially licensed centre, which is bound to follow certain prescribed procedures—is not to be treated as the child's father. But the effect of this provision is to create the possibility—admittedly somewhat remote—that a child will be legally fatherless.

Suppose, for example, that sperm is donated for treatment services in accordance with the provisions of the Act; and that the donor is accordingly not to be treated as the father. In the usual case, the mother's husband (or partner) will be treated as the father.[98] But there could be circumstances in which those provisions would not apply—the husband might, for example, prove that he did not consent to the treatment carried out on his wife, and if he does so, he is not to be treated as the child's father.

The rules so far set out could give rise to difficulties in cases of surrogate parenting, as was dramatically illustrated by a case which came to the courts while the Human Fertilisation and Embryology Bill was being debated:—

[94] Recommendations 54 and 55.   [95] HF&EA 1990, 27(1).
[96] HF&EA 1990, 28(2).   [97] HF&EA 1990, 28(3).
[98] HF&EA 1990, s. 28(6)(b).

In *re W (Minors) (Surrogacy)*[99] a married couple were anxious to have children, but the wife had no womb. She provided eggs which were removed, and fertilised *in vitro* with sperm provided by her husband. The resultant embryo was implanted in a woman ("the surrogate") who agreed that she would hand the child—in fact twins were born—to the commissioning couple; and she did so. The effect of the rules so far set out would have been as follows: first the surrogate would be treated in law as the mother, notwithstanding the fact that she had not provided any of the genetic material which had resulted in the children's conception, that she had never acted as the children's parent, and did not wish to do so; and secondly, the surrogate's husband would, (assuming that he had agreed to the procedure) be treated as the children's father notwithstanding the fact that he had had nothing whatsoever to do with the children's conception or with caring for them.

Adoption could have been used to make genetic and social parenting congruent with the legal parentage; but, perhaps not surprisingly, the commissioning parents considered that to be inappropriate. The legislation was therefore hurriedly amended whilst it was passing through Parliament to incorporate a provision[100] enabling a married couple who have provided the genetic material which has led to a child's conception to apply for a court order—a so called parental order—which will provide for the child to be treated in law as their child. Not surprisingly, the legislation appears to be defective in a number of respects.

5. THE LIMITS OF FAMILY AUTONOMY

The question of defining the circumstances in which an outsider is entitled to intervene and question decisions taken by those who by law have parental authority over a child is a difficult one in all legal systems. Understanding of the position in English law is made all the more difficult because of the existence of the so called wardship jurisdiction and it is necessary, first, to sketch in the main features of that jurisdiction before turning to the statutory provisions.

5.1. Wardship—the Court as the Child's Parent

Wardship originated in the special duty of the Crown to protect minors (and other persons under legal incapacity) against injury of any kind.[101]

---

[99] See HF&EA 1990, ss. 28(2), (3), above.
[100] [1991] Fam. Law 180.   [101] S. 30.

As already noted, any person could invoke this jurisdiction by issuing a summons: thereafter, no important step in the child's life could, so long as the wardship continued, be taken without the approval of the Court; and in deciding any question relating to the ward's care and upbringing the Court would apply the principle that the ward's welfare was the paramount consideration.

This jurisdiction has, for a number of reasons, been extensively used in recent years. The lack of any restrictive rules about standing has meant that it may be invoked (often for the good[102]) by persons whose interest in the child does not derive from any legally recognised relationship; but the absence of rules about standing inevitably led to the possibility of abuse.[103]

Secondly, the fact that all important issues affecting a ward must be referred to the court means that it is possible to have a careful and dispassionate analysis of the most complicated and ethically troubling problems—for example, the questions whether an abortion should be carried out on a ward contrary to the wishes of her parents[104] and whether a handicapped baby should be allowed to live or die.[105] But, once again, although wardship has proved to be of practical value in many cases it could well be argued that the absence of any guiding principles (beyond the assertion of the paramountcy of the child's interests) and in particular the absence of any special protection for the voice of the child could lead to unsatisfactory results and indeed to results which could well be inconsistent with the United Kingdom's obligations under the European Convention on Human Rights. Thus in *re SW (A Minor) (Wardship: jurisdiction)*[106] a seventeen year old girl

---

[102] *Re X (A Minor) (Wardship: jurisdiction)* [1975] Fam. 47, 52.

[103] See e.g. *re D (A Minor) (Wardship: Sterilisation)* [1976] Fam. 185, discussed at p. 51 above.

[104] As in the celebrated case of *re Dunhill* (1967) 111 S.J. 113 where a nightclub owner made his hostesses wards of court in a successful attempt to publicise his activities. (This particular possibility for abuse has now been dealt with—as is so often done in English law—by procedural rules: the rules now require an applicant to state his relationship to the minor, and the proceedings will be dismissed if they are considered to be an abuse of process).

[105] See *re P (A Minor)* [1986] 1 F.L.R. 272.

[106] See *re B (A Minor) (Wardship: medical treatment)* [1981] 1 W.L.R. 1421—severely handicapped baby should be subjected to surgery to prolong her life, notwithstanding parental desire to allow nature to take its course; and *re C (A Minor) (Wardship: medical treatment)* [1989] 3 W.L.R. 240 (where the court authorised a course of treatment which would allow an incurably handicapped child to die with dignity).

had allegedly stolen jewellery from her mother; and she had run away
from home on a number of occasions "after some of which she returned
very much the worse for drink and showing clear signs of having
indulged in sexual intercourse". She had also had her hair shaved, and
been tattooed. The court committed her to the care and control of a
Local Authority on the basis that her welfare so required.

Moreover, the fact that in wardship the court would determine the
issue of the child's welfare afresh led to many parents, whose children
had been committed under statutory procedures to the care of Local
Authorities, seeking to have the Local Authority's decisions investigated
(for example in relation to such matters as parental access to the child)
by warding the child. The outcome of a flood of such cases was a series
of judicial decisions preventing wardship being invoked where legislation had entrusted decisions relating to a child to a Local Authority.[107]

However, the converse was not true: local authorities who failed to
establish the necessary statutory ground justifying the removal of a
child from the family were still able to invoke wardship on the basis
that the child's welfare required intervention.[108]

The inequity of such a situation was manifest; and an attempt has
been made to deal with it by including provisions in the Children Act
1989[109] which effectively prevent Local Authorities from invoking the
wardship jurisdiction save with leave of the Court (which may only be
granted in special circumstances). However, the Children Act does not
affect the right of individuals to bring wardship proceedings; and the
future of the jurisdiction is therefore very much a matter for speculation.
Wardship can be invoked speedily, and has immediate effect; and for
those reasons it may well remain attractive to lawyers advising clients.

5.2. Statutory Procedures—the Children Act 1989

Until the enactment of the Children Act 1989, the statute law governing
relationships between the child, the family and the state were complex
and incoherent. The 1989 Act introduced an orderly scheme, most of
which is based on coherent[110] principles.

---

[107] [1986] 1 F.L.R. 24.
[108] See notably *A* v. *Liverpool City Council* [1982] A.C 263; *re W (A Minor) (Wardship: Jurisdiction)* [1985] A.C. 791.
[109] Re *D (A Minor) (Justices' Decision: Review)* [1977] Fam. 158.
[110] Children Act 1989, s. 100(3), (4).

5.3. Standing

The Act deals with the difficult question of juristic philosophy involved
in determining who is to be entitled to bring issues to the court for
judicial decision by drawing a distinction. First, certain persons—any
parent (whether the child be legitimate or illegitimate) or guardian, and
any person who already has an order (a "residence" order) permitting
the child to live with him or her[111]—are entitled as of right to apply to
the court for orders under the Act. A second group—the person with
whom the child has lived for at least three years, for example—is
entitled to seek orders that the child live with the applicant, or that the
applicant should have contact with the child.[112] Finally, any other person—including the child—may apply for leave to seek an order;[113] and
in deciding whether or not to grant such leave the court is directed to
have particular regard to matters which include the applicant's connection with the child, and any risk there might be of the proposed application disrupting the child's life to such an extent that he would
be harmed by it.[114] (Where the applicant is the child himself, the court
may only grant leave if it is satisfied that the child has sufficient understanding to make the proposed application). This attempt[115] to resolve
the difficult question of standing is undoubtedly ingenious; and it can
be assumed that certain persons (for example grandparents) would readily
be granted leave to apply for orders, whereas the officious bystander is
likely to encounter difficulties. However, there are obvious dangers that
the mere making of an application will be disruptive, and it is not clear
how well the courts will be able to resolve such applications without
carrying out a full investigation into the matter such as would be expected in the case of a substantive hearing.

5.4. When can the State Intervene?

The Children Act restricts the right of the State to intervene in family
life. First, as already mentioned, Local Authorities no longer have the

---

[111] The Government has published an admirably lucid guide to the main principles of
the legislation: *An Introduction to the Children Act 1989* (1989). There are numerous
other texts, eg Bainham, *Children, The New Law* (1990); White, Carr and Lowe, *A Guide
to the Children Act 1989* (1990).

[112] Children Act 1989, section 10(4).

[113] i.e. Residence or contact orders: section 10.   [114] Section 10(1)(A)(ii).

[115] Section 10(9). Certain persons are debarred from making applications (section
9(3)) in order to ensure that where a child has been placed in the care of the Local
Authority the Authority's decisions are, in principle, to be determinative.

unfettered power (which they previously enjoyed and exercised) to make a child a ward of court.[116] Secondly, Local Authorities are not permitted to apply for residence or contact orders: they cannot apply for an order that the child be required to live in a particular place, or that particular persons (such as their own officials) should have contact with the child.[117] These restrictions stem from the fundamental principle of the new legislation that if a Legal Authority wishes to intervene in family autonomy it must seek a care or supervision order under the provisions of the Act; and the court may not grant such an order, even if to do so would be consistent with the child's welfare, unless certain threshold conditions are satisfied.

What are the threshold conditions? It is provided that the court may not make care or supervision orders in favour of a Local Authority unless it is satisfied first that the child concerned is suffering or is likely to suffer significant harm; and secondly that the harm or likelihood of harm is attributable to what can broadly be described as inadequate parenting.

5.5. Orders which the Court can Make

One of the major achievements of the Children Act 1989 is that it goes some considerable way towards demystifying the terminology of court orders. For example, instead of conferring power to make orders for "custody"—a term whose meaning was extremely obscure[118] the Act empowers the court to make a residence order (that is to say an order settling the arrangements to be made as to the person or persons with whom a child is to live). Instead of using the term "access", the court is empowered to make a contact order (that is, an order requiring the person with whom a child lives to allow the child to visit or stay with the person named in the order or for that person and the child otherwise to have contact with each other.[119] The court may also make a specific issue order (that is to say an order giving directions for the purpose of determining a specific question—for example whether a girl's pregnancy

---

[116] It should be said that the court may also make orders under the Children Act whenever proceedings which are (broadly) defined as "family proceedings" (s. 8(3), (4)] have been properly constituted. Thus, to take the most obvious example, the court may deal with the question of the child's residence arrangements in the parent's divorce suit.

[117] Section 100(3). There are exceptional circumstances in which the court may permit a Local Authority to invoke the exercise of its inherent jurisdiction: *ibid.*

[118] Section 9(2).

[119] See Cretney: *Principles of Family Law* (4th ed., 1984), pp. 313–15.

should be terminated—which has arisen or which may arise). Effectively, therefore, it can be said that the scheme of orders under the Act is that the orders will have to spell out what is intended in plain English; and that the orders will mean what they say (and in principle, no more than they say).

5.6. Principles to be Applied by the Court

The Act embodies the general principle that where a court determines any question with respect to the child's upbringing the child's welfare shall be the court's paramount consideration. This does not differ from the law as it was before the enactment of the Children Act. What is different is that the court is specially directed to consider the impact of making an order at all: it is provided that where a court is considering whether or not to make an order, *it shall not make the order* unless it considers that doing so would be *better* for the child than making no order at all. This is a principle which may have the most profound impact on the relationship between the courts and the family; but it is, perhaps, of particular significance in the context of applications for care orders by Local Authorities.

We have already seen that the court cannot make an order effectively enabling the State to interfere in parental arrangements for the upbringing of children merely because the court considers that the State could make a better job of it than can the parents. In the case of applications by a private individual it does suffice that the child's welfare would be best served by intervention taking the effect of a court order; but where a Local Authority seeks a care order—an order giving it the power effectively to control the child's upbringing—it must first satisfy the threshold criteria set out above. Doing so is a *necessary* precondition for intervention, but it is not a *sufficient* condition. After satisfying itself that the "threshold" criteria has been satisfied the court *must* ask whether making an order will be better for the child's welfare than making no order at all. In doing so, it must consider all relevant factors affecting the child's welfare, including certain matters specifically referred to in the Act. It is certainly possible that having heard all the evidence about the effect of entrusting the care of a particular child to the Local Authority the court may decide that it would be better not to make an order; and the court will frequently have to consider very carefully whether the Local Authority could not achieve more for the child by acting in voluntary partnership with the child's parents rather than under the implied coercion of a court order.

The Children Act thus significantly redefines the boundaries between the state and family privacy; and may well tip the balance away from compulsory intervention in a significant number of cases.

6. CONCLUSION

This brief sketch of recent trends in English family law has demonstrated that the subject—like the society to which it applies—is in a state of transition. The lawyer's technical machinery for dealing with cases involving children has certainly been greatly improved by the enactment of the Children Act 1989; but other parts of family law remain full of ambiguity and inconsistency.

3

Law Reform in England and Wales

by the Rt. Hon. the Lord Mackay of Clashfern, the Lord High Chancellor*

I expect you will have heard or read something about the various initiatives which are being taken forward in my Department to reform the
court service and the legal system generally in England and Wales. I
will mention, first, the Legal Aid Act, which was passed last year. This
enabled me to set up a new, independent Legal Aid Board to administer
the provision of financial assistance to people who are unable to pay for
legal advice and representation privately. The Board began operation
on 1 April, and it has now taken over from the Law Society the administration of the existing legal aid schemes, both criminal and civil. In
the longer term the Board will be reviewing the present arrangements
for legal aid and will, I hope, put forward new proposals of its own for
improving the provision of legal services.

Three consultation papers were issued by my Department in January
this year, proposing radical changes in the work and organization of the
legal profession. The proposals, which are aimed at promoting efficiency and competition in legal services, include encouragement of
specialist education and practice, new arrangements for lawyers and
others to qualify as advocates in the courts, and a change in the system
of fees, designed to enable people of limited means to undertake legal
action without fear of excessive cost. Consultation on these proposals
is still in progress. They have already provoked lively discussion and
attracted extensive attention from the media.

Other initiatives are concerned with the structure and procedure of
the civil courts. The Children Bill which is currently before Parliament
provides a single integrated code dealing with the care and upbringing

* This article is a transcript of a speech delivered by the Lord Chancellor at the University of Leiden on 14 April 1989 at the invitation of the Institute of Anglo-American
Law. The text first appeared in 37 *Netherlands International Law Review* pp. 71–8
(1991) and is reprinted by kind permission of the Journal.

of children. It will also contain provisions for a means of matching the weight and complexity of each case to the level of court which will hear it, consolidating proceedings relating to the same child or family, reducing delay and generally providing a more effective system of justice in cases involving children. These measures are the first step in a rolling programme in which the Government will be looking at other areas of family law and related procedures and arrangements.

Last week I announced to Parliament that I am planning further legislation to implement changes in civil jurisdiction and procedure along the lines proposed by the Civil Justice Review in its final report published in June of last year. The proposals of the Review were designed to reduce delay, cost and complexity and to improve access to justice.

I should like to concentrate, in the rest of the time available, on telling you some more about the Civil Justice Review: how it was set up and conducted, its main proposals, and my plans for implementation. But before I move on to this in detail, there is one general point I want to emphasize at this stage. That is that the Civil Justice Review, together with the other initiatives I have briefly mentioned, forms part of a coherent programme of reform with a common aim. The aim is to improve the standard of service offered by the courts and the legal profession to the public. It may seem rather obvious to point out that the civil courts exist for the benefit of the public, but I believe that this is a principle we must always keep firmly in mind. Of course, reform of the court system will also impinge on the judiciary, the legal profession and court staff. Some changes will be welcomed by these professional groups while others may be resisted, but the interests of ordinary court users must never be overlooked in all this.

Let me turn now to the work of the Civil Justice Review, which was established by my distinguished predecessor, Lord Hailsham of St. Marylebone, in February 1985. Its terms of reference were "to improve the machinery of civil justice in England and Wales by means of reforms in jurisdiction, procedure and court administration and in particular to reduce delay, cost and complexity". Although in principle the remit of the Review included all aspects of civil justice, there were in fact certain exclusions. The most significant of these are appeals, administrative law and family cases. The Review was intended to be an enquiry into first-instance justice in ordinary civil cases in the High Court and the county courts. In the course of its work the Review Body itself decided to extend its terms of reference to include access to justice, thus enabling the Review, in its examination of the civil justice system, to give particular emphasis to the perspective of the ordinary litigant.

I do not want to spend too long on the nature and history of the civil justice system in England and Wales. However, if the proposals of the Civil Justice Review are to be fully understood, it is important to have at least some background knowledge of court structure and procedure. It may therefore be helpful at this stage if I attempt to summarize the essential features as briefly as possible.

There are two civil courts of first instance in England and Wales: the High Court and the county court. The High Court, which is a superior court of record, has unlimited jurisdiction in most types of civil cases. Its business is conducted at the Royal Courts of Justice in London and at 26 provincial trial centres. The High Court comprises three Divisions—Queen's Bench, Chancery and Family—which deal with broadly distinct areas of work. The Civil Justice Review was almost exclusively concerned with the work of the Queen's Bench Division, which includes personal injury cases, debt claims and the Commercial Court.

At the lower level there are more than 250 county courts throughout the country. Their jurisdiction overlaps to a limited extent with that of the High Court, but is restricted financially as well as geographically. In contract and tort, for example, the county courts have jurisdiction only up to £5,000. Cases above that level must start in the High Court, although they may be transferred down if they are considered suitable for trial in a county court. Cases below £5,000 may start in either the High Court or a county court, although there are sanctions in costs which are intended to deter smaller cases from starting in the High Court.

In both the High Court and the county courts there are two levels of judiciary. In the High Court, trials are heard by High Court judges, while interlocutory matters are dealt with in the Royal Courts of Justice by judicial officers known as masters and in the provinces by district registrars, who have the same powers as masters and like them are judicial officers. In the county courts, the more substantial trials are heard by Circuit judges. County court registrars, who are also judicial officers, deal with interlocutory matters, arbitrate in small claims proceedings and have a limited trial jurisdiction. Outside London, registrars are appointed to act both in the county courts and as district registrars of the High Court. I have not mentioned family business conducted by judges and registrars, or the involvement of Circuit judges in criminal work, because these matters are beyond the scope of the Civil Justice Review.

The two fundamental features of English civil procedure are that it is adversarial and largely oral. It is the adversarial principle, in particular, which determines the respective role of the court and the parties in civil litigation, both at the pre-trial stage and in the course of the trial itself. In general terms the role of the court is passive and non-interventionist; it is up to the parties (or, perhaps more usually, their legal representatives) to initiate, prepare, conduct and present proceedings, and thus very largely to determine the pace at which they proceed. At the pre-trial stage the timetable for progressing a case is largely in the hands of the plaintiff, while at the trial itself it is the parties who have the primary responsibility for summoning, examining and cross-examining witnesses. The role of the judge is simply to adjudicate between the two sides of the case as they are put to him at the trial. It is not the judge's primary function to determine what are to be the issues in dispute between the parties, nor to promote a settlement or compromise between them, although frequently the judge may seek to clarify the points in the interest of shortening the proceedings, and encourage the parties to negotiate, if this seems appropriate.

Like the adversarial principle, the oral hearing of evidence at trial is a traditional feature, originating when all civil cases were heard by juries. Nowadays the use of civil juries is restricted to defamation, malicious prosecution, false imprisonment and certain cases involving fraud. This means that the vast majority of civil cases going to trial are heard by a judge alone, but the principle of orality in relation to argument and to a lesser extent to evidence still remains prominent in practice.

I shall return to the matters of court structure, jurisdiction and procedure in relation to the proposals of the Civil Justice Review. First, however, let me continue by describing the conduct of the Review. It was carried out by an independent advisory committee whose chairman was a leading industrialist and whose members were predominantly not practising lawyers, working with a small team of officials from my Department. It began its enquiry by commissioning five factual studies from outside consultants to look at the handling of the major areas of civil business: personal injuries, debt, small claims, housing and commercial cases. A consultation paper was issued on each of these topics, based on the results of the consultant's studies and putting forward a number of options for change. These five papers on specific topics were followed by a wide-ranging consultation paper entitled "General Issues" which dealt with matters common to all classes of business, such as court structure, procedure and judicial administration.

Despite the limited period of just three years set aside for the Review to complete its work, careful time-tabling made it possible to ensure that the public had a good opportunity to study and comment on each consultation paper. Over 700 items of evidence, both written and oral, were received from respondents who included solicitors and barristers, judges, trade unions, professional organizations, consumer groups, trading companies and individual members of the public. All these responses were carefully analyzed and considered by the Review Body, and as a result there were significant modifications to many of the proposals put out for consultation. The consultation process and the subsequent efforts to find a workable consensus were, in my view, an extremely important part of the Review process as a whole.

The final report of the Civil Justice Review was delivered to me a few months after I took office. It contains over 90 recommendations, which may conveniently be considered under three main headings. The first of these, which I will call "matching cases to judges", arises from the central finding of the Review that too many relatively unimportant cases were being handled and tried in the High Court. This is obviously wasteful of High Court resources, and causes unnecessary delay for those cases which genuinely need the services of the High Court. It also adds to the length and cost of smaller cases, which could be dealt with more quickly and conveniently at county court level. The problem is most acute in relation to personal injury cases, which make up the greater bulk of cases going to trial in the High Court.

It became apparent, then, in the course of the Review, that the key to reducing delay and cost in civil cases lay in finding a better system for the allocation of cases to the appropriate level of judge. Under the old system, although it is true that most of the weightier cases are already dealt with in the High Court, there was no effective means of preventing small and medium level cases entering and staying in the High Court also. The Review found that existing sanctions in costs, and powers to transfer cases down from the High Court to a county court, had failed to prevent what it aptly labelled "upward drift". Nevertheless, before the Review reported, the High Court judges themselves embarked upon a rigorous course of transfer down once there were facilities available in the county courts for continuous trial of cases that required more than a day for trial.

It was in this context that the Review considered the relationship between the High Court and county courts which, as recorded in the report has been more vigorously debated than any other matter raised in the course of the Review. The consultation paper on General Issues put forward a proposal offering two options: either amalgamation of the High Court and county courts into a single civil court or closer integration of two formally separate courts. Perhaps not surprisingly, the review process has revealed that amalgamation of the High Court and county courts would present formidable obstacles. It would, in the first place, take a number of years to achieve; major legislation would be required, as well as wide-scale administration reorganization.

At the same time it was impossible to ignore the fact that there was no clear consensus in favour of a unified court. Those who favoured retention of a separate High Court did so both on the ground that such a court provides specialist excellence and that its separate existence provides an important constitutional guarantee of the independence of the judges who are its members.

Given the objections I have mentioned, and the commitment to put forward practical solutions to clearly identified problems, the Review Body needed to consider whether there were other measures, short of amalgamating the two courts, by which the crucial objective of improving the service to the public by means of better case allocation could be attained.

In the end the Review did not propose amalgamation of the High Court and county courts but concentrated instead on specific selective measures designed to provide what is needed in a manner which is effective, acceptable, financially viable and requires the minimum of legislation and of implementation time. Amalgamation was not, however, ruled out in the longer term if the selective measures put forward did not prove adequately effective.

The specific measures proposed by the Civil Justice Review are:

1. The High Court to retain exclusive jurisdiction in public law cases and certain specialist types of work.
2. High Court and county courts both to have unlimited jurisdiction in general cases, including tort and contract, which embraces the great mass of personal injury and debt cases.
3. Cases worth less than £25,000 to be tried in a county court, wherever they commence.
4. A flexible band between £25,000 and £50,000 within which general

cases are triable either in the High Court by a High Court judge or in a county court by an appropriate Circuit judge, depending on the nature of the case and the availability of an appropriate judge.

5. County court registrars, that is to say junior judges, to have jurisdiction to try cases up £5,000, instead of £1,000 as now.

6. Informal arbitrations by registrars, instead of full trial, to be obligatory up to £1,000 instead of £500 as now.

7. A special regime for personal injury cases requiring all such cases to commence in a county court, with transfer for trial in the High Court of cases involving more than £25,000 or which are otherwise especially important or complex.

As can be seen these proposals create, for general cases, means to allocate cases to judges flexibly within a single High Court-county court system. The concept of a single system for general cases is further developed by proposals to have a single procedural code for High Court and county court, a uniform set of remedies in each court and a single costs regime for both courts. All of these proposals will remove existing barriers, both legal and psychological, between the two courts and promote maximum flexibility between them.

The second major group of proposals put forward by the Civil Justice Review falls under the heading "speeding up and improving the handling of cases". I have already described briefly the oral and adversarial nature of English civil procedure, and it will be apparent that these traditional features present a number of problems.

The main difficulty with "part prosecution"—the principle that pre-trial case progress is largely the responsibility of the parties—is that it often leads to avoidable delay. There can, I think, be no room for doubt that delay on the scale found by the Civil Justice Review is unacceptable. Delay, as the Review pointed out, undermines justice. It reduces the availability of reliable evidence, withholds compensation at the time of greatest need, and causes continuing personal stress, anxiety and financial hardship. I have already mentioned that a more effective system of case allocation was identified by the Civil Justice Review as the key to reducing delay. To reinforce this, the Review also recommended that the court should play a more active role in controlling the progress of cases before they come to trial. Such a system will not, of course, be effective unless the courts are in a position to guarantee prompt trial of cases which are ready, and that is the objective towards which I am working.

The Review has also proposed that specific steps be taken to ensure more openness in the conduct of litigation and to make greater use of written rather than oral evidence. In particular, it proposes that parties should be required, as a matter of course, to exchange witness statements. This proposal is seen as providing the basis for earlier settlements, where appropriate, and for better conducted trials. Not only the parties, but the judge himself would see the witness statements before trial and the trial could therefore proceed by reference to those matters which are genuinely in dispute. Opening statements by counsel on each side could be limited whilst oral evidence would be taken only from those witnesses who needed to be challenged or whom the court otherwise required to hear.

The third, and final, group of proposals which I wish to discuss falls under the general heading "access to justice". There is a natural tendency for lawyers and judges to concentrate on questions of court structure and changes in jurisdiction and procedure. Nevertheless, as I have already suggested, the objective of changes to the civil justice system must, in the end, be to provide a more effective service for court users. This goes beyond improved conditions for the judiciary and court staff or more convenient working conditions for lawyers, important as these are. It was because the level of "customer satisfaction" was recognised as an important measure of the effectiveness of the court service that interviews with litigants and potential litigants were included in some of the factual studies carried out for the Review. In my judgment it was particularly important that some attempt be made to evaluate quality of service by direct contact with members of the public. At the same time the consultation process played an important part in supplementing information obtained from surveys of litigants and of potential litigants.

In this way the Review Body was able to bring forward proposals to simplify procedure in small cases and to provide assistance to litigants in those cases in such a way as to protect them from the expense of legal representation.

The Review Body was, I have no doubt, encouraged to take this approach by the evident success of the small claims procedure in England and Wales, which has become established over the last 15 years as a highly effective means of deciding civil disputes involving comparatively small sums of money. The essence of the scheme is cheapness, speed and informality; this is why legal representation, although not actually banned from small claims hearings, is discouraged by the rule that no costs are awarded and by the fact that legal aid is not normally available.

The Review did in fact discover inconsistencies of practice in the handling of these small claims, and accordingly recommended that there should be a self-contained set of small claims rules; that cases should normally be disposed of at a single substantive hearing; that hearings should be conducted on an interventionist basis; and there should be a statutory right to lay representation. Perhaps of greatest importance is the recognition that the judges who hear small cases will need more extensive training if these principles are to be carried through consistently.

The Review made other recommendations for the simplification of procedures and for increasing the availability of lay help and representation. These will not, of course, remove the need for legal representation in cases where complex issues of law are at stake. It would plainly be wrong to reduce the scope of legal aid for representation by a qualified lawyer where such issues are involved.

In its recommendations on access to justice, particularly those concerned with lay representation and the standard of service provided by lawyers, the Review foreshadowed my current proposals for consultation on the work and organization of the legal profession. As I indicated in my statement to Parliament last week, the Government's final decisions on the nature and scope of the service offered by the county court to litigants in smaller cases must await the results of this consultation process.

Implementation of the Civil Justice Review will be a complex task, involving primary and subordinate legislation as well as administrative changes. My programme for implementation has been carefully phased to reflect the capacity of the courts and the legal system generally to adapt to change, and the process as a whole is likely to last about five years. Within that time-scale my first priority must be to introduce a new and more effective system for the distribution of cases between the High Court and the county courts. This, as I have said, is the key to providing a service which is better adapted to the needs of litigants in cases at all levels. After careful consideration, I have decided not to adopt the Review's proposal that all personal injury cases, of whatever value, should start in a county court. I think it is preferable to ensure, so far as possible, that cases start in the court in which they will eventually be tried, and for this reason I intend to allow commencement in the High Court for really substantial cases only. Procedural changes to reduce delay will be introduced at the same time, and the later stages of the programme will concentrate on specific proposals designed to encourage participation in the legal process by unrepresented litigants.

By way of conclusion I should like to remind you of my earlier point that the civil justice system exists to serve the interests of ordinary people. It is, I believe, of paramount importance in any civilized society that the State must provide, through the courts, the appropriate machinery for the resolution of disputes between citizens. Deficiencies such as excessive delay, cost and complexity create barriers which make justice inaccessible to the public at large. This undermines the maintenance of law and order and, ultimately, the stability of society itself.

It had become apparent, even before the report of the Civil Justice Review was available, that our system of civil justice in England and Wales had failed to keep pace with the changing needs of modern society. In one of his 1986 Hamlyn lectures, Sir Jack Jacob observed that "for most people English civil justice is a remote, incomprehensible, mystifying and in some ways terrifying area of the law". He went on to say: "What is needed above all today is a breath of fresh air to blow through the corridors of civil justice to de-mystify the process, to render it plain, simple and intelligible, to enable . . . the man in the High Street to understand and appreciate its operation and in this way to bring justice closer to the common people".

I hope that, in the course of the next few years, implementation of the Civil Justice Review will provide just such a breath of fresh air as Sir Jack Jacob had in mind. However, I think it needs to be recognized that a single completed process of reform will not in itself be sufficient to maintain public confidence in the administration of justice. I have no doubt that my successors in the office of Lord Chancellor will need to make further changes in order to ensure that the civil justice system is properly attuned to changing social conditions. I believe they will find that the principles laid down by the Civil Justice Review have provided them with a solid basis for further reform.

4

The English Law of Defamation—
Is Trial by Jury Still the Best?

by the Rt. Hon. Sir Martin Nourse*

You will at once observe that the title of my talk does not ask you to consider whether trial by jury is an ideal mode of trial, nor whether the English law of defamation is ideal or even the best that there is. I rather suspect that Professor Markesinis has already told you that it is not. And certainly it is he and not I who is competent to undertake that wide comparative study. My purpose is simply to take our substantive law as it is and to ask whether, at the end of the 20th century, it is better that civil actions for defamation should be tried by judge and jury or by judge alone.

In the 18th and the 19th centuries it was customary for English lawyers to applaud the system of trial by jury as one of the greatest achievements of their jurisprudence. Blackstone himself said that it would ever be looked on as the glory of the English law. But from Jeremy Bentham onwards there were always doubters. Although in the 17th and 18th centuries it was an incomparable bulwark against aggression by the Crown, as times have become more settled and the transactions of an advanced industrialised society more complex, it now seems natural, notwithstanding the American experience, for the system to have fallen into disfavour insofar as most civil proceedings are concerned. The action for defamation is now one of a minority of civil actions where either party has an absolute right to trial by jury.

The judge, of course, is the sole judge of law. In regard to questions of fact, the relative functions of judge and jury are well expressed in these words of W.F. Craies, a barrister and lecturer at London University, writing in the early years of this century:

* This is the text of a lecture delivered at the University of Leiden on 27 April 1990 at the invitation of the Leiden Institute of Anglo-American Law. The text was first published in 37 *Netherlands International Law Review* and is reprinted here by kind permission of the Journal.

While the jury is in legal theory absolute as to matters of fact, it is in practice largely controlled by judges. Not only does the judge at the trial decide as to the relevancy of the evidence tendered to the issues to be proved, and as to the admissibility of questions put to a witness, but he also advises the jury as to the logical bearing of the evidence admitted upon the matters to be found by the jury. The rules as to admissibility of evidence, largely based upon scholastic logic, sometimes difficult to apply, and almost unknown in Continental jurisprudence, coupled with the right of an English judge to sum up the evidence and to express his own opinion as to its value, fetter to some extent the independence or limit the chances of error of the jury.

That said, the jury is still supreme. And actions for defamation are as good an example of that supremacy as any other. Not only do the jury decide whether the defendant is liable to the plaintiff. If they hold that he is, they also decide the amount of the damages which the plaintiff should receive. Remember also that they have the inestimable advantage, regrettably denied to judges, of never having to give reasons for their decisions. And their decisions can only be upset on appeal if it can be shown that no jury, acting rationally, could have arrived at the same conclusion.

Although recent public interest in this question has centred on the jury's role in assessing damages, their role in determining liability is of equal interest and of greater historical importance. In most early systems of law injuries committed by the spoken or written word were treated as remediable not by compensation to the injured but by punishment of those who committed them. As I am sure that you will know from your learning in the Roman law of the XII Tables the composition of scurrilous songs and gross noisy public affronts was punishable by death. In the course of time punishment often came to include the payment of compensation to the injured. And from there it was but a short step to develop a civil remedy, either as an incident of the criminal proceedings or by way of separate action.

In England the civil action was developed out of the criminal and has virtually replaced it. Prosecutions for criminal libel are now extremely rare. But in the latter part of the 18th and the early part of the 19th centuries they were very common. And for the most of the 18th century the lawyers were at odds amongst themselves as to respective functions of judge and jury on the trial of such an indictment. Since the case out of which the dispute arose was both the most stirring trial in our constitutional annals and one of the principal causes of the Glorious Revolution and the union between our two nations under the Prince and

Princess of Orange, William and Mary, I hope that I may dwell on it for a short while.

In April 1688 James II, apart from Mary I the only self-confessed Roman Catholic English Sovereign since the Reformation, issued his second Declaration of Indulgence, in which, having announced his intention to protect Catholics in the free exercise of their religion, he authorised them to perform their worship publicly and without molestation. He also purported to abrogate the Test Acts, which imposed religious tests as a qualification for any civil or military office under the Crown. No constitutional lawyer, either then or now, has ever doubted that this purported dispensation with acts of Parliament was illegal at the time and it led directly to the provision of the Bill of Rights of 1689 which so declared.

Throughout the constitutional struggle which followed, the freely declared opposition of William and Mary to the Declaration of Indulgence was of immense political significance and moral value. But the immediate problem was that the King directed the Declaration to be read in all churches throughout the Kingdom at morning service on two successive Sundays in May. And he directed the bishops to distribute copies throughout their dioceses for that purpose. Sancroft, the Archbishop of Canterbury, and six other Bishops having signed a petition to the King stating that they could not, in prudence, honour or conscience, be parties to the solemn publishing of an illegal declaration in the house of God, were arraigned before the Court of King's Bench on an information that they had published a false, malicious and seditious libel.

I have read again the account of this celebrated proceeding in the eighth chapter of Macaulay's *History of England*. While I am no doubt more aware of the partisanship of the great Whig historian, I have felt the same schoolboy thrill at discovering a love of history and a passionate commitment to our constitutional freedoms. It was the jury, the people of England, who were the heroes of that day. Of the four judges of the King's Bench, Wright C.J. and Allibone J. directed them that the petition was a libel. Holloway J. said that is was not. None of those three expressed an opinion as to the legality of the dispensing power. But Powell J. went further. He said that there had been no libel and, moreover, that the Declaration of Indulgence was illegal (12 St. Tr. 427):

In short, if there be such dispensing power in the king, then that can be no libel which they presented to the king, which says that the declaration, being founded upon such a pretended power, is illegal. . . . If this be one allowed of, it will need no parliament; all the legislature will be in the king, which is a thing worth considering, and I leave the issue to God and your consciences.

The jury were locked up all night without fire or candle, not such a hardship as it might have been, since the day was the 29th of June. When they delivered their verdict of not guilty the next morning, there were, as the report in the State Trials records, several great shouts in the court and throughout Westminster Hall, shouts which, as Macaulay records, were taken up by the crowds thronging outside and echoed throughout the City of London.

The dispute which arose out of the trial of the Seven Bishops was whether it was for the judge or for the jury to say that the writing was libel or not. It is a matter of some interest that even in those servile times all four judges of the King's Bench seem to have assumed that it was a decision for the jury. But the preponderance of judicial opinion after the Revolution, affirmed by Lord Mansfield, C.J., was that it was a decision for the judge, the questions to be decided by the jury being confined to the fact of publication and the truth of the innuendos (*see Rex.* v. *Woodfall* (1770) 5 Burr. 2661 and *Rex* v. *Shipley* (1784) 4 Doug. 73). In the latter case Lord Mansfield simply ignored the case of the Seven Bishops and referred only to the post Revolution decisions.

The chief proponents of the contrary view were Lord Camden and, as advocate for the defendant in the case of *Rex* v. *Shipley*, Thomas Erskine. Their view was adopted by Parliament in Fox's Libel Act of 1792, which, by providing that the jury should give a general verdict, ensured that the question of libel or no libel would also be left to them. Although the Act was in terms confined to criminal proceedings, it was expressed to be declaratory of the common law and soon came to be treated as definitive of the functions of judge and jury in civil actions for defamation as well, subject only to the power of the judge to withdraw the case if the material complained of is not reasonably capable of bearing a defamatory meaning (see *Capital and Counties Bank Ltd.* v. *George Henty & Sons* (1882) 7 App. Cas. 741).

The objective of those who secured the passing of the 1792 Act was to protect the freedom of the press by ensuring that the question of libel or no libel was not left to judges who might be favourably disposed towards the Crown. As I have said, prosecutions for criminal libel are now extremely rare, so that, even supposing that the protection was still necessary, the need for it in practice would be very limited. But civil actions are very common, perhaps more common than ever before, and their trial by jury is still very much the rule and not the exception. Under section 69(1) of the Supreme Court Act 1981, the present position is that either party is entitled as of right to trial by jury, unless:

the court is of opinion that the trial requires any prolonged examination of documents or accounts or any scientific or local investigation which cannot conveniently be made with a jury.

The irony of the present position is that, whereas the jury was originally the means by which the press was protected against the Crown, it is now seen by many, not least by juries themselves, as the means by which the private citizen is protected against the press. The freedom of the press is one thing, its licentiousness another; a distinction which was made by Lord Mansfield himself in *Rex* v. *Shipley*, at p. 170:

The liberty of the press consists in printing without any previous licence, subject to the consequences of law. The licentiousness of the press is Pandora's box, the source of every evil.

And so I come to the burning question of the day. Assuming that liability ought still to be determined by the jury, is there nevertheless a case for saying that damages ought to be assessed by the judge?

It was natural in a system where the civil action had been developed out of the criminal that juries should have tended to include a punitive or "exemplary" element in their awards of damages. This tendency had first been clearly observed in the 18th century for trespass and false imprisonment which arose out of the illegality of general warrants to search premises and seize goods (see *Wilkes* v. *Wood* (1763) Lofft. 1 and *Huckle* v. *Money* (1763) 2 Wils. 205). Similarly, until 1964 it was thought to be the law that an award of general damages in defamation cases could include an exemplary element if the conduct of the defendant had been so wanton as to merit punishment. But in *Broome* v. *Cassell & Co. Ltd.* (1972) A.C. 1027, the House of Lords, affirming and applying to defamation cases their earlier decision in *Rookes* v. *Barnard* (1964) A.C. 1129 (an intimidation case), authoritatively held that exemplary damages can only be awarded in three instances, of which the only one with any practical relevance to defamation cases is where the defendant, either with knowledge of the tort or recklessly, decides to publish because the prospects of material advantage to him outweigh the prospects of material loss. In all other cases the damages may be compensatory only.

It might have been thought that this restriction on the power of jury to award exemplary damages would not have had a significant effect on libel actions against newspapers, where it could be supposed that it would often not be difficult to prove that the defendant had calculated that the profits from publishing the libel would exceed the damages revocable by the plaintiff. However, it is now generally recognised that exemplary damages cannot be, or at any rate are not, claimed in the great majority of libel actions, even in those which are brought against tabloid newspapers. And so the plaintiff's remedy is usually restricted to his feelings at having been written or spoken of in defamatory terms, injury which can be aggravated by the defendant's subsequent conduct. Compensatory damages may also include a sum sufficient to vindicate the plaintiff's reputation.

The current interest in the level of damages awarded by juries really started in July 1987 when Mr. Jeffrey Archer, the well-known author and then a vice-chairman of the Conservative Party, was awarded £500,000 in an action against a tabloid newspaper which had falsely alleged that he had a casual relationship with a prostitute. There was no claim for exemplary damages in that case. That was followed by a number of other very high awards. But it was not exceeded until 1989 when a jury awarded £600,000 to Mrs. Sonia Sutcliffe, the wife of a mass murderer known as "the Yorkshire Ripper" against the proprietors of *Private Eye*, a satirical magazine with a relatively small circulation. The essence of the libel was that Mrs. Sutcliffe had made a deal worth £250,000 with a tabloid newspaper for her story as the wife of the Yorkshire Ripper. The sting of the libel was that she was the sort of person who was prepared to make a fortune out of her husband's wickedness. Although there was no claim for exemplary damages, the plaintiff alleged that the injury to her feelings had been much aggravated by the defendants' subsequent conduct, which included a repetition of the libel one year later, the publication of further libels in two articles in 1989, being articles calculated to frighten her from going on with her action, and her subjection to a three day cross-examination designed to prove the truth of the libel, which was not in the end supported by any evidence called on behalf of the defendants.

In that case there was, for the first time in recent years, an appeal to the Court of Appeal against the jury's award of damages. My membership of the court which heard that appeal is both my qualification for talking to you today and an assurance that, in accordance with convention, I will say no more about the case than can be gathered from the report in (1990) 2 W.L.R. 271. But I must tell you straightaway that the presiding judge, Lord Donaldson, M.R. said that the jury had been entitled to regard the persistent wrongs which had been done to Mrs. Sutcliffe by the defendant "as prolonged and vicious persecution".

As I have said, it is well established that an appellate court can only interfere with a jury's award of damages if it is so large or so small as to be irrational; that is to say, incapable of having been arrived at by a process of reason and necessarily arrived at through emotion, prejudice, caprice or stupidity, or simply on a wrong basis. That means that the Court of Appeal will very rarely interfere and there have been many cases in the past where they have declined to do so. The case on which Mrs. Sutcliffe's counsel most relied was *Youssoupoff* v. *Metro-Goldwyn-Meyer Pictures Ltd.* (1934) 50 T.L.R. 581, where the wife of the Russian prince who killed Rasputin was falsely portrayed in a film as the victim of a rape by him. The jury awarded her what was then the enormous sum of £25,000, which we were told might now be worth about £900,000, but the Court of Appeal refused to set it aside. That case, however, was decided at a time when the old rule as to exemplary damages was still in force.

One of the criticisms of the level of defamation awards which is most frequently voiced is that they vastly exceed the general level of awards for pain and suffering and loss of amenity in personal injury cases, for which a sum of about £100,000 may be taken to be an absolute maximum at the present time. In dealing with this question in *Sutcliffe* v. *Pressdram Ltd.* the Master of the Rolls said, at page 286F:

There are two reasons why the scale of damages in the two categories of case are quite different, notwithstanding that in both the law is attempting the same impossible feat, namely, to put a monetary value on something which can neither be evaluated in money terms nor fully compensated by a monetary award.

uu The first is that under the law as it stands at present, what it called the "measure of damages" is or may be different in the two cases. In relation to claims for personal injury the law calls for compensation to be assessed by reference to the pain and suffering caused by the injury itself. In cases of libel, the law calls for compensation to be assessed by reference not only to the pain and suffering caused to the plaintiff by the publication of the libel, but also to the extent to which this pain and suffering is aggravated, or reduced, by the defendant's subsequent conduct. It also requires account to be taken of the plaintiff's need to receive an award which will vindicate his or her reputation in the eyes of the public.

uu The second is that Parliament has decreed that damages shall be assessed by judges in cases of personal injury and by juries in cases of libel and has confirmed this decision as recently as 1981 in section 69 of the Supreme Court Act of that year. As Parliament well knew, the approach of a jury to any assessment of damages is different from that adopted by judges. It is not for me to express any view on which is better, but they *are* different. Judges are trained, and bound by precedent, to have regard to awards made by other judges in similar cases. Juries are not. It is a necessary consequence that awards by judges tend to conform to conventional scales which may or may not represent what the public would regard as appropriate. Judges analyze claims and give reasons for their decisions. Juries may or may not analyze claims, but they are certainly free to give effect to what may be described as a "gut reaction" to an extent which judges are not. Juries do not give reasons for their awards and it is the common experience of judges that having to give reasons is something which puts a substantial premium on ensuring that the head rules the heart.

uu Accordingly, it is to be expected that awards in personal injury cases will be in no way comparable with awards in libel cases. In considering any appeal of this nature, an appellate court is bound to disregard its experience of the assessment of damages in personal injury cases: see the speech of Lord Hailsham of St. Marylebone LC in *Broome* v. *Cassell & Co. Ltd.* (1972) A.C. 1027, 1070–1071 and notwithstanding the views of Diplock, L.J. in *McCarey* v. *Associated Newspapers Ltd. (No. 2)* (1965) 2 Q.B. 86, 109.

The essence of the decision in the *Sutcliffe* case can be taken from the headnote in (1990) 2 W.L.R. 272:

. . . taking the fullest account of the extent to which the jury considered that the plaintiff's initial injury had been aggravated by the defendant's conduct and of the extent to which they considered a large sum necessary for unequivocal vindication in the eyes of the world, the size of the award indicated that they had failed to appreciate the real value and effect of so large a sum; and [by two members of the court] that they had wrongly included in the award an amount in respect of exemplary damages; and that, accordingly, damages being very substantially in excess of what could be considered reasonable to compensate the plaintiff, the award would be set aside and damages re-assessed by a fresh jury.

That last passage discloses one of the main objections to the current system, which is that the Court of Appeal has no right to assess the damages themselves. However, immediately after judgment the parties agreed that the court should substitute its own figure and the hearing was adjourned for further argument as to that matter. In the end it was disposed of by agreement. I will return later to the present inability of the Court of Appeal, in default of agreement to the contrary, to substitute its own figure for the jury's.

The feature of the judgments in the *Sutcliffe* case which may have some permanent value is the court's view on the guidance which should be given to juries in the future. Following its earlier decision in *Ward* v. *James* (1966) 1 Q.B. 273, the court was against any change in the practice that juries are not referred, either by counsel or by the judge, to awards which have been made in other cases. But they did say that in his summing-up the judge could usefully ask the jury to consider the real value to the plaintiff of any sum which they were thinking of awarding. The Master of the Rolls pointed out that the jury had awarded Mrs. Sutcliffe a sum which, prudently invested, might well provide her with an income before tax of over £1,000 per week and still leave her with the original sum of £600,000 to bequeath to whomsoever she wished to benefit on her death. Having said that it was understandable that the jury did not appreciate the true size of the award which they were making, he continued:

What is, I think, required, is some guidance to juries in terms which will assist them to appreciate the real value of large sums. It is, and must remain, a jury's duty to award lump sums by way of damages, but there is no reason why they should not be invited notionally to "weigh" any sum which they have in mind to award.

Whether the jury did so, and how it did so, would be a matter for them, but the judge could, I think, properly invite them to consider what the result would be in terms of weekly, monthly or annual income if the money were invested in a building society deposit account without touching the capital sum awarded or, if they have in mind smaller sums, to consider what they could buy with it.

The Court of Appeal decision in the *Sutcliffe* case was given in October of last year. Just before Christmas another jury, having been given the *Sutcliffe* guidance, awarded a plaintiff a sum of £1.5 million, again in a case where there was no claim for exemplary damages. Many people might have thought that that was a severe set-back for the hopes which had been expressed in *Sutcliffe*, although that could probably be described as a wholly exceptional case. Beyond that I ought to say no more, because the jury's award is currently under appeal.

In general I am pleased to be able to tell you that my information from those who participate in defamation trials is that the new guidance is beginning to have some effect. Another recent development is the Government's proposal, which is included in the Courts and Legal

Services Bill now going through Parliament, that in a case where the Court of Appeal sets aside a jury's award it shall have power to substitute its own figure. That proposal would have the desirable effect of cutting out the expense, delay and anxieties of a retrial, without replacing the jury as the tribunal of first instance. Moreover, I would think it clear that the Court of Appeal would have to cast itself in the role of the jury and not that of a judge in a personal injuries case.

I have referred to the irony of a system which originated as a protection to the press having become one by which a protection is erected against the press. It cannot be doubted that many of the large awards in recent years have been expressions of the abhorrence of ordinary citizens at the cynical and unprincipled behaviour of certain sections of the tabloid press. Such behaviour is made the easier by the failure of the English law to provide any right to personal privacy, in particular by no general right to restrain the publication of true private facts, a topic of which there is a valuable treatment in the second edition of Dias and Markesinis' *Tort Law*. Thus an unscrupulous editor can freely publish gratuitous facts about an individual's life, health or associations which, because they are true, cannot found an action for defamation, but whose publication is nevertheless hurtful to the individual and his family and likely to reduce him in the esteem of others. It is, I think, because so many articles in the tabloid press are intrusive in this way that when a jury finds one which is also false, especially if it is deliberately or recklessly false, it marks its loathing of the newspaper's conduct by making a huge award of damages. And who are judges to blame those ordinary men and women simply because they have not heard of the rule in *Broome* v. *Cassell* or, if they have, because they have not understood it or, if they have both heard of it and understood it, because they have not been able to see the justice of it?

A brief diversion on the law of privacy is here desirable, more especially in the light of the decision of the Court of Appeal on 23rd February of this year in the case of *Kaye* v. *Robertson*. The plaintiff, Mr. Gorden Kaye, is a well-known actor and the star of a popular television series called *'Allo 'Allo*. On 25th January there was a storm of hurricane proportions in London and, while Mr. Kaye was driving in it, a piece of wood smashed through the windscreen of his car, causing severe injuries to his head and brain. He was taken to a nearby hospital where he was on a life support machine for three days, followed by another four or five days in intensive care. On 13th February, while Mr. Kaye was still in no fit condition to be interviewed or to give any valid consent to be interviewed, a journalist and a photographer from a tabloid newspaper, acting on their editor's instructions, gained unauthorized access to his private room in the hospital, where he apparently agreed to talk to them and did not object to a number of flashlight photographs being taken, including some showing the substantial scars to his head. About 15 minutes after the journalist and photographer had left his rooms, Mr. Kaye had no recollection of the incident.

The newspaper having made it clear that it intended to publish an article about the interview on the following Sunday, using one or more of the photographs which had been taken, Mr. Kaye's next friend, Mr. Kaye himself being still incapable of managing his own affairs, applied for an interlocutory injunction restraining the publication. An injunction was granted by the High Court, the form of the injunction being modified on an appeal by the newspaper to the Court of Appeal.

All three members of that court observed that there was no right to privacy in English law and certainly two of them, perhaps all three, regretted that state of affairs. Bingham, L.J., having said that any reasonable and fair-minded person who had heard the facts of the case would conclude that the newspaper had wronged Mr. Kaye, continued:

This case nonetheless highlights, yet again, the failure of both the common law of England and statute to protect in an effective way the personal privacy of individual citizens. This has been the subject of much comment over the years, perhaps most recently by Professor Markesinis (*The German Law of Torts*), second edition, 1990 page 316) where he writes: "English law, on the whole, compares unfavourably with German law. True, many aspects of the human personality and privacy are protected by a multitude of existing torts but this means fitting the facts of each case in the pigeon-hole of an existing tort and this process may not only involve strained constructions; often it may also leave a deserving plaintiff without a remedy".

Leggatt, L.J. added some observations about the way in which the common law has developed in the United States in order to meet the need which English law was unable to fulfil satisfactorily. In passing, I hope you will note that these judgments are some evidence of the interest, not much apparent in the past, which English judges are beginning to take in comparative law.

Kaye v. *Robertson* is itself a telling example of Professor Markesinis' thesis that an English court, when faced with the facts of such a case, will strive to fit them into the pigeon-hole of an existing tort. Mr. Kaye's claim for an injunction was based on alleged rights of action in no less than four different torts: libel, malicious falsehood, trespass to the person, and passing off. The Court of Appeal thought that the claim in passing off was hopeless and that those in libel and trespass to the person were not sufficiently made out to justify the grant of an interlocutory injunction. But with a certain amount of flair they were able to hold that the claim in malicious falsehood was sufficiently established for that purpose, although Bingham, L.J. acknowledged that that cause of action could not give Mr. Kaye the breadth of protection which he would have wished and which would have been available if there had been a cause of action in invasion of privacy. That was soon demonstrated when the newspaper was able to publish the article under a headline proclaiming that Mr. Kaye had *not* given his consent to the interview.

The justification which I seek to make for this diversion into the law of privacy will soon appear. I am now ready to give my own answer to the question which I asked that we should consider. In my opinion it is still better that civil actions for defamation should be tried by judge and jury and not by judge alone. As to liability, I have already said elsewhere that the question whether someone's reputation has or has not been falsely discredited, no less than this innocence or guilt in a criminal proceeding, ought to be decided by ordinary sensible men and women. And judges are not, at any rate for this purpose, ordinary sensible men and women. I would add that in recent years there has been little agitation for a change in the system of deciding liability, and I would expect Parliament to see very great objections, so far as concerns that matter, to any further restriction of the right to trial by jury beyond that for which provision is made by section 69(1) of the 1981 Act.

As to the more controversial question of damages, I am firmly of the opinion that we would need a far greater experience of error on the part of juries before such a radical change ought to be made. We can never know when a system which has been of critical importance in the past and which, with hiccups from time to time, works as well as any other at the present, will not become of critical importance in the future. With the improved guidance which is now available to juries and the prospect of the Court of Appeal's ability to substitute its own figure where a jury has gone badly wrong, there is I believe some cause for hope that the present trend of awards at a more sensible level will continue.

The behaviour of the press cannot be omitted from the equation. It is here that the statutory creation of a tort of unlawful invasion of privacy is in the long term desirable and probably essential. If there was such a tort, much of the offensive but unactionable material which is now published would become actionable, with a consequential improvement in the standards of behaviour. If that did not work, it is not beyond the bounds of possibility that the House of Lords might one day reconsider the rule in *Broome* v. *Cassell.* Anyone who wishes to see good grounds for their doing so need only consult the judgments of the Court of Appeal in that case ((1971) 2 Q.B. 354). But that in turn would give rise to the familiar objection that, if there is to be an exemplary element in an award, it ought to go to the State or to charity and certainly not to the plaintiff, who, if he has been properly compensated, deserves no more. And then it would be objected that the exemplary damages were a penalty, which should not be exacted without a greater protection to the defendant; i.e., the criminal standard of proof. And so on. On the whole, there is much to be said for a system which ensures that compensatory damages only are awarded because compensatory damages only are needed.

5

The English Criminal Trial:
The Credits and the Debits

by the Rt. Hon. Sir Thomas Bingham,
*the Master of the Rolls**

The story is familiarly told that when Oliver Cromwell sat for his portrait to the great Dutch painter Peter Lely he desired the artist to "remark all these roughnesses, pimples, warts, and everything as you see me, otherwise I will never pay a farthing for it".[1] To most British citizens of my generation it was a hereditary article of faith that the English criminal trial, if subject to occasional roughnesses, was notably free of anything that could be called a wart. Indeed, uniquely so, for uncritical and ill-informed comparisons were habitually drawn with what was thought to prevail everywhere else. The Americans were felt to have some of the right ideas, but to have allowed the criminal trial process to degenerate into something of a circus. In continental Europe, it was confidently thought, defendants were treated as guilty until they established their innocence. Happily, through the labours of comparative lawyers such as your distinguished Director, such misleading insular assumptions in this and other legal fields have been tempered by exposure to the realities of law and practice elsewhere. The invincibility of ignorance has been challenged. And a series of shocks have in recent times caused us to ponder, not whether the English criminal trial process is subject to warts but whether in truth the disfigurements are more deep-rooted and serious—carbuncles, perhaps.[2] The old certainties

---

* This is the text of a lecture delivered at the University of Leiden on 26 October 1990 at the invitation of the Leiden Institute of Anglo-American Law.

[1] Walpole's *Anecdotes of Painting*, ch. 12.

[2] The topic has been addressed by the Home Affairs Committee of the House of Commons in 1982 (1982 H.C. 451); by *JUSTICE* in a report later referred to; by much journalistic discussion; by at least one political party at its conference; and in learned journals.

have come to look much less secure. My purpose this morning is to discuss, in a practical not a formal way, how the process is *meant* to work, to consider how miscarriages (or alleged miscarriages) of justice have occurred, and to touch on possible solutions. But I fear, under this last head, I have rather meagre fare to offer. Perhaps this experienced audience will come to my aid and suggest an answer.

I would like to approach the subject by considering the roles of the leading players in the English criminal jury trial even if I cannot guarantee, like the playwright, to list them in the order of their appearance.

First, prosecuting counsel. He is an advocate in private practice who in the ordinary way will appear sometimes to prosecute, sometimes to defend. His duty when prosecuting is, unsurprisingly, to present the prosecution case. But very well-established rules make it clear that it is not the duty of prosecuting counsel to obtain a conviction by all means at his command. He should not regard himself as appearing for a party. Rather, he must lay before the jury fairly and impartially the whole of the facts which comprise the case for the prosecution and see that the jury are properly instructed in the law applicable to those facts. Where he holds statements from witnesses he does not propose to call he should make them available to the defence, so that the defence can call the witnesses if they want to. If prosecuting counsel finds that a witness' oral evidence differs markedly from a written statement in his possession, he should show the statement to the defence. If a witness called by the prosecution is known to have previous convictions the defence must be informed. If the judge's direction to the jury is felt to be deficient in its treatment of the facts or the law, the prosecutor should draw the deficiency to the judge's attention. He may not seek by advocacy to influence the court in regard to sentence, and if the defendant is unrepresented he should tell the court of any mitigating circumstances.[3] Overall, he has a duty to be fair. I have indeed known judges to complain that prosecutors are so anxious to be fair that they fail to present the case against the accused with sufficient vigour.

Secondly I come to counsel for the defence. He also will be an advocate in private practice. The best account ever given of his role is, in my opinion, Samuel Johnson's, given during his tour of the Scottish Hebrides in August 1773 and recorded by James Boswell. (I digress to express regret that I cannot refer to Boswell, the greatest biographer in

---

[3] See *Code of Conduct for the Bar of England and Wales*, Annex H, and Archbold, *Criminal Pleading Evidence and Practice*, 43rd edn (1988) vol. I. paras. 4–178, 180.

the English language, as an alumnus of this university. Scottish law being based on civil law principles, it was the practice for aspiring Scottish advocates in the eighteenth century to visit the continent of Europe in order to study the best European models. Thus it was that Boswell's father and grandfather studied here at the University of Leiden. When Boswell's turn came, there was anxious consideration whether he should follow in their footsteps, but in the end he went to the University of Utrecht. I hope, however, that honour will be regarded as satisfied when I record that Utrecht was preferred on social, not academic, grounds and that Boswell was no sooner installed at Utrecht than he bitterly regretted not being here at Leiden).[4] I hope that Boswell's record of Johnson's exposition, long though it is, may be felt to merit quotation:

We talked of the practice of the law. Sir William Forbes said, he thought an honest lawyer should never undertake a cause which he was satisfied was not a just one. 'Sir, (said Mr. Johnson), a lawyer has no business with the justice or injustice of the cause which he undertakes, unless his client asks his opinion, and then he is bound to give it honestly. The justice of the cause is to be decided by the judge. Consider, sir; what is the purpose of courts of justice? It is, that every man may have his cause fairly tried, by men appointed to try causes. A lawyer is not to tell what he knows to be a lie: he is not to produce what he knows to be a false deed; but he is not to usurp the province of the jury and of the judge, and determine what shall be the effect of evidence,— what shall be the result of legal argument. As it rarely happens that a man is fit to plead his own cause, lawyers are a class of the community, who, by study and experience, have acquired the art and power of arranging evidence, and of applying to the points at issue what the law has settled. A lawyer is to do for his client all that his client might fairly do for himself, if he could. If, by a superiority of attention, of knowledge, of skill, and a better method of communication, he has the advantage of his adversary, it is an advantage to which he is entitled. There must always be some advantage, on one side or other; and it is better that advantage should be had by talents, than by chance. If lawyers were to undertake no causes till they were sure they were just, a man might be precluded altogether from a trial of his claim, though, were it judicially examined, it might be found a very just claim.

"This", Boswell comments, "was sound practical doctrine, and rationally repressed a too refined scrupulosity of conscience".[5] So the duty of

---

[4] *Boswell in Holland* 1763–1764, ed. Pottle, pp. 3, 9, 10, 16.
[5] Boswell, *Journal of a Tour to the Hebrides* (OUP, 1974, p. 175).

counsel for the defence is, within the limits prescribed by practice and propriety, to do the best he can for his client according to his instructions.

Thirdly, the defendant. He may play as large or as small a part in his trial as he chooses. (I hope it will not be regarded as sexist to cast this villain as a male). Until 1898 he had no general right to give evidence at his own trial. There were several, somewhat illogical, reasons for this: partly it was thought that as an interested party evidence was of no value; partly it was to protect him against incriminating himself, partly it was a reaction against the oppression of the Court of Star Chamber which had, in the seventeenth century, obliged those brought before it to answer questions on oath.[6] During the nineteenth century the defendant was given the right to make an unsworn statement from the dock—a valuable right, because it enabled him to appeal to the emotions of the jury while not exposing him to the hazards of cross-examination by counsel for the prosecution. It was, however, a right capable of abuse, and this led to its abolition in 1982.[7] Although since 1898 the defendant has been free to testify in his own defence if he wishes,[8] the choice whether to do so rests with him and his advisers. They have to balance the chances of weakening the prosecution or strengthening the defence cases against the risk that the defendant when subjected to skilful and searching questioning may make damaging admissions. It might be thought that an honest man, charged with an offence he did not commit, would leap at the opportunity to establish his innocence before the jury through his own mouth, but the defendant's right to remain silent is jealously protected. The prosecution may not comment on the defendant's failure to give evidence.[9] If the judge comments on the defendant's failure in his direction to the jury, he must be very circumspect in doing so: he must tell the jury that the defendant is fully entitled to give no evidence, and his failure to give evidence must not be taken as evidence of guilt; stronger or less balanced comment may lead to a conviction being quashed.[10] The rule in The Netherlands and Germany is, as I understand, rather similar. So the defendant may play the role of mute observer or active participant: to advise which is often the most anxious and difficult decision the criminal defender has to make.

In turning, fourthly, to the criminal jury I am anxious to stress the

[6] Cross on *Evidence*, 7th edn (1990) pages 203–204.
[7] Criminal Justice Act 1982, s. 72.   [8] Criminal Evidence Act 1898, s. 1.
[9] Criminal Evidence Act 1898, s. 1(b).
[10] See, e.g. *R* v. *Sparrow* (1973) 57 Cr. App. R. 352.

central and also the extraordinary role of this body, quite different from the lay judges seen in the German criminal courts or the jurors found in the French *cours d'assises*. Unqualified by legal knowledge or forensic experience, jurors are nonetheless entrusted, in any major trial, however momentous, with the sole decision on whether the case is established against the dcfcndant or not. The judge will instruct the jury on the relevant law, but the jury may acquit in disregard of his direction with impunity. The judge must tell the jury that its task is to decide the disputed issues of fact, ignoring any views of his which they do not accept. Any decision by the jury to acquit is final, any decision to convict (after a properly conducted trial and a correct direction on the law is exceedingly hard to challenge. They need give no reasons for their decision. They enjoy full judicial privilege and are not accountable for anything said or done in the discharge of their office. Any attempt to influence their decision by abuse, threats or media pressure is punishable as a contempt.[11] So it is to obtain, disclose or solicit any details of the jury's deliberations after verdict, a provision which makes academic enquiry into the working of the jury system virtually impossible.[12] Lord Devlin was reflecting popular sentiment when he wrote:

So that trial by jury is more than an instrument of justice and more than one wheel of the constitution: it is the lamp that shows that freedom lives.[13]

The jury is seen as a guarantee of freedom for, as Lord Dvelin also says, "no tyrant could afford to leave a subject's freedom in the hands of twelve of his countrymen".[14] So when, as happens from time to time, it is proposed to limit a defendant's right to choose jury trial in more minor cases, or when, as happened in 1986, it is proposed to conduct complex cases of serious fraud without a jury,[15] there is a storm of popular and parliamentary protest and the proposal founders. I stress both the finality of the jury's verdict and the very deep popular attachment to jury trial because both are directly germane to the problems I shall shortly discuss and the difficulty of finding a solution.

Fifthly, I come to the judge. He will until appointed to the judicial bench in middle age, have spent his career in private practice, almost certainly as an advocate. It is customary to speak of the judge presiding over the trial, and in the case of a criminal trial the expression is particularly apt. For the judge takes (or should take) no part in the

---

[11] Lord Devlin, *Trial by Jury* (revised edn 1976), p. 41.
[12] Contempt of Court Act 1981, s. 8.   [13] Devlin, *op cit.*, p. 164.
[14] *Ibid.*, p. 164.   [15] Fraud Trials Committee Report (1986).

adversarial contest between prosecuting and defending counsel. He will have played no part at all in the investigation or preparation of the case. He will usually have had nothing whatever to do with the case until he receives the papers very shortly before the trial begins. He is above the battle. But this detachment from the fray does not mean that he has no important role to play. His function is three-fold. First of all it is his duty to see that the trial is regularly conducted according to settled legal rules. Thus if, to take just one example, either party objects to the admissibility of evidence which the other party wishes to call, it is for the judge, applying the established law of evidence, to rule whether the evidence is admissible or not. Secondly, and perhaps more importantly, the judge has many discretionary powers, that is, powers which he is not required by law to exercise in a certain way but which he exercises in accordance with what justice seems to him to require, his overriding duty being to ensure a fair trial for the defendant. Some of these discretionary powers have grown up at common law, others have been conferred by statute. They are far-reaching in their scope and may have an important impact on the outcome of the trial. Thus where two or more defendants are accused jointly, the judge may order them to be tried separately if he thinks it may be unfairly prejudicial to one defendant to be tried at the same time as another. Where several charges are joined in one indictment against a defendant, the judge may order different charges to be tried separately if he is of opinion that a person may be prejudiced or embarrassed in his defence by reason of being charged with more than one offence in the same indictment.[16] Or, to take another important example, the judge may exclude evidence which is technically admissible if its prejudicial effect in blackening the conduct or character of the accused in his judgment outweighs its value in proving the case against him. This discretion, which originally grew up at common law,[17] has recently been embodied in a statute[18] which provides:

In any proceedings the court may refuse to allow evidence on which the prosecution proposes to rely to be given if it appears to the court that, having regard to all the circumstances, including the circumstances in which the evidence was obtained, the admission of the evidence would have such an adverse effect on the fairness of the proceedings that the court ought not to admit it.

[16] Indictments Act 1915, s. 5(3).
[17] It is traceable back to *R* v. *Christie* [1914] A.C. 545.
[18] Police and Criminal Evidence Act 1984, s. 78.

A learned author has recently identified literally dozens of discretionary powers exercisable by the criminal judge.[19] I cannot of course mention them all, but I do wish to stress the range of powers available to the judge: he will exercise them constantly bearing in mind that the final decision rests with the jury, and so his concern will be to ensure that the case reaches the jury in a form fit for their fair decision. The proper exercise of these powers is often an anxious matter for the judge. He cannot simply protect the defendant against prejudice, since of course the prosecution evidence and the cross examination of defence witnesses including the defendant himself will ordinarily be prejudicial to the defendant, and the whole purpose of the prosecution is to prejudice. So the judge has to distinguish that which is unfairly prejudicial from that which is simply prejudicial, and that is not so easy.

The Judge's third important role is to direct and sum up the case to the jury. So far as the law is concerned, he will instruct the jury as simply and accurately as he can on the principles of law applicable to the case. Thus he will, for example, tell the jury what mental intention must be proved before they can convict of murder, or what are the ingredients of theft. He will tell the jury to accept the law as accurately stated by him and this the jury should do although, as I have already said, if the jury choose to defy the judge's ruling on the law in order to acquit there is nothing anyone can do about it. When he turns to the facts the judge must tell the jury that all factual issues are for their decision alone. While a judge may, within limits, make his own views on the facts and the credibility of witnesses (including the defendant) clear, a resulting conviction will be quashed if he fails to emphasise that it is for the jury, not him, to decide what evidence to accept and whether guilt is established to the requisite standard. When dealing with the facts the judge's real task is to dissect and analyse the issues which the jury must decide, in the light of his ruling on the law, to help them in their task. He must also instruct them, as a matter of law, that they must not convict the defendant unless they are all (or, after a long period of deliberation and a further judicial direction, by a majority of not less than 10–2[20] sure that he is guilty.

I shall say nothing of the judge's further function—of passing sentence on a defendant convicted by the jury—since that has no relevance to the subject of this lecture.

---

[19] R. Pattenden, *Judicial Discretion and Criminal Litigation* 2nd edn, 1990.
[20] Juries Act 1974, s. 17.

Lastly I should mention the Criminal Division of the Court of Appeal which is, in all save a handful of cases raising points of pure legal principle, a defendant's final court of appeal following a jury trial. The Court of Appeal's powers are statutory and the Court must allow an appeal against conviction if they think

(a) that the conviction should be set aside on the ground that in all the circumstances of the case it is unsafe or unsatisfactory;
(b) that the judgment of the court of trial should be set aside on the ground of a wrong decision of any question of law; or
(c) that there was a material irregularity in the course of the trial.

But the Court may dismiss the appeal, even if they think one of these conditions might be made out, if they consider that no miscarriage of justice has actually occurred.[21] The Home Secretary, acting for this purpose as if he were a minister of justice, may refer a case to the Court of Appeal for its consideration, and this is a power regularly exercised.[22] It is an important power to which I shall return. But if there has already been an unsuccessful appeal the Home Secretary will ordinarily refer a case to the Court of Appeal only if new evidence has come to light, not presented to the jury, and possibly capable of throwing doubt on the soundness of the conviction.

It is not altogether easy for me, as one bred up in this system of criminal justice, to know how this brief and impressionistic glimpse of how the system is meant to work will strike those not so conditioned. The audience may be wondering how such a system, combining the certainty which is required of the law with the flexibility needed for ensuring justice in the individual case, and rooted in the necessity to convince a jury randomly drawn from the general public of the defendant's guilt, can give rise to miscarriages of justice. Or the audience may be wondering how a system so deficient in the fundamental safeguards which a citizen is entitled to expect ever enjoyed the confidence which the British public traditionally placed in it. I must hope to have provoked, at least tentatively, the first of these reactions, for if not there will be rather less interest in what I have to say about how miscarriages have occurred and what may be done to prevent them. I suppose a purist might argue that a miscarriage of justice occurs as much when a guilty man is acquitted as when an innocent man is convicted. It is not, however, the acquittal of the guilty which on the whole gives rise

---

[21] Criminal Appeal Act 1968, s. 2.   [22] *Ibid.*, s. 17.

to public disquiet, and the occasional acquittal of guilty defendants is, I think, generally accepted as the price which has to be paid for observance of the beneficial principle that the defendant shall enjoy the benefit of any doubt. No doubt the courts of the Netherlands, France, Germany and elsewhere which observe the same principle do so for the same sort of reason. By miscarriages of justice, therefore, I mean and mean only cases in which a defendant later established to be innocent or about whose guilt there is later shown to be real doubt is tried and convicted for a crime he did not commit or may well not have committed. If the wrong is corrected in the ordinary process of appeal, the case is not in my view to be regarded as a miscarriage, for the ordinary machinery of justice has correctly operated to deliver the right result. The archetypal miscarriage of justice occurs where the defendant's appeal against conviction is unsuccessful and he has served a sentence, perhaps of years, before the error or doubt becomes apparent.

It seems probable that the most fruitful source of miscarriages, in the sense I have just defined, arises from the honest but mistaken identification of a suspect as the author of a crime. Typically, a crime is committed; a witness or witnesses of the crime, most frequently the victim, has only a brief glimpse of the criminal; a suspect is arrested; the witness confidently identifies the suspect as the criminal; the jury convict; an appeal fails; it is later—perhaps much later—established, perhaps because of new evidence, perhaps because another man confesses (demonstrably truthfully) to having committed the crime, that the convicted man could not or may not have committed it.

This is not a new problem. After years of agitation by weighty authorities, notably Sir James Fitzjames Stephen,[23] the Court of Criminal Appeal (as it was then called) was finally set up in 1907[24] as a result of public disquiet concerning the case of Adolf Beck. At a trial in 1896 ten women identified Beck as the man who had defrauded them. He was convicted and served a sentence of seven years penal servitude. In 1904 he was tried again for further offences of the same kind and five women identified Beck as the man who had defrauded them. He was again convicted. It was later proved that all fifteen witnesses, although honest and party to no conspiracy against Beck, had been mistaken. It was doubtless hoped that the Court of Criminal Appeal would be effective to prevent repetition of such miscarriages.

---

[23] See K.J.M. Smith, *James Fitzjames Stephen* (1988).
[24] Criminal Appeal Act 1907.

Unhappily, this has not proved to be so. In 1969 Laslo Virag was convicted of a shooting offence. He was convicted and his appeal failed. Only after he had been in prison for some years did it emerge that he had been wrongly convicted, another man having confessed to the crime and been found in possession of the gun from which the bullet in question had been fired. Luke Dougherty was convicted of stealing curtains from a shop in 1973. His defence was that he had been on a coach outing to the sea at the time of the crime. Two shop assistants identified him as the thief. Two others who had been on the coach trip gave evidence supporting Dougherty's defence. They were not believed by the jury, who convicted. An appeal failed. It was only later, when further statements were taken from those on the coach, that the truth of Dougherty's account became clear. The Home Secretary referred the case back to the Court of Appeal and the conviction was quashed.[25]

Shortly after the quashing of this conviction a committee under the chairmanship of Lord Devlin was established to consider evidence of identification in criminal cases. It recommended that save in exceptional circumstances convictions should not be permitted to rest on eyewitness evidence of identification alone. It wishes this requirement to be statutory. This recommendation has not been followed. Instead, the Court of Appeal in *R* v. *Turnbull*[26] laid down detailed rules for the guidance of trial judges directing juries in eye-witness identification cases. Thus juries must be told to consider the circumstances in which the witness saw the defendant, the length of time the witness saw the defendant, the lighting conditions, the opportunity for close observation, the previous contact between the parties (if any), and so on. Above all, the jury must be told in clear terms that a mistaken witness may be a very convincing witness and that an entirely honest witness may nonetheless be mistaken. These rules fall somewhat short of Lord Devlin's recommendation, but the Court of Appeal is likely to quash a conviction if a full *Turnbull* direction is not given to the jury in a case where it should have been.

The *Turnbull* directions, again, have failed to prevent miscarriages. The case of Anthony Mycock is a good example. He was convicted in 1983 and sentenced to 5 years imprisonment for attacking a woman late at night in the course of a burglary at her home. She gave a detailed description of her assailant. Mycock did not fit this description but she

---

[25] For information on this and other cases I am very greatly indebted to a report *"Miscarriages of Justice"* published by JUSTICE in 1989.

[26] [1977] Q.B. 224.

identified him at a parade some weeks after the attack. The jury convicted and an appeal failed. The conviction was later quashed on a reference back to the Count by the Home Secretary after it came to light that the woman had herself sold many of the items she claimed to have been stolen in the burglary and had, immediately after the incident, identified a different man (also, curiously, called Mycock) as the culprit.

It may well be asked why, in these and perhaps other cases, the Court of Appeal did not, as its founding fathers intended, detect the error and put the matter right. In part at least the answer is to be found in the tradition, on which I have already commented, of regarding the verdict of a properly directed jury as almost sacrosanct. From the outset the Court of Criminal Appeal made it clear that its function was not to re-try cases properly left to the jury.[27] As the Lord Chief Justice put it in 1949.

Where there is evidence on which a jury can act, and there has been a proper direction to the jury, this Court cannot substitute itself for the jury and retry the case. That is not our function. If we took any other attitude it would strike at the very root of trial by jury.[28]

The judgment of the Court of Appeal when dismissing Mycock's original appeal illustrates the point very clearly. The Court held, as counsel for Mycock accepted, that the trial judge had directed the jury strictly in accordance with the *Turnball* guidelines. He had warned the jury against the danger of relying on the identification of a single eye witness. He had forcefully told them that a convincing witness could be mistaken. He had pointed out the discrepancies between the woman's description and Mycock's appearance. The Court of Appeal acknowledged the difficulties and dangers inherent in evidence of this sort, but held that they were overcome by a proper direction to the jury. Since the matter had been fairly left to the jury, the jury were entitled to convict and there was (the Court of Appeal held) nothing unsafe or unsatisfactory in the conviction.[29]

It would seem that present procedures provide inadequate protection. Steps to tighten police practice in identifying suspects at the investigatory stage have already been taken.[30] There is, however, as I think, force in the suggestions made that the Devlin Committee's recommendations should be given statutory force, superseding the *Turnbull* guidelines,

---

[27] *R* v. *Williamson*, The Times, 16th May 1908.
[28] *R* v. *McGrath* [1949] 2 E.R. 495.
[29] See *JUSTICE* report, *supra*, at pages 87–88.
[30] Pursuant to Code of Practice D under the Police and Criminal Evidence Act 1984.

and that the Court of Appeal should be more ready to interfere where it has doubts about the correctness of the jury's verdict.[31]

I should mention, although I do not wish to linger on, a further serious source of miscarriages: the voluntary but false confession. The best known cases are those of Timothy Evans, who was hanged in 1950 for murdering his child and later pardoned, and the case of three young men convicted in 1972 of murdering Maxwell Confait, their convictions being later quashed. In each case the convictions rested on confessions which were made voluntarily but were false. To the ordinary person, and to the juries who tried these cases, it would seem unreasonable that anyone of sound mind should voluntarily confess to a crime he had not committed, and no doubt the incidence of such confessions is small. But a growing body of evidence[32] shows that certain people will for psychological and other reasons, in the absence of any improper pressure, threats, inducements, fraud or violence confess to crimes they have not committed. The most constructive proposals for remedying this problem are, I think, that interrogations should be video-taped so that the manner in which a confession is made may be assessed; that defendants should have an early opportunity of disavowing a confession before a judicial officer; that the truthfulness of a confession should require to be corroborated by independent evidence; and, perhaps, that a defendant's suggestibility should be accepted as a proper subject for expert evidence.[33]

These cases are in themselves serious enough, but it is not they which have in recent years and months caused our English criminal procedures to be the subject of serious questioning and concern. That has been very largely provoked by cases arising from the activities of Irish terrorists on the mainland of Britain. The setting has unfortunately become familiar enough. A bomb is placed, often in a public house, timed to explode during the evening when the public house is crowded. The bomb explodes, killing and injuring members of the public. There is a widespread reaction of public outrage. The situation is fraught with difficulty, because the responsible police forces come under the strongest pressure to bring the perpetrators of such atrocities to justice and jurors would be less than human if, despite the strongest judicial warnings, they were not tempted to reflect the sense of outrage felt by the community as a whole.

[31] See the *Justice* report, *supra*, pages 74–75, paras. 6 and 13.
[32] See the *Justice* report, *supra*, pages 27–30, paras. 3.13–3.19.
[33] See the *Justice* report, *supra*, pages 74–75, paras. 3, 7 and 8.

The three cases which have really excited public concern have become popularly, and sometimes officially, known as the Birmingham Six, the Guildford Four and the Maguire Seven.

Of these three cases I put on one side the Birmingham Six, which is not to be regarded as a miscarriage of justice. The Birmingham Six were arrested, tried and convicted following the detonation of bombs in public houses in Birmingham causing multiple deaths and injuries. Their appeal failed. Following public agitation, including press comment and the publication of at least one book, the Home Secretary referred the case back to the Court of Appeal. A long and detailed hearing then took place before the Lord Chief Justice and two senior Lords Justices, who delivered a lengthy judgment dismissing the appeals and holding that the convictions were not unsafe or unsatisfactory. Since then new evidence has come to light and the Home Secretary has referred the case back to the Court of Appeal yet again. The further hearing has not yet taken place. There remain some sections of the public which continue to challenge the correctness of the convictions, but as matters stand the Court of Appeal's decision is that the convictions were sound and it would be quite improper of me to question the Court of Appeal's decision, which in any event I do not. I express no personal opinion one way or the other but simply record what has happened.

So I pass to the Guildford Four. On 5th October 1974 a bomb exploded in a public house in Guildford, during the evening, killing 5 people and injuring over 50. Less than an hour later, another bomb exploded in another public house in Guildford, injuring 11 people. Two days later a bomb was thrown through the window of a public house in Woolwich, killing 2 people and injuring 27. Investigations were made by the Surrey and Metropolitan Police forces and the Guildford Four were arrested, tried and convicted of causing these explosions. The case against them rested solely on confessions which they were said to have made while in the custody of the Surrey police. The defendants disputed the truth of these confessions and denied that they were freely given but these issues were decided against them. That was for many years the end of the matter. Further investigation, however, threw doubt on these convictions, which aroused expressions of concern at the highest level,[34] and the Home Secretary referred the case back to the Court of Appeal. Three results followed. First, the prosecuting

---

[34] From, among others, Lord Devlin, Lord Scarman and the Cardinal Archbishop of Westminster.

authorities accepted in the Court of Appeal that they could not seek to uphold the convictions, which were accordingly quashed last October. Secondly, Sir John May, a recently retired Lord Justice of Appeal, was appointed to inquire into the convictions of the Guildford Four and the related convictions of the Maguire Seven. And thirdly, criminal proceedings were begun against certain officers of the Surrey police.

These criminal proceedings have caused Sir John May to defer, until their conclusion, his inquiry into the case of the Guildford Four. But it is clear that the convictions were quashed because it had become clear that Surrey police officers had seriously misled the court when they gave evidence in respect of the confessions. There are, I think, two points worthy of note even at this interim stage.

First, in England the investigation of any crime up to the time a suspect is charged with an offence is exclusively in the hands of the police. Thereafter, since 1985,[35] the preparation of the case is handled by a body, the Crown Prosecution Service, under the direction of the Director of Public Prosecutions and ultimately the Attorney General. But during the very important period when suspects are arrested and interrogated the police, although now subject to detailed statutory rules,[36] are not in any way supervised by any independent, let alone judicial, authority. This lack of supervision presents no danger if the probity of the investigating police officers and the experts they consult can be relied on without question. But it may be thought to present the gravest dangers if these police officers or experts are or even may be dishonest, unscrupulous, overzealous or willing to cut corners to secure the conviction of a suspect of whose guilt they are, for reasons good or bad, convinced.

The second point again concerns the appellate jurisdiction. Where a defendant challenges the voluntariness and truth of a confession, the issue of voluntariness is tried by the judge alone because if the confession was involuntary evidence of it cannot be placed before the jury. If, having heard the conflicting evidence in the absence of the jury, the judge rules the confession to have been voluntary, evidence of it is placed before the jury[37] who, having in their turn heard the conflicting evidence, must decide whether the confession was truthful or not. This situation is very far from unusual, since in a significant proportion of criminal trials defendants who have made damaging confessions seek

[35] Prosecution of Offences Act 1985.
[36] Under the Police and Criminal Evidence Act 1984.
[37] Unless the judge, in the exercise of his discretion, rules that it should not.

to renounce or disown them, frequently contending that they never made them at all. Save in an extreme case, or a case where the judge has fallen into legal error, the Court of Appeal judges will be very slow to reverse the trial judge's decision on voluntariness, he having enjoyed the opportunity denied to them of seeing and hearing the witnesses and forming a first-hand impression of where the truth lay. On grounds now familiar, the Court will be even slower to reverse the jury's decision on credibility where the issue has been fully and fairly laid before it. One must question whether the Court of Appeal is an effective sensor to detect miscarriages of justice involving no error of law or irregularity of procedure.

It would be rash to suggest solutions when Sir John May's inquiry into the Guildford Four has not begun. The remedies already mentioned—a requirement that confessions be corroborated, an early hearing before a judicial officer—will no doubt be considered. So, perhaps, will be a suggestion made by Lord Scarman that the investigation of offences be the subject of judicial oversight, a proposal tentatively favoured by one political party.

Sir John May has made an interim report on the case of the Maguire Seven.[38] Of the Seven, four (two parents and two children, the youngest aged 13 on arrest) belonged to the Maguire family and two more were related. The seventh was a family friend. One of the Seven was the father of one of the Guildford Four, and it was (it seems) as a result of statements said to have been made by the Guildford Four that the Seven were arrested, on the evening of the 3rd December 1974. All their hands and fingernails were swabbed and scraped that same night as the first step in a scientific investigation and the police took possession of a large quantity of plastic gloves found in a kitchen drawer. The personal samples and the plastic gloves were sent for examination to a government scientific laboratory where they were subjected to a testing procedure technically known as thin layer chromatography (or TLC).

The Maguire Seven stood trial at the Old Bailey on an indictment which charged each of them with having had in his or her possession or control an explosive substance, namely nitroglycerine, in circumstances giving rise to a reasonable suspicion that it was not possessed or controlled for a lawful object.[39] The trial lasted some seven weeks

[38] 12th July 1990. My summary of the facts, necessarily somewhat over-simplified, is entirely based on Sir John May's report.
[39] Explosive Substances Act 1883, s. 4.

and they were all convicted. Their attempt to challenge these convictions in the Court of Appeal proved unsuccessful.

The prosecution case against the Seven rested in the main on the following points:

1. The samples taken from six of the Seven were shown by the TLC tests to contain small traces of nitroglycerine.
2. In the case of the seventh, Annie Maguire, although the personal samples proved negative, the gloves which were hers were shown by the TLC tests to contain small traces of nitroglycerine.
3. The TLC testing carried out was specific to identify nitroglycerine, that is, the positive results could not have been given by any other substance, whether explosive or non-explosive.
4. The finding of nitroglycerine under the fingernails of all the Seven save Annie Maguire showed that the explosive had been handled or kneaded as a baker dough and could not have been the result of innocent contamination.

At the eleventh hour of the trial, when the judge was on the point of beginning to sum up, a document came to light (emanating from the laboratory which had carried out the TLC testing, and dating from before the Guildford explosions) showing that these tests as carried out did not distinguish between nitroglycerine and another explosive substance, PETN. Coming when it did, this document placed all parties in a quandary. On its face the document contradicted the third prosecution point I have summarised, although the prosecution still believed that they could show (because of the colour development of the samples) that the samples were nitroglycerine and not PETN. The defence for their part, believing the closing speeches for the defendants to have been effective, were reluctant that witnesses should be re-called for further questioning and the issues re-opened afresh. Accordingly, and with the judge's agreement, the new document was placed before the jury with a short written statement agreed by all parties which concluded:

It is clear that there is no suggestion by either the prosecution or the defence that PETN was a substance either on the swabs or the gloves.

In his interim report Sir John May expressed the personal conclusion that the convictions were unsound, that the Home Secretary should refer the cases to the Court of Appeal and that the Court should be invited to set aside the convictions.[40] The cases were duly referred but the further appeals have yet to be heard by the Court.

For the purpose of Sir John May's inquiry further scientific tests were ordered to be carried out by a distinguished independent chemist. These tests showed that the TLC technique used in 1974 could not distinguish between nitroglycerine and PETN. Even more importantly, they showed that significant and detectable amounts of nitroglycerine could be picked up, and found under the fingernails, as a result of handling a contaminated object such as a towel. Plastic gloves could similarly become contaminated if they came into contact with a hand which was itself contaminated. These findings destroyed the scientific premise upon which the prosecution case had been founded, because the evidence did not suffice to show that the defendants had possessed or controlled any explosive substance, innocent contamination remaining a possibility, or that the contaminating substance was nitroglycerine rather than PETN.

In his report Sir John May criticised almost all the parties whose roles I earlier described. He implicitly criticised counsel for the prosecution and the defence for dealing with the last minute document in the way they agreed to do without recalling witnesses. He criticised the judge for giving that agreement his blessing. He criticised the prosecution for failing to make the government scientists' original notes available to the defence on their request. He criticised the judge for failing fully to appreciate and explain to the jury that the TLC testing carried out was not, as the prosecution had contended almost throughout the trial, specific to identify nitroglycerine. He also criticised the judge for allowing evidence to be given of TLC tests being carried out on a large number of members of the public, with negative results, when there was no evidence of how the tests had been conducted. He criticised the Court of Appeal for upholding the judge's direction to the jury on the significance of the last-minute document and for upholding the judge's admission of the evidence of random testing.

But the main weight of Sir John May's criticism was directed at the government scientists who appeared for the prosecution. They had known throughout, he found, that the TLC tests were not specific to nitroglycerine, but had failed to say so. They had testified that second tests were not necessary or practicable although second tests had in fact been carried out and proved negative. They had failed to disclose the results

---

[40] Pages 50–1, paras. 14.3 and 14.5.

of the tests carried out during the trial. They had spoken as if with firsthand knowledge of tests which had in fact been carried out by others. Sir John concluded that if all these matters had been known to the jury the trial might have turned out differently. So once again one is confronted by a miscarriage of justice deriving, certainly in the main, not from defects in the trial process as such but from failure of the trial procedures to detect and neutralise error or malpractice in the preceding investigatory stages.

The cases which have given rise to concern are, relatively speaking, few in number but the results have been serious and unacceptable.[41] Many solutions have been suggested. I fear this lecture would be of even more intolerable length were I to do more than touch, and that superficially, on four of the more important.

For many years it was the practice of the Court of Appeal, in an appeal when new evidence was before it,[42] to ask itself the question whether the new evidence might have led the original jury to entertain a reasonable doubt about the guilt of the accused.[43] This of course reflected the principle I have ventured to emphasise that guilt and innocence are questions for jurors not judges. In 1973–1974 the Court of Appeal and the House of Lords adopted a new line, of asking whether the new evidence caused them to entertain a reasonable doubt about the conviction.[44] This change of front has been passionately and authoritatively criticised,[45] as many would think justly. Not only does it involve an usurpation by judges of the jurors' role, but it involves great practical problems, because although the appellate judges have heard and considered the fresh evidence, given orally, they have only the written record of the evidence originally given, so they have to compare the impression given by live witnesses against the record of what was said before, not of course knowing why the jury decided to convict or where, if anywhere, their hesitations lay. The jury might, for example, have accepted a confession as true at the original trial when, with the new evidence before them, they would not. How can the judges tell? A reversion to the former practice has much to commend it.

---

[41] One need only mention the case of *R* v. *Cooper and McMahon* in which there were five separate appeal hearings before the Home Secretary exercised his prerogative power to release the men.

[42] Under the Criminal Appeal Act 1968, s. 23 and its predecessor section.

[43] See, e.g. *R* v. *Parks* (1961) 46 Cr. App. R. 29.

[44] *R* v. *Stafford & Luvaglio* [1974] AC 878.

[45] Notably by Lord Devlin, "The Judge and the Jury: Sapping and Undermining", published in *The Judge* (1981).

The second suggestion is closely linked: that the Court of Appeal should be much readier to exercise its power to order a re-trial. These powers have existed since 1964 where a conviction has been quashed following the admission of fresh evidence on appeal[46] and since 1988 on the quashing of any conviction.[47] But the power has been very sparingly exercised,[48] no doubt because of the difficulty of conducting a fair and effective trial years after the event. It may, however, be that greater readiness to order re-trials, in cases where judges have real doubts about how new evidence would have affected the jury's minds or about the soundness of the conviction, would offer a partial solution.

A more radical proposal which has attracted considerable support[49] is that there should be an independent body with the responsibility of reviewing alleged miscarriages of justice. This has been rejected by the Government as violating the constitutional principle that the administration of justice is a matter for the courts. This principle is not, however, rigidly observed, as shown by the Home Secretary's power to release convicted prisoners whose appeals have been dismissed, and the proprieties could be preserved if the tribunal were composed of members, such as members of the Judicial Committee of the Privy Council, who although judges stand (or sit) somewhat outside the ordinary court system.[50] If lay membership were thought to be important, the Privy Council could no doubt supply suitable members, although judicial hackles might predictably rise.

The most radical proposal of all is that recently adopted by the Liberal Democrats at their recent party conference that a Royal Commission be appointed

to consider the advantages and/or disadvantages of a change from the adversary system of criminal justice to the inquisitorial system as practised on the continent. . . .

Of course it may be said that there is nothing radical about considering something, and all possibilities should doubtless be considered.

But those who call for proposals to be considered often view consideration as a halfway house on the road to implementation and I would

---

[46] s. 1 Criminal Appeal Act 1964; s. 7 Criminal Appeal Act 1968.

[47] s. 43 Criminal Justice Act 1988.

[48] See P. O'Connor, "The Court of Appeal: Re-Trials and Tribulations" [1990] *Cr.L.Rev.* 615 at 622.

[49] E.g. from the *Justice* report at p. 75; the Home Affairs Committee of the House of Commons; O'Connor, *op cit.*, at 624–6.

[50] This has been suggested informally by Lord Scarman.

have great reservations about implementing this change. I give three brief reasons. First, I simply do not think that human institutions can be lifted out of one society which has grown up round them and adapted itself to them and transplanted into another quite different society whose other organs are not adapted to receive them. Secondly, as our system operates in our society—I make no comparison with any other system in any other society—it has great strengths which we should be slow to sacrifice. Thirdly, serious though these warts, or carbuncles, that I have described undoubtedly are, I think they can be treated by medical means. I do not think they call for heroic transplant surgery. But there I fear I reveal the invincible conservatism traditionally associated with the legal, and particularly the judicial, profession. I will plead guilty if I must.

6

Problems Confronting the Administration of Justice in England

by the Rt. Hon. the Lord Donaldson of Lymington*

When I was invited to deliver this lecture, I accepted with alacrity. I am no stranger to the Low Countries, but this is the first time that I have had the privilege of visiting in the capacity of a lawyer. My first visit was on an occasion of greater historic importance, although it was by no means as comfortable. It was undertaken by road from France and I spent one night under canvas in a public park in Brussels before moving on to Nijmegen. The time was the summer of 1944 and I was a young signals officer attached to the British Guards Armoured Division. The welcome which we received from the people of Brussels on the first day of the liberation of that city was unforgettable. So too was the crushing disappointment when the Arnhem operation failed and the Division found itself halted on the Rhine.

When I left the Army and became a practising lawyer, my wife and I took up sailing as a hobby and it was as an amateur yachtsman that I have continued to visit your country until about 2 years ago when we ceased to own a boat.

My first task when invited to give this lecture was to decide upon a topic upon which to speak. This is not as easy as it might seem at first. I say this because I am not a comparative lawyer and it is therefore difficult to know what subject, which would interest English lawyers, would also interest those from your country. However, over the years when I have visited a number of foreign countries whilst attending legal conferences, I have been struck by the fact that however much our substantive laws and our procedures may differ, the underlying problems confronting the administration of justice in a civil, as opposed to

* The lecture was delivered at the University of Leiden on 16 April 1991.

a criminal, context are the same. They are cost, speed, accessibility and achieving and maintaining public confidence in the system.

In these circumstances I decided to tell you something of the problems which are at present confronting us in England. Since I understand that this lecture may be printed and might even be read by a Welshman, I should perhaps make it clear that in speaking of England I really mean England and Wales, because of course we enjoy a common system of justice. It is, however, tiresome to have continually to refer to both countries and I can only hope that my hypothetical Welsh reader will forgive me. Scotland and Northern Ireland have their own systems upon which I am not competent to speak.

I have also been encouraged to talk about the administration of justice, because I am firmly of the view, which is I know heresy to many lawyers and indeed I suspect to some of my brother judges, that if a choice has to be made, you can do more good for people as a whole by improving the administration of justice—the systems and procedures whereby it is administered—than by reform of the substantive law itself.

Last, but not least, I have chosen this theme because I have personally always derived great benefit from talking to foreign lawyers about the problems which confront them in the administration of justice and about the solutions which they have been exploring. The problems are never the same in detail, but there is almost always an underlying similarity. The solutions can never be the same for them as for us, because solutions do not transplant. This is true even of common law systems which are derived from the same source as ours, such as the United States of America and the older Commonwealth countries. Nevertheless I have always found that such discussions have sparked off ideas of what could be done in my own country in our different context.

It is a curious feature of reforms in the administration of justice that they seem to go in spasms—in fits and starts. The judges are always interested in the subject and do suggest small reforms from time to time. Occasionally they institute major reforms of their own initiative. This was the case at the end of the last century when they and the merchants of the City of London thought that major reforms which had been effected 20 years before by the Judicature Acts still did not go far enough. They instituted the Commercial List, now the Commercial Court, which has grown into an international court. In only 2 out of 10 cases are all the parties English. Of the remaining 8 cases, in 6 of them there are no English parties.

Another reform which was judge-driven occurred in 1979 when Parliament was persuaded to alter the law relating to the supervisory jurisdiction of the courts over arbitration and, in particular, London-based international arbitration. But these are exceptions. The basic reason for this lack of smooth progress is, I think, the fact that it is difficult for the judiciary to introduce reforms without changes in statute law, which is a matter for Parliament, and without the allocation of greater resources, which is a matter for the government of the day. If the judiciary were servants of the state responsible to a Ministry of Justice it might be easier, but I have no doubt whatsoever that the judges' independence of Parliament and of the Executive Government is a benefit which far outweighs any disadvantages.

The particular spasm of reform which is in progress at the moment is without doubt the greatest for a century. I am not quite sure what inspired it. It may be that it was an increase in litigiousness amongst the population leading to a greater interest in the law and its workings. I should be interested to know whether you have experienced the same phenomenon. It may be that it was inspired by increased expectations of what dispute resolution services ought to be provided by a civilised country. It may have stemmed from dissatisfaction with the high cost and apparent slowness of litigation.

What brought it to a head was two initiatives. The first was a Government decision in 1985 to set up an independent body in the nature of a Royal Commission whose terms of reference were to make recommendations to improve the system of civil justice in England and Wales by means of reforms in jurisdiction, procedure and court administration with a view in particular to reducing delay, cost and complexity. This body was known as "The Review Body on Civil Justice". It reported in June 1988.

Meanwhile Mrs. Thatcher's Government which had been re-elected in July 1987 had what most judges regarded as a rush of blood to the head. Based upon its philosophic attachment to competition and what it believed to be the beneficial effects of the market place, without any research and with only limited consultation it produced proposals for major changes in the organisation and functions of the two branches of the English legal profession. Those two branches are, of course, the solicitors who form the retail branch of the profession dealing directly with the public and, if they wish, providing advocacy services in the lower courts and the barristers who form the wholesale or referral branch of the profession and have exclusive rights of audience in the higher courts, acting only on the instructions of solicitors. In particular the Government proposed to take power to alter the professional rules of the two branches and to alter or abolish the division of function between them. The Government also proposed to give competing rights to professional groups who were not lawyers at all. The object of the exercise was said to be to introduce competition as a spur to providing a better service to the public.

Suffice it to say that in the face of very determined, and sometimes rational, opposition from the judiciary and others, who rightly or wrongly saw the proposals as a real threat to the independence of justice in England, the Government modified its proposals. Instead we now have machinery which in due course will produce desirable changes in the different spheres of activity of the two branches of the legal profession and will in appropriate situations enable non-lawyers to play a part, but will preserve the independence of the administration of justice by, amongst other things, giving the four senior judges, of which I am one, a right of veto over Government proposals. As there has as yet been no time for changes to take place, I say no more about this aspect of the matter, than that it is a continuing problem and that some changes will without doubt occur.

Much more interesting for present purposes, were the proposals of the Civil Justice Review Body, with almost all of which I am in total agreement.

The first question which it asked itself was whether there should be any alteration in the hierarchy of the courts. At the time we had a number of local or County Courts whose jurisdiction was in general limited to claims of under £5,000. We also had a national or High Court with unlimited jurisdiction. Unlike most European countries we do not have a career judiciary. Our professional judges are drawn from the practising profession in middle age and either become County Court judges or High Court judges. There is very little movement from one to the other.

The Review Body took the view that whilst we ought not to have a single national court, which might have the effect of eroding the paramount authority of the High Court, there should be no jurisdictional divide. Instead each court would, with certain very limited exceptions, have an unlimited jurisdiction, but cases of lower value should be directed administratively to the County Courts and those of higher value or special complexity to the High Court. It suggested a flexible cut-off band whereby claims worth below £25,000 would normally be tried in the County Courts with those over £50,000 or of special importance or difficulty being tried in the High Court. It also recommended raising the level of claim which qualified for being decided under the simplified small claims procedures of the County Courts (of which there are 268 in England and Wales) in which the parties are not usually represented by lawyers. In a word what was being recommended was a major devolution of work from the High Court to the County Courts and from the County Courts to the Small Claims Courts.

This reform which is eminently sensible brings its own problems with it. Circuit Judges, who try civil cases in the County Courts, are also (like most High Court Judges) charged with the duty of trying criminal cases in what is called the Crown Court. Their existing workload is considerable and it is not clear how they are going to be able to handle the increased volume of work. Nor is it clear whether initially all of them have the necessary training and experience to deal with the much heavier and more complex claims with which they will now be faced.

Next the Review Body turned to consider how procedures could be simplified and costs reduced. So far as costs are concerned, the devolution of work to the County Court should of itself produce some savings, because traditionally lawyers' fees for taking cases in these courts have been lower. But the Review Body rightly wished to go much further. The outstanding feature which it identified was that the vast majority of civil cases never get as far as the stage of being heard and decided by a judge. Before that stage is reached the claims are abandoned or the parties reach an agreed settlement. The Review Body therefore concluded that the procedures should be altered with a view to encouraging settlement at a much earlier stage than occurs at present and at a time when much fewer costs have been incurred.

The chief obstacle to early settlement, apart from incurable and inconsistent optimism by both sides, is ignorance of the strength of your opponent's case. What the Review Body therefore recommended was, in essence, that the parties should be compelled to disclose their hands at the earliest possible moment by an exchange of witness statements and full disclosure of all documentary evidence which was relevant, whether or not it assisted their respective cases. This will enable each party to make a realistic assessment of their chances of success. This reform may seem small, but I have no doubt that in the long run it will be found to have been one of enormous significance.

The Review Body made a vast number of other recommendations, some in respect of matters of detail, some of more general application, but if I were to go into all of these I should not be delivering a lecture, but a complete course of lectures. There is, however, one other recommendation which I believe to be of fundamental importance. This was that the courts should actively manage and control the progress of litigation—"case management" as it is called. Traditionally the English courts have taken the line that whilst they are happy to resolve disputes, it is for the parties, or more accurately their lawyers, to dictate the pace at which litigation should proceed. Where lawyers were busy or incompetent or both—and I fear that this fatal combination does occur—the delays can be horrifying. I need hardly say that when the clients complain, it is the courts which get the blame.

The sheer number of cases in progress at any one time would make active case management difficult were it not for the arrival of small computers. In the Civil Division of the Court of Appeal, for which I am responsible, we have some 1,600 appeals in progress at any one time and we can find out at the press of a button what stage each has reached. If progress is not being maintained, we summon the lawyers and ask for explanations. This approach is being developed for use in the courts of first instance and I hope that in due course the vast majority of cases will be computer-controlled. If either party fails to take the appropriate procedural step within the fixed time table and does not ask the court for an extension of time, the computer will automatically generate a warning letter. If this is ignored and the defaulter is the claimant, he will find that the computer dismisses his claim. If it is the defendant, the computer will give judgment for the claimant.

We have not quite reached that stage in the Court of Appeal, but we do use the computer to monitor our own performance. One of the reforms which we have introduced is a system whereby the court decides the order in which appeals should be heard based upon its assessment of relative urgencies. Thus it is not unknown for the court to hear and determine appeals within a few days, and occasionally a few hours, of the decision being given by the court of first instance.

This results from a firm policy decision that, whatever the difficulties, every appeal must be heard before the passing of time makes it pointless. If, for example, a trial judge makes an order on a Friday morning forbidding the showing of a television programme on Sunday, any appeal has to be determined on the Friday or the Saturday and preferably the Friday because of the problems of re-programming. This is all to the good, but it has a down side. Appeals which have no claim to urgent treatment can go on being displaced by urgent appeals and never get heard at all. To meet this problem each new appeal is given a "hear by" date, like the "sell by" dates on goods in supermarkets. The computer warns the listing staff when the "hear by" date is approaching.

But however much we improve the efficiency of the courts, two problems remain. They are the accessibility and availability of civil justice. The obstacle to accessibility is the cost of legal advice and representation. The obstacle to availability is the lack of sufficient courts to hear the cases.

Let me take first the question of cost. To some extent this can be reduced by simplifying or altering procedures with a view to saving lawyers' time. For example, a few years ago the English Court of Appeal decided to try to reduce the length of oral argument. Such argument is costly because all the lawyers concerned have to be present and the clients may also wish to attend. We did it by requiring the delivery to the court of skeleton arguments for study by the judges in advance of the hearing. This has made it unnecessary for the lawyers to waste time telling the court what the appeal was about and has enabled the judges to adopt a much more interventionist approach than had been traditional with a view to making the lawyers deal at once with the central point or points in the appeal.

But there is no escape from the fact that legal professional advice is expensive. This is not a criticism of lawyers, although a few are undoubtedly very highly paid and arguably overpaid. However the fact is that they have undergone a long and exacting training and they have considerable overhead expenses. Whilst on the subject of expenses, let it be said that modern methods of documentary reproduction, storage and communication have much to answer for in the context of the problems which face the courts not only in England but, I suspect, throughout the Western world. Lawyers, like other professional and business men, have to make large investments in information technology and this cost has to be recovered somehow. Furthermore the ease with which documents can be produced generates mountains of paper which were unheard of in the days of the quill pen. Even the simplest of cases threatens to drown the courts in paper and, when judges protest, lawyers have been known to suggest that it is cheaper to drown the court in paper than to use expensive professional skills in sorting the relevant from the irrelevant. I am not sure that this is right, but if a failure to reduce the quantity of paper saves money, it certainly also contributes to delay in the form of longer and more complex hearings.

But I digress. If legal professional advice and representation is necessarily expensive, something must be done if justice is not to be denied to all but the rich. There are two possible answers. The first, to which I think too little attention is paid, is to make the courts more "layman friendly". In other words, when dealing with cases where the cost of employing lawyers would be disproportionate to the amounts at stake, the courts must be so organised as to be able to deal quickly and efficiently with litigants who seek to argue their own cases and must encourage them to do so. This is the policy in the County Courts when faced with small claims. But I think that the concept of a "small claim" —at present defined as one for less than £1,000—needs looking at again with a view to bringing considerably larger claims within its scope.

The second possible answer is for the state to pay for legal advice and representation, where the litigants cannot afford to do so. There are two ways of doing this. You can have state salaried lawyers who make their services available to litigants who qualify for help, either free or at limited cost. Alternatively you can leave the litigants to engage lawyers of their choice and meet the whole or part of the bills from public funds. In England we have adopted the second alternative, known as the Legal Aid Scheme. It covers legal costs in both criminal and civil cases and has run into deep trouble on three grounds. First, from the point of view of the public purse, it is becoming prohibitively expensive—£852 million last year and expected to rise to £1,150 million this year. Second the lawyers complain that the scale of fees paid under the scheme is wholly uneconomic and many are refusing to act under it. Third, the relatively low level of income and capital at which a litigant ceases to be eligible for civil legal aid leads to a large number of people being in a litigation poverty trap. They are not poor enough for state aid, but cannot afford to litigate any but the simplest of claims.

My own view is that there has to be a fundamental re-appraisal of the whole basis of legal aid, not least because litigants are expected to repay the costs incurred by the state out of any money recovered in the litigation. In practical terms this means that those who are successful and are justified in litigating get loans. Those who are unsuccessful and should not have been litigating get grants. But this is really a subject on its own. Suffice it to say that it is a major political issue at the present time.

The second problem is that we have nothing like enough judges or courts to deal with all the civil disputes which arise. We have only 86

High Court judges or roughly 1 for every 600,000 of our population of slightly over 50 million. We have only 467 circuit judges or roughly 1 for every 100,000. In fact we employ a number of lawyers who are in private practice as part time judges, but the problem still remains and is acute. There are limits to the extent to which it is possible to find suitable lawyers who are prepared to become whole time professional judges, particularly as they can never return to private practice and the pay is not regarded as particularly attractive. Similar problems arise in relation to finding part time judges.

There are two solutions which need to be explored. The first is to expand the already large number of specialist tribunals which deal with disputes about employment law, taxes, welfare payments and the like into the field of consumer claims, landlord and tenant disputes and indeed any largely self-contained area of the law where the members of the tribunal do not need the wide ranging knowledge of the law called for in the case of professional judges. Experienced laymen would be as good as and perhaps better than professional judges. The second is the adoption of what is coming to be called "Alternative Dispute Resolution" or "A.D.R.".

A.D.R. is much under discussion in England at the present time and seems to have considerable marketing appeal. Leaving aside the packaging, which is not unimportant in selling it to the public, each form of A.D.R. involves introducing an independent third party into the dispute, but the intended outcome is different in the two main categories. The intended outcome in the first category is that the third party shall reach a decision which will be binding upon the parties. I personally regard this as neither more nor less than consensual arbitration, which has been with us for well over a century, but it is marketed as something novel and is acquiring new names such as "Rent-a-Judge" where retired judges are employed as the independent third party. In the second category the object of the exercise is different. It is that the intervention of the independent third party shall cause the parties themselves to settle their dispute. This again is not novel and has been known for years under the description of "mediation" or "conciliation". But here again the packaging is sometimes different. For example it is claimed that, particularly in the case of commercial disputes, more cases would settle if senior executives of the parties were more directly involved instead of leaving it all to their lawyers. This has led to the evolution of what is known as a "mini-trial". Essentially what happens is that the arguments and the evidence are put forward in summary form in the presence of the lay clients at a hearing before the independent third party. It is then pointed out to the lay clients that they face a long and expensive trial with inevitable damage to their commercial relationship if they do not settle and, so it is claimed, they usually take the hint.

A.D.R. is very much a growth industry in England and consideration is being given to an experiment designed to show whether it can be incorporated into the formal justice system starting with a small group of County Courts. Whilst I regard the claims made for novelty as largely bogus—judges have for years been persuading parties to settle their disputes—I welcome anything which will assist in the process of disposing of disputes more cheaply and swiftly than is the case at present.

As I have said, we have comparatively few whole time professional judges in proportion to the size of our population—28 Appellate judges, 86 High Court and 467 Circuit Judges. As part of the current reforming mood, it is being suggested that the present system for appointing these judges is unsatisfactory. All are appointed by the Queen. In the case of the more senior appointments—Lord Justice of Appeal and above—she acts on the advice of the Prime Minister. In the case of High Court and Circuit Judges, she acts on the advice of the Lord Chancellor, who is a member of the Government. There is one further difference between the way in which appointments are handled at the different levels in that whereas those who wish to be appointed Circuit Judges apply to the Lord Chancellor for appointment, appointments at more senior levels are by invitation only.

You might be forgiven for thinking that this system would be criticised as likely to lead to the appointment of political judges or their appointment on the basis of political considerations. You would, however, be wrong. No one suggests that it has any such effect and indeed it does not. What is suggested is that it is capable of overlooking suitable or better qualified candidates and that the confidentiality which surrounds the process of selection undermines public confidence in the judiciary.

It is also suggested that it leads to the appointment of too few women judges.

Critics of the system suggest that it should be replaced by one in which a Judicial Appointments Board, with a significant lay element in its membership, makes the necessary recommendations to the Queen. I personally disagree with this suggestion because I do not think that a Commission would or should recommend different appointments from those recommended at present and in my view there would be a risk that, as happens in the United States, the appointment of particular judges would become a matter of public controversy. This would without doubt damage public confidence in the judiciary as a whole.

The fact that lawyers can apply for appointment as Circuit Judges ensures that no suitable applicants for that level of appointment are overlooked. In the case of appointments to the High Court and above, the pool of potential candidates is much smaller and the risk of someone being overlooked is I think negligible. Furthermore the final recommendations by the Prime Minister and the Lord Chancellor are preceded by very wide, although confidential, discussions with judges and lawyers. That there is no consultation with representatives of the general public is understandable, for they would not be in a position to make an informed judgment.

The fact that there are so few women judges in England is a rather different problem. There is 1 Lord Justice of Appeal, 3 High Court Judges and 22 Circuit Judges. In the High Court and below cases are heard by a single judge, who must necessarily be either a man with a man's experience and attitude towards life or a woman with a woman's. I can think of no way in which disputes can be divided into those which should be tried by men and those which should be tried by women. The fact that the judge is a man rather than a woman or *vice versa* should be irrelevant.

But this does not dispose of the real gravamen of the criticism, which is that women who want to become judges are being discriminated against. As one who is directly involved in the process of consultation, I can say firmly that there is no conscious discrimination. We recommend the appointment of whoever we think is the best candidate, whether it is a man or a woman. We may, of course, be mistaken, but that is all that we can be expected to do. However it is said that the figures speak for themselves. I do not think that they do. It must be remembered that appointments are made from lawyers who have been in practice for about 20 years. Twenty years ago there were far fewer women entering the legal profession than men. Furthermore by the stage in their careers at which appointments fall to be made, a lot of women lawyers have left the profession still further reducing the number of women available for appointment and others have taken time off to raise families as a result of which they do not have the experience of their male contemporaries.

I have no doubt that the proportion of women judges will rise, but I see no advantage in changing the present system of selection and great disadvantages in introducing positive discrimination in favour of women. This would discredit *all* women judges.

One further suggestion which is beginning to be made is that we should have a career judiciary as is, I believe, common throughout the Continent. This attracts few supporters. Our starting point is different from that which prevails on the Continent in that our magistrates who try the less serious criminal cases are lay people and not lawyers. Accordingly it would be impossible to become a judge soon after qualification. Furthermore the Circuit Judges as a body are not in terms of a career structure the junior branch of the High Court. They are a quite separate body. Although there have been a few transfers from the Circuit Bench to the High Court Bench, as a general proposition if you become a Circuit Judge you cannot expect to become a High Court Judge at a later stage in your career. High Court Judges are appointed direct from the practising profession. Last, but by no means least, and in this we may be quite wrong, many of us feel that a career structure in which promotion would be something which reflected Government thinking would be destructive of the English judiciary's reputation for independence and willingness, or as the Government would say "enthusiasm", for finding the Government to be in the wrong. We also think, and again I accept that we may be wrong, that authority of English judges in controlling the conduct of hearings depends in large measure upon the fact that the advocates appearing before them know that the judges have themselves been experienced and successful advocates before their appointment to the Bench.

I began this lecture by saying that I had always found it interesting and profitable to learn of the problems which are confronting foreign lawyers and the solutions which they have adopted or are considering. I only hope that in listening to this lecture, you have had the same experience. However that may be, it has been a great privilege and pleasure to be able to talk to you.

7

Fundamental Issues in Privacy Law

*Professor David A. Anderson**

Most legal systems offer some protection from unwanted disclosure of information about a person's private life. Although the form of these remedies varies widely, as do the limitations imposed on them to protect freedom of speech, the underlying issues are universal. Every system must decide what information is private, and how much privacy to sacrifice in the interest of public discussion. I offer some thoughts here on the issues that these decisions raise.

I deal here with only one of the many aspects of privacy. There are vast areas of privacy law dealing with the government's power to search one's person or home or seize one's papers, or demand that one furnish information about one's private life. The power of technology that enables commercial entities to store, process, and distribute information raises important privacy issues that most legal systems are attempting to address. In America, at least, reproductive freedom is treated as a privacy issue, and has generated its own body of constitutional law. I am not here addressing any of these issues. Rather, I address only the problems that arise when media or other private parties disclose truthful information, obtained by legal means, for journalistic purposes. I believe this is the area where privacy issues are toughest, because the conflict between privacy values and free speech values is sharpest here. If privacy issues can be resolved in this context, I believe they will be comparatively easy to resolve in other cases, such as those where private information is obtained by objectionable means, or presented inaccurately, or used for commercial purposes. Resolving the toughest privacy issues may be more difficult, however, than we on either side of the Atlantic have recognised.

In some European legal systems the law of defamation offers some protection for privacy. In the Netherlands, for example, the unintentional

* This article is adapted from a lecture given on 27 November 1992 at the Institute of Anglo-American Law, University of Leiden.

defamation statute[1] provides a cause of action for the publication of truthful information if it causes damage and there was no good reason for the harmful manner in which the defendant published. In the United States the law of defamation provides little protection for privacy, because the First Amendment has been interpreted as requiring the defamation plaintiff to prove the falsity of the publication.[2]

The European Convention on Human Rights states that "Everyone has the right to respect for his private and family life, his home and his correspondence."[3] It allows these rights to be interfered with, however, when necessary "for the protection of the rights and freedoms of others."[4]

In the United States, disclosure of private facts is a tort if the disclosure would be highly offensive to a reasonable person and the information disclosed is not a matter of legitimate public concern. The law of privacy has been developing for 100 years in the United States, and this particular tort is recognised by almost all the jurisdictions. But in practice victims of invasion of privacy almost never succeed. Although there are hundreds of reported cases involving disclosure of private information, only a handful of plaintiffs have prevailed.

Perhaps I can best explain why privacy plaintiffs usually lose by describing three well-known American privacy cases.

Robin Howard's Case

As a teenager in Iowa, Robin Woody was a behaviour problem. She also may have been mentally retarded, but that is unclear. Eventually she was committed to the Jasper County Home for the mentally disabled. The staff described her as aggressive and irresponsible. When Robin was 18, the home's psychiatrist concluded that "she would be a very questionable risk, as far as having and rearing a baby went," so he ordered her sterilized, against her will but with her parents' consent. Not long after the operation she was discharged from the home. Apparently she married and led a more or less normal life.

Five years later, after several deaths and other incidents at the Jasper County Home, the State of Iowa initiated proceedings to revoke the home's licence on the ground that it had a long history of health, safety,

---

[1] Art. 1401, Civil Code.
[2] *Philadelphia Newspapers Inc.* v. *Hepps*, 475 U.S. 767 (1986).
[3] Art. 8, sec. 1, European Convention on Human Rights.
[4] *Id.*, art. 8, sec. 2.

and management problems. Some members of the staff came forward with reports about questionable practices at the home.

The Des Moines Register, one of America's respected regional newspapers, investigated the allegations and published a long article about the home and its history of problems. Deep in the story, the writer included seven paragraphs about the involuntary sterilization of Robin Woody five years earlier. It quoted the psychiatrist's reasons for ordering the surgery, a nurse's recollection of Robin's anguish, and Robin's mother's confirmation that she and Robin's father had consented to the operation. The newspaper said it was unable to locate Robin herself.

Robin, whose surname was now Howard, saw the story, engaged a lawyer, and sued the newspaper for invasion of privacy. Howard's lawyer conceded that the disclosures about her were true, and that her mental or behaviour problems and her commitment to the home were not private facts. He also conceded that the fact of her involuntary sterilization was a matter of legitimate public concern. Ultimately Howard's case rested on a single proposition: that the public's legitimate concern over practices at the home, including involuntary sterilization of young women, did not require or justify the use of her name.

Robin Howard lost. The Iowa Supreme Court held that the newspaper's inclusion of the story of her sterilization

offered a personalized frame of reference to which the reader could relate, fostering perception and understanding. Moreover, it lent specificity and credibility to the report.... The editor also had a right to treat the identity of victims of involuntary sterilizations as a matter of legitimate public concern. The matter is one of grave public interest.... [T]he editors also had a right to buttress the force of their evidence by naming names.... [A]t the time when it was important to separate fact from rumour, the specificity of the report would strengthen the accuracy of the public perception of the merits of the controversy.[5]

Howard's lawyer appealed to the United States Supreme Court, but the Court declined to hear the case.

Hilda Bridges' Case

Hilda Bridges was kidnapped from her workplace in Florida by her estranged husband. At gunpoint he took her to an apartment they had

---

[5] *Howard* v. *Des Moines Register and Tribune Co.*, 283 N.W. 2d 289, 303, cert. denied 445 U.S. 904 (1980).

once shared. Police surrounded the place. The man beat her and forced her to disrobe to discourage her from escaping. Finally he shot himself in the head. Upon hearing the gunshot, the police stormed the apartment and rushed Bridges out. Still naked, she held a dish towel in front of her as police led her out of the apartment.

Waiting outside with the police were reporters and photographers. A photographer took several pictures of Bridges as she emerged. The next day the local newspaper published one of them. It was a dramatic photograph and won several awards for news photography.

Bridges sued for invasion of privacy on a theory similar to Howard's, and originally won a $10,000 judgment. But the Florida Court of Appeal reversed the judgment and dismissed the case. The court said the photograph was not sufficiently offensive to be an invasion of privacy:

The photograph revealed little more than could be seen had [Bridges] been wearing a bikini and somewhat less than some bathing suits seen on the beaches. There were other more revealing photographs taken which were not published. The published photograph is more a depiction of grief, fright, emotional tension, and flight than it is an appeal to other sensual appetites . . .

Just because the story and the photograph may be embarrassing or distressful to the plaintiff does not mean the newspaper cannot publish what is otherwise newsworthy.[6]

Mike Virgil's Case

Sports Illustrated decided to do a story about the daredevil sport of body surfing. The writer contacted surfers at the Wedge, a particularly dangerous beach in California, and soon learned that Mike Virgil was considered by his peers the most fearless of all the body surfers there. The writer contacted Virgil and at first Virgil co-operated, allowing himself to be interviewed and photographed.

But when a fact checker from Sports Illustrated telephoned his home to confirm details of the story, Virgil learned that the story was not just about his prowess as a surfer, but also about his personal peculiarities. The story described Virgil's surfing feats and also contained numerous facts and anecdotes to help explain Virgil's psychological makeup. His wife was quoted as saying "Mike also eats spiders and other insects and things." He was quoted as saying he once dived headfirst down a flight

---

[6] *Cape Publications Inc.* v. *Bridges*, 423 So. 2d 426, 427–8 (*Fla. App.* 1982), cert. denied 464 U.S. 893 (1983).

of stairs at a party, that he sometimes took construction jobs and then dived off billboards or dropped loads of lumber on himself so he could collect unemployment and surf at the Wedge, and that he once bit off the cheek of a man in a gang fight. The article stated that Virgil never learned to read and that he was considered somewhat abnormal by other surfers.

When he learned that the magazine intended to publish these facts he told them he did not want to be mentioned in the story. Sports Illustrated published the story anyway, under the title "The Closest Thing to Being Born."

Mike Virgil sued on the same theory that Howard and Bridges had used. He might have lost on the ground that he had consented, or had himself made public the facts about which he complained. Unlike Howard and Bridges, he had himself provided many of the details of which he now complained. The magazine argued that people who co-operate in the preparation of a story about themselves ought not to be allowed to censor the resulting story by withdrawing consent on the eve of publication. But the courts held that Virgil was entitled to withdraw his consent when he learned the direction the story was taking, because he acted early enough to avoid any unfair burden on the magazine. He was thus in no worse position legally than if the magazine had obtained the information without his cooperation.

But Mike Virgil lost anyway. The court granted the magazine's motion for summary judgment on the ground that no reasonable jury could conclude that the facts revealed about Virgil were sufficiently offensive. The judge said disclosures are not actionable unless they reach a very high level of offensiveness, such as "a morbid and sensational prying into private lives for its own sake."

The above facts [about Virgil] are generally unflattering and perhaps embarrassing, but they are simply not offensive to the degree of morbidity or sensationalism. In fact they connote nearly as strong a positive image as they do a negative one. On the one hand Mr. Virgil can be seen as a juvenile exhibitionist, but on the other hand he also comes across as the tough, aggressive maverick, an archetypal character occupying a respected place in the American consciousness. Given this ambiguity as to whether or not the facts disclosed are offensive at all, no reasonable juror could conclude that they were highly offensive.[7]

---

[7] *Virgil v. Sports Illustrated*, 424 F. Supp. 1286, 1289 (*S.D.Cal.* 1976).

As an alternative ground of decision, the court said even if the disclosures were sufficiently offensive, no reasonable jury could deny that they were a matter of legitimate public concern. The court said it could not be doubted that body surfing in general and Mike Virgil's prowess in the sport were both matters of legitimate public concern. The facts about his personal peculiarities were also of legitimate public concern unless their disclosure was "for its own sake".

Any reasonable person reading the Sports Illustrated article would have to conclude that the personal facts concerning Mike Virgil were included as a legitimate journalistic attempt to explain Virgil's extremely daring and dangerous style of body surfing at the Wedge. There is no possibility that a juror could conclude that the personal facts were included for any inherent, morbid, sensational, or curiosity appeal they might have.[8]

In my view all three of these cases are wrong, but they show how privacy law works in the United States today. They are tough but not aberrational cases. They were decided by respectable courts, and most other courts would have reached the same results. People who sue for unwelcome media disclosures about their private lives almost always lose, usually for the same reasons that Howard, Bridges, and Virgil lost.

In any legal system, the key issues in a privacy case are the same as they were in these three cases:

1. What matters are private?
2. Under what circumstances does the public interest require that media and others be allowed to disclose the facts that normally would be private?

Trying to answer these questions quickly leads us to two more profound issues:

1. Is the concept of privacy normative or empirical? Should the law attempt to reflect what the society in fact considers private, or should it try to tell the society what it ought to consider private?
2. Is it permissible—in a system that values freedom of speech and press—to allow courts to substitute their judgment for that of editors as to what the public is legitimately interested in?

To decide whether privacy is empirical or normative, we have to ask what is the purpose of protecting it. I agree with Robert Post; the

---

[8] *Virgil* v. *Sports Illustrated*, 424 F. Supp. 1286, 1289 (*S.D.Cal.* 1976).

purpose of privacy law is the preservation of norms of civility.[9] It is a means by which society defines its relationship with the individual, just as the law of battery or the laws of property do. The law says up to a point I am public property and others can touch me or enjoy my land or satisfy their curiosity about my life, but beyond that point I am autonomous and I have a right to control others' use of me.

If the law merely protects so much privacy as the society is accustomed to protecting, it abdicates this defining role. It fails to protect either the individual or the society from the brutalising effects of subjugating individual autonomy to the appetites of the group. I therefore believe that privacy law must be normative as well as empirical. It has to take account of community expectations regarding privacy, to be sure, but it cannot surrender entirely to the mores of the moment.

In the United States the law's approach to privacy is almost entirely empirical. Courts rely principally on their perception of contemporary mores in deciding what kinds of disclosures would be "highly offensive", and they accept virtually any rational argument that a matter is of "legitimate public concern." This approach has two weaknesses.

The first is that the empirical approach tends to be self-defeating, or at least self-eroding. If the law protects what the mores of the community view as private, then the more privacy is invaded the less privacy is protected. Public expectations as to what is public and private are shaped by what is in fact made public. People, including jurors and judges, react to claims of invasion of privacy in the light of their experience: "this cannot be an invasion of privacy, media say such things about people all the time."

The second weakness of the empirical approach is that it submerges the individual in the sea of commonality. Privacy is intensely personal. To an exhibitionist, publication of a nude photo might be of no great concern, but to another it could be deeply hurtful. Some people delight in discussing their medical problems—matters that others would find embarrassing or humiliating.

Privacy is also highly contextual. We have very few secrets that are secret from everybody. We take off our clothes in front of some people but not others. We discuss medical matters with some family members and friends, but not with others. The essence of privacy is not that some things are intrinsically private and others public, but that the individual

---

[9] See Robert C. Post, "The Social Foundations of Privacy: Community and Self in the Common Law Tort", 77 *Calif. L. Rev.* 957 (1989).

should have the power to decide what things to make public, and to whom.

Of course the law cannot provide a remedy for the hypersensitive, and cannot be tailored to each person's sensibilities. But it has to take some account of differences both in context and in individual sensibilities. Treating privacy as purely an empirical question—what do reasonable people find highly offensive—does not protect either the individual's interest or the society's interest in establishing and enforcing civility norms through law. It is one of the reasons that American privacy law does so little to protect privacy.

The other reasons courts rarely provide a remedy for invasion of privacy in the U.S. is that they are reluctant to decide what are matters of legitimate public concern. Judges are reluctant to substitute their own judgment for that of editors, and they are even less inclined to submit the matter to the judgment of the jury. Some courts have gone so far as to assert that they must accept the editor's judgment that the matter in question is of legitimate public concern unless the judgment is one no reasonable editor could reach.[10] Others accept the argument that media must be allowed to include in a report about a matter of legitimate concern any fact that adds credibility or specificity to the report[11]—an argument that protects publication of rape victims' names and most other private facts that media are likely to be interested in disclosing.

This deference to editorial judgment eviscerates privacy. It means that the law of privacy protects only such matters as the media themselves cannot rationally consider public. But editors quite rationally can and do view all information as being of legitimate public concern. It is their role in our system to discover and disclose information, not suppress it. We look to them to vindicate our right to know, not safeguard privacy. We look to the media to scrutinise government, but we do not concede that it is for the media to decide what information the government must give them. We expect the media and the government to disagree as to what information should be public, and we accept that the law must resolve those conflicts. Similarly, we should recognise that the law, not the media, must ultimately decide how much private information is of legitimate public concern.

If courts are not to reflexively defer to editors, how are they to decide

---

[10] See, e.g. *Gilbert* v. *Medical Economics Co.*, 665 F. 2d 305 (10th Cir. 1981).

[11] See, e.g. *Howard* v. *Des Moines Register and Tribune Co.*, 283 N.W. 2d 289, cert. denied 445 U.S. 904 (1980).

when the public interest justifies disclosure of private facts? I believe the justifications fall into three principal categories.

One justification is that the matter disclosed is improper behaviour which is itself a matter of public concern. The most obvious example is disclosure of criminal activity. By defining the activity as criminal, the society arguably has decided it is of public concern, and the person engaged in it should not be able to complain when media disclose it. The principal area about which there may be disagreement involved activity that many people believe should not be prohibited but which may be criminal in some jurisdictions, such as abortion or certain sexual acts by consenting adults. An argument can be made, certainly, that not all criminal activity is of public concern. For the sake of bright lines, however, it may be fair to say any disclosure of criminal activity should be protected and the privacy problems that arise from such disclosure should be addressed by decriminalising the conduct.

It is not enough, however, to protect disclosure of criminal conduct. The "improper behaviour" justification should also cover non-criminal improprieties. Historically the press has performed an invaluable service by exposing practices that are not criminal but have consequences that deserve public attention. Such disclosures should be protected. The Calcutt Committee in Britain suggested that the law might do so by recognising a justification for exposing "seriously anti-social conduct."[12]

In my view this suggestion is inadequate. Some of the finest moments of journalism have been crusades against practices that at the time were not recognised as anti-social. It is at this point that the press may play its most valuable role in making an issue of something the public has chosen to ignore. Child labour, racial discrimination, destroying rain forests, whaling, and sexual harassment were not considered "seriously anti-social conduct" until after the press and others made them an issue. It is often in these early stages of a public controversy that the press is most likely to be "chilled" by threats of litigation, so it is important to protect such disclosures even before the conduct is recognised as seriously anti-social.

The law should not sacrifice privacy to every crusader who sees something he or she considers anti-social, but it at least should protect disclosure of conduct that could be reasonably expected to have serious consequences for a significant portion of the public.

---

[12] Par. 3.26a., Report of the Committee on Privacy and Related Matters, David Calcutt QC Chairman, June 1990.

A second category of justification is disclosure of a matter that reflects on the person's ability to perform public duties. Where the disclosure is clearly relevant to the duties, such as disclosure that a public official has a debilitating disease or is engaging in conduct that invites blackmail, these are relatively easy cases. Unfortunately, this justification often is merely a cover for less elevated motives. Disclosures of sexual peccadillos, in particular, are often accompanied by solemn assurances that the discloser is interested only in the effect on the subject's public responsibilities—assurances that are belied by the salacious treatment of the details disclosed. But clearly a disclosure that is relevant to the ability of a candidate or official to perform public duties has to be protected, and the law should not blanch if the story happens to be titillating as well as significant.

The most difficult type of justification is the argument that the disclosure exposes the hypocrisy of the subject or someone else. This is the justification given for disclosing that the clergyman is having an affair or the screen sex symbol is a lesbian. We live in a cynical age. We widely suspect that people and institutions are corrupt, and we seem to relish disclosures that confirm our suspicion.

But here is the real heart of the problem with privacy. We value privacy largely because it enables us to be hypocritical—to pretend to be something we are not. We do not want our physical abnormalities known because we want people to think we are normal. We do not want our moral lapses known because we want people to think we are moral. To protect privacy is to protect hypocrisy. The values of privacy are fundamentally at odds with those of candour and openness. Privacy exists to subvert those values, to allow us to misrepresent ourselves, passively if not actively.

If we are to protect privacy, we have to be prepared to say that exposing hypocrisy is not by itself a sufficient justification for disclosure. The Calcutt committee recognised this, suggesting that disclosure should be protected when necessary to prevent a real risk that some section of the public would be materially misled by some previous statement by the subject.[13]

I think this formulation is too narrow, because it focuses only on a person's words, not deeds. Media should be free to disclose that a noted television evangelist consorts with prostitutes even if he has not made

---

[13] Par. 12.23c., Report of the Committee on Privacy and Related Matters, David Calcutt QC Chairman, June 1990.

previous statements on the subject. A better approach might be to allow disclosure when necessary to evaluate the person's public life or evaluate the person's credibility with respect to a public issue.

So far I have said nothing about the special difficulties that the law encounters in protecting privacy of public figures (I use that term as shorthand for public officials, candidates, people caught up in public events, and celebrities—categories that sometimes require separate consideration, but which may be lumped together for present purposes).

I do not believe that privacy is for private people only. If we are serious about it, we must protect some privacy for public figures as well. I have emphasised privacy in the context of private people only because until we appreciate how difficult it is to protect even them it is impossible to fully appreciate the difficulty of protecting some sphere of privacy for public figures. Saying "the law ought to protect privacy of private people, but not public figures", is like saying the law ought to prohibit rape, but not if the victim is female. By and large, private people are not the parties at risk of invasion of privacy. Media are not interested in ordinary people because the public is not. They do not care who we are sleeping with, or what diseases we have. But they have an insatiable appetite for details of the lives of celebrities.

There is no doubt that the lives of public figures are in large part matters of legitimate public concern. The issue is whether some aspects of their lives are not. I believe the law must reject the notion that public figures are *ipso facto* entitled to less privacy than private individuals. Their privacy should be evaluated by the same criteria that are applied to private people, though of course the results will often be very different. Public figures more often will be held to have waived their privacy by inviting publicity about matters that otherwise would be private. Those who seek or hold public office open themselves to scrutiny of their ability to perform the duties of the office. People who seek to influence the public must endure disclosures that affect their credibility with respect to the matters that they seek to influence. People who seek public approval of their vision of life—writers and artists, for example—cannot complain about disclosure of matters the public needs to know to evaluate the artist's public life or work. The conduct of people who have great power is more likely to have serious consequences for the public than the conduct of the weak.

But none of those considerations justifies disclosure merely because the person is a public figure. Even when the plaintiff is a public figure, the touchstone is still legitimate public concern: the media are entitled to disclose an otherwise private matter about a public figure only if it relates to a matter of legitimate public concern—not merely because it tells us more than we previously knew about a public figure.

It is here that the need for a normative approach to privacy is clearest. There is virtually nothing about a celebrity that the public is *not* interested in, and there is very little that contemporary public mores place off-limits. There are very few matters that one could say no reasonable editor would disclose, because there are few that editors are not in fact disclosing more or less routinely. Public figures today have almost no protection against unwanted disclosure of private facts; a scheme of law that takes an empirical view of what should be protected will change nothing.

It is here also that the law can do the most for the cause of civility. Egregious disclosures about private people remain the exception rather than the rule. Media do not normally disclose names of rape victims, or embarrassing medical details or sex lives of private people. The civility norms that discourage such disclosures thus remain largely intact. It is important to have an effective law of privacy to reinforce those norms, but in the area of private individuals the role of the law is primarily defensive, to prevent the destruction of fairly stable and widely observed norms.

With respect to public figures, however, the law's role must be more affirmative. In the United States, at least, and increasingly in England, privacy of public figures is invaded routinely and egregiously. We have come to expect and accept ruthless exploitation of the lives of certain types of public figures, such as film stars and athletes, and what civility norms remain with respect to other types, such as candidates for public office and prominent business people, are under immense pressure. In the area of public figure privacy, the law can have a restorative, rather than merely preservative, effect on the society's obligation to protect individual integrity and dignity from the brutalisation of unbridled public curiosity.

8

Adjudication and Interpretation in the Common Law: A Century of Change

Peter Birks (Hon.), D.C.L., F.B.A.*

There are close ties between the University of Leiden and the University of Oxford, especially between our two law faculties. It is a pleasure today to be able to add one more link to that strengthening relationship. It is also a great pleasure to be drawn within the gravitational field of Professor Basil Markesinis and the Institute of Anglo-American Law which he has built up. It is, as I believe, a unique venture and one which has the first importance, intellectually, legally and politically. Its success reflects the energy and optimism of its founder. Professor Markesinis has sought out for his Institute many who have been willing to offer material support, among them Clifford Chance who have established this lecture and in whose debt I therefore stand today. At this time above all, in the infancy of the European Union, the work of the Institute deserves support, both moral and material. The energetic spirit which greets the visitor justifies the conviction that it will continue to find the help which it needs.

This lecture is concerned with one hundred and ten years of legal history. Its theme is also optimistic—a success story. But it runs into, not an unhappy ending, for the end is in the future, but an unhappy present. Markers put down in 1883 and 1983 define a century which saw the intellectual transformation of the common law. Case-law, ever-increasing in quantum and kept in shape first by the forms of action and then by a hardening of the doctrine of precedent, required to be more rationally ordered; and, as the century wore on, it found in the universities the means of achieving that more rational structure. Analysis, definition and classification, the familiar tools of the university, were brought to bear for the first time on the raw materials of the common

* The text of a lecture delivered on 3 December 1993.

law. And the thought of the new university law schools issued in the innumerable books and periodicals which we now take for granted.

This intellectual transformation of the common law took place at two levels, in the literature of the law and in legal education. There is, as Dicey saw, a systematic link between the two. A poorly educated legal profession will produce unthinking literature and law which will often be caught looking asinine. Correspondingly, enlightening literature and rationally defensible law can only be produced where lawyers are seriously committed to the business of understanding their subject and communicating that understanding to the next generation. Although England managed for centuries without any, university law schools turn out, in modern society, to be essential engines of rationality.

This development does not diminish the priority of the judges in the making of the common law. The energy for change comes from the litigants themselves. It is the demands of plaintiffs and defendants which shift the frontiers of liability. The judges are the umpires. It is for them to gauge the pressure on the existing lines. The common law could not remain the common law if this were otherwise. Moreover, England has by and large been very fortunate in its jurist-judges. Adjudication, always difficult and sometimes agonizing work, these days comes in almost insupportable quantities. At least for the higher judiciary, every decision requires the composition of something like an article in a law journal or a chapter in a book; some require whole books. Then there is the machinery of critical review: it is essential to the health of the system that the work be done under the eager eyes both of the media and a hardly less predatory horde of academic lawyers. Despite these pressures and a critical literature which can only feed on lapses and rumours of lapses, what the law reports chiefly attest is the judges' remarkable intellectual and personal qualities.

It takes nothing from the judges to recognize that adjudicators who must also interpret the law cannot now function satisfactorily without the support of the organizing and analysing legal science in the law schools. Though the balance between the two is different, there is in the English common law, just as there is in the civilian jurisdictions of the continent, an indispensable extrajudicial branch of interpretative authority.

I. CONTRASTING PARADIGMS?

Gaius lists the sources of Roman law in these words: "The laws of the Roman people are based on acts, plebeian statutes, resolutions of the

Senate, imperial enactments, edicts of those having the right to issue them, and the answers of the learned."[1] The list reaches through history and hence through constitutional change. Interpretation is represented by *responsa prudentium*, the answers of the learned, and, within the category of imperial pronouncements but still with most of their history in front of them, by their nationalized successors, the rescripts of the emperor. Legislation accounts for the rest of the list. Except perhaps for the emperor's own interventions, again hidden in the generic reference to imperial utterances, there is no trace of adjudication. Classical Roman law is thus the paradigm of a system which divides the essential functions of authoritative interpretation and adjudication.

The exclusion of Roman judgments from the interpretative stream was not formal or artificial; that is, they were not excluded despite being fit to be admitted. They were simply unfit. Issues were tried by judges who were of course bound by the law but who more often than not would have no special legal expertise, and judgment was given inscrutably, without reasons. The latter point is very important. It would never be clear quite why a *iudex* had decided as he did. He did not reveal his findings of fact any more than he stated his understanding of the law. The literature of the law, the developing library of interpretative utterance, was therefore built up outside the process of adjudication, although focused very much upon it, by those who made themselves learned in the law.

The common law is extraordinarily similar to classical Roman law, uncodified, pragmatic and casuistic. The great figures of the common law such as Lord Mansfield and Baron Parke, who became Lord Wensleydale, or, nearer our own time, Lord Devlin, would all have found themselves entirely at home in the shoes of Labeo, Celsus or Ulpian. And these in turn, if they could come back, would happily set to work in the House of Lords. They would be more at home in England than in any continental jurisdiction, knowing as they did nothing of the exercise of subsumption and the other intellectual tyrannies of a code.

And yet our law is perceived even now as paradigmatically opposed to Roman law. In one matter, institutionally striking but substantially trivial, it has been so. We combined adjudication and interpretation. Our jurists sit in court. A common law judgment must stabilize the facts, interpret the law and, finally, apply that law to the facts. The judicial exposition of the law, its focus sharpened by the application to

---

[1] Gaius, *Institutes* 1.2 as translated in W.M. Gordon and O.F. Robinson, *The Institutes of Gaius* (London, 1988) 20–1.

the facts, is our principal form of juristic utterance. As Roman law was to be found in the writings of the learned, so the common law is to be found in the law reports.

For centuries that was all there was to it. There were no other jurists of the common law, and there was precious little legal utterance that was not done from the bench. Until Charles Viner's benefaction to Oxford which, in 1758, brought Blackstone to the first ever chair of common law, there was no competition from the universities. And one swallow does not make a summer. More than a century was to pass before there was any real change.

Just as judgements were naturally excluded from the sources of classical Roman law, so in these conditions there was no artificiality, no hint of restrictive practice, in the judicial monopoly of interpretative authority. Some systematising ideas were imported, usually unacknowledged, from abroad. Pothier, for example, was influential.[2] If there was any competition at home it came from learned practitioners. It was unimaginable that anyone who was not a barrister could ever write anything serious about English law, and it was almost equally inconceivable that the pre-eminence of the judges who had risen through the ranks of the barristers could be rivalled.

Sheer learning occasionally leaped the gap. In 1814, for example, in *Johnes* v. *Johnes*[3] Lord Eldon, L.C., allowed himself to rely on an opinion of Serjeant Williams:

> [T]hough one who held no judicial situation could not regularly be mentioned as an authority, yet he might say that to anyone in a judicial situation it would be sufficiently flattering to have it said of him that he was as good a common lawyer as Mr. Serjeant Williams, for no man ever lived to whom the character of a great common lawyer more properly applied.

However, in the last hundred or so years, and with growing momentum in the last fifty since the Second World War, the picture has changed dramatically. The paradigm of the common law as solely judge-made, so far as it survives, has become grossly misleading. Outside the law reports there is now a mountain of legal literature—journals, textbooks and monographs, pitched at every level. The lion's share is written in the university law schools. Many of the writers are still technically

---

[2] A.W.B. Simpson, "Innovation in Nineteenth Century Contract Law," (1975) 91 L.Q.R. 247, esp. 255 *et seq.*

[3] (1814) 3 Dow. 1, 15. Serjeant Williams (1757–1810) is best known for his notes on Saunder's Reports (*Williams' Saunders*).

barristers, although it is as university jurists that they write. Many of the books are aimed primarily at teaching and learning. In the university their authors' teaching not only forms legal minds but, in doing so, lays down future paths of change and development. But university juristic influence is not only exercised through teaching. Many books are aimed directly at practitioners, and there is no important case nowadays in which counsel do not use the work of academic jurists in both books and periodicals.

Exemplification cannot but be invidious, and examples are therefore best kept small in number. Contract is on any view a central subject and, within it by way of examples of specific contracts, sale and agency. Every practitioner depends on the two volumes of *Chitty on Contract*, on *Benjamin's Sale of Goods* and on *Bowstead on Agency*. The recent fourth edition of *Benjamin*[4] has 25 chapters and runs to nearly 2,000 pages. *Bowstead*[5] is less vast; its 560 pages are divided into 9 chapters. The 26th edition of *Chitty*[6] has, in the first volume, 30 chapters and, in the second, 12 chapters. That makes, in *Benjamin, Bowstead* and the two volumes of *Chitty*, 76 chapters in all. All but three are the responsibility of university jurists: Professor H.G. Beale (Warwick), Professor J. Beatson (Cambridge), Professor A.G. Guest (London), Professor E.P. Ellinger (Singapore), Mr. D.R. Harris (Oxford), Professor C.J. Miller (Birmingham), Professor C.G.J. Morse (London), Dr. P.M. North (Oxford), Professor D.D. Prentice (Oxford), Professor F.M.B. Reynolds (Oxford), Professor L.S. Sealy (Cambridge), Professor G.H. Treitel (Oxford), Dr. S.J. Whittaker (Oxford). The three remaining chapters, all in volume 2 of *Chitty*, are contributed by four practitioners, G.D. Kinley, S. Moriarty, S. Richards and V. Rose. All of these have strong university connections.

Besides these books there are many others in the same field, of which at least four can claim to have formed the minds of judges and practitioners, namely Treitel's *Law of Contract*,[7] Cheshire and Fifoot and Furmston's *Law of Contract*,[8] *Anson on Contract*,[9] and Atiyah's *Sale of*

---

[4] A.G. Guest (General Editor), *Benjamin's Sale of Goods*, 4th edition (London, 1993). This book is the successor of Judah Benjamin, *Treatise on the Law of Sale of Personal Property* (London, 1868) which had eight editions between 1868 and 1950.

[5] F.M.B. Reynolds, *Bowstead on Agency*, fifteenth edition (London, 1985).

[6] A.G. Guest (General Editor), *Chitty on Contracts*, 26th edition (London, 1985).

[7] G.H. Treitel, *The Law of Contract*, 8th edition (London, 1991).

[8] M.P. Furmston, *Cheshire and Fifoot and Furmston's Law of Contract*, 12th edition (London, 1991).

[9] A.G. Guest, *Anson's Law of Contract*, 26th edition (Oxford, 1984).

Goods.[10] Special and separate mention should be made, because of the cardinal importance, at this point in legal history, of knowledge of other jurisdictions, of Professor Treitel's superb comparative study of remedies for breach of contract.[11] There are many others. Some are, so to say, remedies against complacency. They probe existing concepts and classifications, and they set out to shake accepted orthodoxies.[12]

This pattern could be repeated for one subject after another, but it will suffice to mention more quickly just three. Criminal Law has been utterly transformed by the books of Professor Glanville Williams,[13] Professor Sir John Smith and Professor Brian Hogan.[14] Again the books of a relatively small group of university jurists have created and developed administrative law, especially those of Professor Sir William Wade,[15] Professor S.A. de Smith,[16] Professor Garner[17] and, more recently, Mr. Paul Craig[18] and Professor Denis Galligan.[19] Private International Law has likewise been created and shaped by Professor A.V. Dicey,[20] Dr. J.H.C. Morris,[21] Professor G.C. Cheshire and Dr. P.M. North.[22] It would be foolish to claim a law school monopoly. We have already noticed four practitioner contributors to *Chitty*. *Dicey and Morris* is now edited by Lawrence Collins, a partner in the same firm as was the late Dr. Francis Mann, the leading authority on money.[23]

Van Caenegem, reflecting on the differences between English and German interpretative techniques, recalls that the great Savigny in his Berlin days (when Lord Eldon occupied the woolsack[24]) organized his

---

[10] P.S. Atiyah, *The Sale of Goods*, 8th edition (London, 1990).

[11] G.H. Treitel, *Remedies for Breach of Contract* (Oxford, 1988).

[12] As, for example, H.G. Collins, *The Law of Contract*, 2nd edition (London, 1993).

[13] Glanville Williams, *Criminal Law*, The General Part, 2nd edition (London, 1961); *A Textbook of Criminal Law*, 2nd edition (London, 1983).

[14] J.C. Smith and B. Hogan, *Criminal Law*, 7th edition (London, 1992); J.C. Smith, *The Law of Theft*, 6th edition (London, 1989).

[15] H.W.R. Wade, *Administrative Law*, 6th edition (Oxford, 1988).

[16] S.A. de Smith, *Judicial Review of Administrative Action*, 4th edition (London, 1980).

[17] B.L. Jones, *Garner's Administrative Law*, 7th edition (London, 1989).

[18] P. Craig, *Administrative Law*, 2nd edition (London, 1989).

[19] D. Galligan, *Discretionary Powers: A Legal Study of Official Discretion*, revised edition (Oxford, 1990).

[20] A.V. Dicey, *The Conflict of Laws* (London, 1896).

[21] Dr. Morris edited *Dicey*, see previous note, from the 6th edition (London, 1949) to the 10th (London, 1980).

[22] G.C. Cheshire and P.M. North, *Private International Law*, 12th edition (London, 1992). Dr. North has been editor since the 8th edition (1970), in conjunction with Professor J.J. Fawcett since the 11th edition (1987).

[23] F.A. Mann, *The Legal Aspect of Money*, 5th edition (Oxford, 1992).

[24] Savigny was called to Berlin in 1810 and held his chair to 1842. Lord Eldon was Lord Chancellor from 1801 to 1806 and 1807 to 1827.

faculty to deliver opinions on questions put by the courts: "just the sort of role he found suitable for a professor."[25] "Who," he asks, "could imagine the High Court, the Court of Appeal or the Law Lords asking the teachers in a law faculty what judgment they ought to give?"[26] Nobody. At least not directly. But the modern courts and practising lawyers depend indirectly on the law faculties more than they realize, and more than they care to admit. The law school's responsibility for the bulk of the literature of the law and hence for its analysis and rational structure is a fact evidenced throughout the law library. All the same it is a fact with a relatively shallow history and, as we shall see, a fragile present.

2. 1883 TO 1983

In the early eighteenth century, even before Blackstone, Thomas Wood described the judge-made law of England as a "heap of good learning" and, in his *Institute of the Laws of England*, he hoped to have taken a step towards putting it in order.[27] That work did not get properly under way until the late nineteenth century.

Although other great figures immediately clamour to be named, perhaps Austin, Maine and Maitland above all,[28] the three who, by reason of their contributions to the central substantive subjects, have some claim to be the founding fathers of the modern juristic tradition of the common law are Dicey, Anson and Pollock. They were born within a decade of each other, Dicey in 1835, Anson in 1843 and Pollock in 1845. Dicey and Pollock in fact delivered their inaugural lectures in Oxford in the same year, 1883, Dicey as Vinerian Professor, Pollock as Corpus Professor of Jurisprudence. Anson at the same time was Warden

---

[25] R. Van Caenegem, *Judges, Legislators and Professors* (Cambridge, 1987) 65.

[26] *Ibid.*

[27] T. Wood, *An Institute of the Laws of England, or the Laws of England in their Natural Order* (London, 1720), p. ii.

[28] John *Austin*, 1790–1859, was the first professor of jurisprudence at University College London, 1826–1832, far ahead of his time in his pursuit of intellectual order in the law. Sir Henry *Maine*, 1822–1888, held chairs in both Oxford and Cambridge. His interests were chiefly in historical jurisprudence and in explaining the development of law from its primitive beginnings. F.W. *Maitland*, 1850–1906, was Downing Professor of Laws at Cambridge. His prodigious output created the discipline of legal history as we know it. For the contributions of *Dicey, Pollock* and *Anson*, see A.W.B. Simpson, "The Rise and Fall of the Legal Treatise" (1981) 48 U. of Chicago L.R. 632, esp. 651–74. Simpson notes that Plucknett took the treatise tradition as starting from Joseph Story's first treatise, on bailment, in 1832 (T.F.T. Plucknett, *Early English Legal Literature* (Cambridge, 1958), 19).

of All Souls.[29] Though old habits of mind adjust rather slowly to sub-
structural changes, the judicial monopoly of interpretative law-making
was broken with the publication of their books.

2.1. Dicey's Programme

Dicey's famous inaugural lecture, given on 21st April, 1883, was entitled "Can English Law be Taught at the Universities?"[30] He did not
doubt that there was some advantage in the existing practice of learning
law in the Inns of Court by sitting at the feet of an established barrister:

> The merits, in short, of the present system may be summed up in the one word
> 'reality.' It brings a student in contact with the real actual business, and fosters
> in him qualities which cannot be produced by any theoretical teaching, however
> excellent.[31]

Against that had to be weighed great disadvantages; the learning acquired
in chambers was fragmentary, negligent of principle and unsystematic.
Disordered learning also wasted time and obstructed understanding:

> The gravest fault of the present system is that, while it involves untold waste
> of effort, it robs the learner of half the gains which he ought to derive from the
> invaluable experience to be gained by the observation of practice.[32]

Dicey's lecture was not simply about legal education. It was about
the intellectual condition of the common law, to which he saw legal
education as being systematically connected. By 1883 the materials of
the common law had multiplied. It was impossible any longer to emu-
late the example of "[a] man of strenuous industry, such as Lord
Campbell, [who] could even half a century ago read through something
like the whole compass of the law."[33] This problem, one might inter-
ject, must now be stated to something like the power of 10, the energy
of the modern legislator being compounded by the supersession, through
information technology, of the benificently selective censorship exercised by the law reporters.

Dicey's anxiety arose from the fact that the massive increase in the
corpus of material had as yet barely begun to be matched by a production of analytical or systematic literature. In the available books he

---

[29] Sir William Anson's *Principles of the Law of Contract* was first published in 1879,
his *Law and Custom of the Constitution* in 1886, with later parts in 1892 and 1908. He
was Warden of All Souls from 1881 to 1898, thereafter sitting in Parliament.
[30] A.V. Dicey, "Can English Law be Taught at the Universities?" (London, 1883).
[31] *Ibid.*, 8.   [32] *Ibid.*, 11.   [33] *Ibid.*, 15.

found divisions which, "for absolute uninstructiveness, may be compared to an attempt to classify animals by dividing them into dodos, lions and those which are not dodos or lions."[34] And, while describing them as among "our best works," Dicey castigated the influential annotated anthologies of leading cases, such as *Smith's Leading Cases*. His words on this topic highlight the link between legal education and legal literature:

They are deficient in all general conceptions, in all grasp of principles, in all idea of method. Authors who have learned their trade by rule of thumb have never aimed at the accurate analysis or definition of legal ideas. Hence the technical terms of the law are as bad as any technicalities can be; they are technical without being precise, or, when apparently popular, are full of latent ambiguity. Attempt to define, in accordance with received authorities, such terms as "chose in action," "personal property," a "void" contract, an 'implied agreement,' and you will not only assent to my criticism, but will soon discover the cause of all this hopeless confusion. Generations of practitioners have neither concerned themselves with definition, nor indeed have understood its nature or necessity.[35]

Dicey's view was that lectures in the university necessarily compelled rational analysis and that it was therefore the universities which must answer for "the much-needed reform, I had almost said creation, of legal literature." By way of incentive to those who would undertake the task, he emphasized that they would be doing a great deal more than teaching:

By teaching and by literature they can influence not only the form but also the substance of the law. The rules of law which are supposed to be so inflexible are, for the most part, in fact enactments of judicial legislation, and nothing is more remarkable or more intelligible than the ease with which judicial legislation is swayed by the pressure of authoritative opinion. Busy magistrates, dealing with cases as they occur, take their principles from text-writers. Particular authors have notoriously, even in recent times, modelled, one might almost say brought into existence, whole departments of law.[36]

2.2. Pollock's Life and Work

By 1883 Sir Frederick Pollock was already one whose work was putting in train the intellectual transformation for which Dicey looked. Properly and unsurprisingly, he himself faithfully taught the doctrine of

---

[34] *Ibid.*, 13.   [35] *Ibid.*, 12–13.   [36] *Ibid.*, 22, 23–4.

judicial supremacy in the interpretative development of the law. In 1896, when *The Principles of the Law of Contract at Law and in Equity* (1876) and *The Law of Tort* (1883) were already in every lawyer's hands, his *First Book of Jurisprudence* instructed the beginner in, inter alia, the use of authority:

Let the student, above all, remember that in our law textbooks are not authorities, with the exception, which in usual practice is seldom material, of the limited number of old books by private writers to which authority in the proper sense has been ascribed.[37]

The reverential exceptions, which he does not enumerate, were Glanvill, Bracton, Littleton, Coke and Blackstone. He appended a footnote in which he recorded the views of his grandfather, Chief Baron Pollock:

When I was beginning the study of the law my grandfather, who had lately resigned the office of Chief Baron, wrote to me as follows: "I myself read no treatises: I referred to them as collecting the authorities." (It must be remembered that in the early part of the nineteenth century very few textbooks aimed at either systematic arrangement or independent criticism.) "I learned law by reading the reports and attending the courts and thinking and talking of what I had read and heard."[38]

Pollock's parenthesis conceded that his grandfather's contempt for treatises was no doubt justified in his time. However, the judiciary could not be expected to give up long-standing habits of mind just as soon as the quality of the literature began to improve. Rather to the contrary, the old outlook was indeed protected by the hazy convention that living authors should not be cited in court. That convention sometimes had to cope with the inconvenient fact that some influential textbooks were written, not by outsiders, but by very learned judges. *Fry on Specific Performance* was such a one. The weight of its authority did not inhibit Kekewich, J.'s outspoken comments in *Union Bank* v. *Munster* in 1887:

The argument, however, has been almost entirely rested upon one passage in the work of Lord Justice Fry on Specific Performance. It is to my mind much to be regretted, and it is a regret which I believe every judge on the bench shares, that textbooks are more and more quoted in court—I mean of course textbooks by living authors—and some judges have gone so far as to say that they shall not be quoted.[39]

---

[37] Sir Frederick Pollock, *A First Book of Jurisprudence* (London, 1896) 319.
[38] *Ibid.*, fn. 2.   [39] (1888) 37 Ch.D. 51, 54.

This is not quite as bold as it sounds, since, as Kekewich, J., observes, Lord Justice Fry was himself anxious that the authority of textbooks by judges should not be overestimated:

> There is one notion often expressed with regard to works written or revised by authors on the Bench, which seems to me in part at least erroneous—the notion, I mean, that they possess a quasi-judicial authority. It is hardly enough remembered how different are the circumstances under which a book is written and a judgment pronounced, or how much the weight and value of the latter are due to discussions at the bar which precede the judgment.[40]

However, Lord Justice Fry was there saying only something which everyone would admit, namely that law books cannot be safely relied upon as a simple alternative to cases, to do the same work which is normally done by cases. That does not exclude other roles important in the interpretation of cases, such as the identification of principles, relationships and latent contradictions.

There is certainly nothing to suggest that Sir Edward Fry would have supported Vaughan Williams, L.J.'s nice doctrine which combined the suppression of attributed citations of living writers with acknowledgment that counsel might wish to adopt the opinions of such authors as part of their argument:

> No doubt Mr. Odgers's book [on *Libel and Slander*] is a most admirable work, which we all use, but I think we ought in this Court to maintain the old idea that counsel are not entitled to quote living authors as authorities for a proposition they are putting forward, but they may adopt the author's statements as part of their argument.[41]

Pollock's long life saw marked changes in attitude. By the time he died in his ninety-second year, in 1937, some judges had come to recognize the necessity of the extra-judicial contribution to interpretative authority. An appreciation *in memoriam* appeared immediately after Pollock's death in the *Law Quarterly Review*, of which he was a co-founder in 1885[42]—it was followed within two years by the *Harvard Law Review*—and first editor, an office which he had held for thirty-five

---

[40] Sir Edward Fry, *A Treatise on the Specific Performance of Contracts*, 2nd edition (London, 1881), preface.

[41] *Greenlands Ltd.* v. *Wilmshurst* (1913) 29 T.L.R. 685, 687.

[42] "It was the first of its kind in England. It has remained in the forefront ever since. It has been followed all over the world by hundreds of other law reviews" Lord Denning, M.R., writing in the centenary edition, (1984) 100 L.Q.R. 513. With just severity he went on a few lines later, "They are baskets full of the fruits of research. Some of the fruit is good and fit to pick. Some of it is full of maggots. It is only fit for the humus heap."

years.[43] The obituary was written by the then Master of the Rolls, Lord Wright of Durley, one of the greatest of our jurist-judges.[44]

Lord Wright recalled that in the Court of Appeal, only very shortly before Pollock died, a judgment of his own had relied on a passage from the thirteenth edition of *The Law of Torts*. He had referred to it as "fortunately not a work of authority"[45] (a humorous tribute which, playing on the exclusion of living writers, both recognized the authority which the book did undoubtedly enjoy and expressed pleasure in its author's longevity). Lord Wright went on to point out that Pollock's works were in fact constantly before the courts. Having made some observations on Pollock's interpretation of the distinction between written and unwritten law, he said, recognizing the change that had overtaken the current of interpretative authority:

This at least is clear, that he has vindicated to this generation the vital importance of extra-judicial writing in the law. . . . The writings of a lawyer like Pollock, constantly cited in the Courts and quoted by the judges, are entitled to claim a place under his category of unwritten law, even in a system like ours which does not normally seek its law from institutional writers.[46]

One might have thought, with books and journals proliferating, that the rest would be plain-sailing. Pollock was not the only jurist whose name crept into the law reports,[47] and the best prediction would have been, about the time of his death, that academic works would gradually be more and more cited and their role in the provision of analysis and organizing concepts would be rather easily recognized. Ten years after

---

[43] Soon exceeded: Arthur Goodhart was editor of the L.Q.R. for fifty years, from 1925 to 1975.

[44] (1937) 53 L.Q.R. 151.

[45] *Nicholls* v. *Ely Beet Sugar Factory Ltd.* [1936] Ch. 343, 349.

[46] (1937) 53 L.Q.R. 151-2.

[47] In 1920 Dicey's teaching on the royal prerogative was accepted in *A.-G.* v. *De Keysers's Royal Hotel* [1920] A.C. 508, esp. 526, where however Lord Dunedin withholds his name, preferring "a learned constitutional writer". In the court of Appeal, arquendo, the name had been mentioned: [1919] 2 Ch. 197, 205. In 1934 Greer and Maugham, L.JJ., though they had the excuse that they were considering a point of American law, had relied on A.L. Goodhart, "Rescue and Voluntary Assumption of Risk," (1933–5) 5 C.L.J. 192: *Haynes* v. *Harwood* [1935] 1 K.B. 146, 156, 162. Later, in *Re Cleadon Trust* [1939] Scott, L.J., discussing the nature of quasi-contract referred to the works of Winfield, Jackson and Allen. In the same volume, in *Shenton* v. *Tyler* [1939] Ch. 620, 633–41, Sir Wilfrid Greene, M.R., reviewed the doctrine of some ten works on evidence. In *Re Ellenborough Park* [1956] Ch. 131, 163 *et seq.*, a famous case raising the question whether a *ius spatiandi* could exist as an easement, the Court of Appeal, through Lord Evershed, M.R., founded its judgment on G.C. Cheshire's exposition of the nature of an easement in *Modern Real Property*, 7th edition (London, 1954).

Pollock's death Denning, J., reviewing the third edition of *Winfield on Tort*, did indeed declare that the notion that academic works had no authority except after the jurist's lifetime had "long since been exploded:" "The influence of academic lawyers is greater now than it ever has been and is greater than they themselves realize."[48]

This was too sanguine. In fact the change has been slower and more patchy than could have been foreseen. When I was a law student some twenty-five years after Pollock died, I remember that we still took in the message that it was only exceptionally that a living author might be cited in court, something which I accepted without question as part of the natural order.[49] The convention, though weakening, retained a curious educative force, enough to create in us an altogether different reverence for the judicial utterance from any that we might display towards juristic literature. And, more importantly, it allowed counsel to behave in the same way, without any sense of guilt. It allowed them, even encouraged them, to make no mention in court of the very books from which they culled their arguments.

2.3. Lord Goff's Maccabaean Lecture[50]

It was not until 1983 and Lord Goff's Maccabaean Lecture[51] that I myself began to see the vestiges of the old convention in a crueller

---

[48] (1947) 63 L.Q.R. 516.

[49] Sir Robert Megarry seemed to express both the beliefs and practice of most judges when he vigorously opposed the notion that the old rule had been "exploded": R.E. Megarry, *Miscellany at Law* (London, 1955) 325 ff. Cf. by the same author, *Lawyer and Litigant in England* (London, 1962) 119 ff. Despite being President of the Society of Public Teachers of Law in 1965–66, he continued to take a hard line against academic writing. Such authors were "exposed to the peril of yielding to preconceptions" and obliged to form ideas "without the aid of the purifying ordeal of skilled argument on the specific facts of a contested case. Argued law is tough law" *Cordell* v. *Second Clarfield Properties* [1969] 2 Ch.D. 9, 16. This outburst later led Professor Hein Kötz to observe with some justification that judges shared the peril of yielding to preconceptions and often could not see the woods of principle for the trees of precedent. Perhaps, he concluded, the best way to develop the law would be by a "joint effort of judges and academics acting in partnership" (cf. Lord Goff, immediately below): H. Kötz, "Scholarship and the Courts: a Comparative Survey," in D.S. Clark (ed.) *Essays in Honour of J.H. Merryman* (1990) 183, 190.

[50] The British Academy's Maccabaean Lecture in Jurisprudence is given at the Academy once every two years. It was endowed in 1956 by the Maccabaeans to mark the tercentenary of the Jewish resettlement in England, permitted by Oliver Cromwell in 1656.

[51] Robert Goff (Lord Goff of Chieveley), "In Search of Principle" (1983) 69 Proceedings of the British Academy 169.

light, as a bizarre, unjust and unnecessary fiction designed to suppress an important change which had overtaken the making of our law. Indeed law schools themselves, especially those outside the magic triangle of Oxford, Cambridge and London, were comprehensively taken in by the innocent but ungenerous practice of the Bar, and to this day their self-image has suffered from the conviction, quite contrary to the facts, that their work has no real importance in the progress of the law. They have found it difficult to accept Dicey's accurate perception of the jurist as law-maker.[52]

Lord Goff's Maccabaean Lecture in 1983 was an event which would have gratified the founding fathers of the university juristic tradition. While rightly insisting on the priority of the judges as essential to the flexible, litigation-led character of the common law, he went out of his way to recognize, and to assert the necessity of, a division of labour:

[One of my principal themes tonight] is that different though judge and jurist may be, their work is complementary: and that today it is the fusion of their work which begets the tough, adaptable system which is called the common law.[53]

Lord Goff's thesis was that, in a world which required us to accept change and adaptation as the order of the day, the judges necessarily had to work under great pressure at the front line of legal development and always with a very close focus on the facts of particular disputes, that the universities, standing further back with more time for the critical and comparative analysis of doctrine, were better placed to make sense of the battle and to identify strategic options. The search for principle, which was the key to flexible stability in a changing world, therefore had to be conducted through a partnership between the courts and the law schools.[54]

The impact of this important lecture contains a powerful comment on the conservatism of legal thought. In the law libraries the partnership between jurists on the bench and jurists in the universities is now so obviously a fact, as witness the example of the literature on contract set out above,[55] that it is difficult to recapture, ten years on, the originality

---

[52] See above, text to n. 36.   [53] *Op cit.* n. 50 above, 171.

[54] *Ibid.*, 186. At a recent seminar in Edinburgh (Parliament House, 23 October 1993) Lord Prosser made the same point, from a rather different perspective. Taxed with judicial failure to sort out problems in the Scots law of unjust enrichment, he turned the tables on the critics by observing that the judges could not discharge their interpretative function effectively if supplies of academic literature were not forthcoming.

[55] Text from n. 4 above.

of the picture which Lord Goff presented or the novelty of his insights into the late twentieth century working of the interpretative machine. For all that the library was full of books and journals, most of them written in the universities, it was still difficult to see, in 1983, that English law was not, and without sacrificing its rational structure could not be, wholly judge-made.

2.4. Educational Underpinnings

Dicey's inaugural lecture was a manifesto for an intellectual transformation of the law in the universities, through new literature and a new pattern of legal education. A decade before Lord Goff's Maccabaean lecture there had been what seemed to be an irreversible breakthrough on the educational front. In December 1967—it is worth remarking that the date takes us only thirty years from the death of Sir Frederick Pollock—the Labour Lord Chancellor, Lord Gardiner, set up a Committee on Legal Education under the chairmanship of Mr. Justice Ormrod. In March 1971 the Ormrod Committee reported to Lord Gardiner's Conservative successor, Lord Hailsham.[56] The Committee came down in favour of the proposition that the law should be a graduate career and that "normally but not necessarily" the graduate's degree should be a law degree.[57]

The committee appreciated that there would have to be a expansion of the existing law schools and, at greater expense, the establishment of some new law schools, but it was clear that the extra expense was justified in the public interest:

Although, in general, we favour expansion of existing law schools, we would not wish to discourage the creation of one or two new law schools, particularly if the universities concerned have fully developed schemes in hand. In any event, we consider that the public interest in having at its disposal an adequate supply of properly trained professional lawyers is sufficiently great to justify, as a matter of priority, a substantial expansion of the facilities at present available for the teaching of law in the universities and in a limited number of colleges of higher education.[58]

The view was taken that a law degree should not be absolutely necessary, although the Committee clearly envisaged that the bulk of the entry would come in through the law degree. It recommended two

---

[56] *Report of the Committee on Legal Education*, Cmnd. 4595 (H.M.S.O., 1971).
[57] *Ibid.*, #103, p. 44.   [58] *Ibid.*, #104, p. 45.

special routes. First, graduates with non-law degrees, and some others, should be allowed to take instead a two-year course, covering eight subjects, five obligatory and three options;[59] second, a mixed degree, for which a candidate studied both law and another subject, should be sufficient provided that the course included eight law subjects, again with the same provision for five obligatory areas and three optional slots.[60]

On the continent of Europe the Ormrod scheme will not seem to have been ambitious. Perfectly implemented it would still have left England and Wales with a shorter legal education than any other European jurisdiction. Nevertheless, Ormrod took a large step towards completing the transformation of our law foreseen, not as an option but as a necessity, by the great English jurists of the late nineteenth century.

If the Ormrod recommendations had been fully implemented almost every practitioner would now have a law degree following a course of at least three years' study or else a degree in another subject followed by two years' study of the law. However, some parts of that scheme were never secured. In the climate now prevailing, that failure threatens real damage to the Diceyan project for the intellectual transformation of the heap of good learning that used to be the common law.

3. THE LAST DECADE 1983–1993

The optimism of a century of progress must now give way. The account of the very recent past cannot but slip into a minor key. The English autumn this year has been cold and dark. For days on end the country was obliged to contemplate its shortcomings in the mirror of a horrible trial which seemed to spring from the depths of William Golding's pessimistic imagination. That, and other events of great sadness, have drained our lives of gaiety. Anti-intellectualism hangs in the atmosphere. At the centre, the Rt. Hon. Michael Howard, Q.C., has taken to pooh-poohing theory. The Home Secretary appears to have decided that the gut, not the brain, is the place in which criminal policy should be formed. In another department of government the same organ is excogitating a pogrom against single mothers, surely the most miserable scapegoats a gut-conviction ever hit upon. And knowledge is for the moment a commodity. It has to be marketed like any other. Cut-price

---

[59] *Ibid.*, #113, p. 50.   [60] *Ibid.*, #111, p. 49.

stores are to be expected and encouraged. Lines which do not sell are discontinued.

This is not a climate in which Dicey's project could be expected to flourish. Law is a line which by and large does sell. Law schools will not be discontinued. But they are exceptionally vulnerable to cost-cutting and down-market commercial strategies. The two legal professions, the barristers and the solicitors, might have been expected to exercise a veto on short-cuts, even if only from an instinct for self-protection. The reality is the contrary. They, or at least those who speak for them, have joined the anti-intellectual, anti-Diceian cause. Their position is, in effect, that the university law school is a luxury that a lawyer can largely do without.

The grim decade has seem some bright intervals. Occasionally in the courts the old suppression of juristic sources has seemed a thing of the past. In *Woolwich Equitable Building Society* v. *IRC*,[61] where the question was whether tax demanded *ultra vires* had to be given back and the answer was yes, Lord Goff's speech from the outset expressly acknowledged the importance of the vigorous academic debate:

I shall be referring to the academic material in due course. But I wish to record at once that, in my opinion, it is of such importance that it has a powerful bearing upon the consideration by your Lordships of the central question in the case.[62]

Another recent example is *White* v. *Jones*.[63] A father had fallen out with his daughters. The quarrel gave the Court of Appeal the opportunity to reconsider *Ross* v. *Caunters*,[64] a first instance decision of Sir Robert Megarry, V.C., holding that a solicitor could be liable to an intended beneficiary disappointed by his negligence in the preparation of a will. In *White* v. *Jones* the quarrel had led the father to make a will which cut his two daughters out. A reconciliation followed. He gave instructions for a new will, leaving them both substantial legacies. The solicitors dragged their feet. The father went off on holiday, had an accident and shortly afterwards died. The daughters who had lost their legacies were allowed to recover their loss from the solicitors guilty of negligent delay.

[61] [1993] A.C. 163.   [62] *Ibid.*, 163–4.
[63] *White* v. *Jones* [1993] 3 All E.R. 481. Cf., in the same volume, *Re G* (*a minor*) [1993] 3 All E.R. 657, in which Butler-Sloss, L.J., cites and relies, in relation to the Hague Convention on the Civil Aspects of International Child Abduction, 1980, on work by J. Eekelaar and by Professor A.E. Anton.
[64] [1980] Ch. 297.

The judgment of Steyn, L.J., is quite exceptional. It looks at German law and at the academic literature. It draws on work by Professors Markesinis, Lorenz, Atiyah and Dugdale. It adopts a passage from an article by Peter Cane.[65] Of particular interest, but also betraying the habitual attitude of the Bar, is Steyn, L.J.'s general comment on the nature of the submissions which had been made to the court:

Pages and pages were read from some of the judgments. But we were not referred to a single piece of academic writing on *Ross* v. *Caunters*. Counsel are not to blame: traditionally counsel make very little use of academic materials other than standard textbooks. In a difficult case it is helpful to consider academic comment on the point. Often such writings examine the history of the problem, the framework into which a decision must fit and countervailing policy considerations in greater depth than is usually possible in judgments prepared by judges who are faced with a remorseless treadmill of cases that cannot wait. And it is arguments that influence decisions rather than the reading of pages upon pages from judgments.[66]

A judgment in this style is still the exception rather than the rule.[67] This is now an English peculiarity, not a characteristic of the common law.

---

[65] *Ross* v. *Caunters* [1980] Ch. 297, 502 f, quoting from P. Cane, *Negligent Solicitors and Disappointed Beneficiaries* (1980) 96 L.Q.R. 184. The author is Law Fellow of Corpus Christi College, Oxford, and has written, inter alia, a major treatise on economic torts: *Tort Law and Economic Interests* (Oxford, 1991).

[66] *Ibid.*, 500.

[67] For example, the preface to the 8th edition of *Treitel on Contract* (London, 1991) observes with perfect restraint, at page v, that its pages take account of important changes entailed, in relation to consideration, by *Williams* v. *Roffey Bros.* [1991] 1 Q.B. 1 and, in relation to contributory negligence, by *Forsikringsaktieselskapet Vesta* v. *Butcher* [1989] A.C. 852. What it does not say is that, though there is no citation of the source, counsel in those cases appear to have derived their arguments from the pages of the 7th edition, 74–5 and 759–61. Again, although *Woolwich Equitable Building Society* v. *IRC* [1993] A.C. 70 contains, in the House of Lords, Lord Goff's generous acknowledgment of the role of academic literature, the majority judgments in the Court of Appeal, reported with the decision of the House of Lords, pioneering as they are, are typically English in making no mention at all of the copious literature on the point, even though the arguments are clearly derived from it. A rather different complaint might be made about the recent important appeal to the Privy Council from New Zealand, *A.-G. for Hong Kong* v. *Reid* (JCPC, November 1993, as yet unreported). The issue was whether the victim of bribery acquires a property in the bribe received by his agent and in assets bought with it. *Lister* v. *Stubbs* (1890) 45 Ch.D. 1, in rather careful judgments of a strong court, said no. The JCPC treated *Lister* as wrong. It cited an important article by Sir Peter Millett, writing extrajudicially: "Bribes and Secret Commissions" [1993] Restitution Law Review 7. It mentioned none of the other juristic support for that position and, more worryingly, apparently took no account of Professor Goode's support for *Lister* (R.M. Goode, "Ownership and Obligation in Commercial Transactions" (1987) 103 L.Q.R. 433, 441–5; "The Recovery of A Director's Improper Gains," in E. McKendrick (ed.), *Commercial Aspects of Trusts and Fiduciary Obligations* (Oxford, 1992) 137, 144 ff.) nor of the criminal

In, for instance, Australia and Canada the reports are full of the citation of juristic literature from outside the cases.

The persistence of a difference in England has to be put down to two causes. One is the cultural fact that barristers still learn, from the echo of the old convention, that it is ethical not to cite their sources unless those sources are cases. This is a complex phenomenon which is only partly explained by the fact that some barristers have made little or no academic study of the law and others are overtly hostile to law schools and academic legal education generally.[68] There are many other factors. One, no doubt, is that the practice of not citing academic authority reduces the range of the research which is regarded as obligatory and the kinds of argument in which it is necessary to be competent, and another is that the traditional self-image of the barrister as materially and intellectually independent, just as it resists partnership in professional practice, also dislikes overt signs of help from outsiders in the construction of arguments. As Steyn, L.J., says, counsel are not to blame; but a visitor from Mars, alien to the inwardness of the tradition, might be forgiven for finding the externalities discreditable.

The other cause is the very small amount of help available to judges. In Australia, for example, senior judges can call on the services of the very best law graduates to provide regular research assistance. The library and research resources of the High Court in Canberra would be the envy of most law schools. Nothing similar is found in England, even at the very highest level. Our judges therefore have no direct line to the recent literature. Steyn, L.J., to whom no literature was cited, will have had to find it for himself.

On the educational front there are blacker clouds. The English professions—it is necessary to emphasize that the Scots have not followed suit—have renounced the Ormrod principle that people should by and

---

consequences of overruling it: *Attorney-General's Reference* (No. 1 of 1985) [1986] Q.B>491; J.C. Smith, *The Law of Theft*, 6th edition (London, 1989) 43-4; cf. (1956) 19 M.L.R. 39; see also A.T.H. Smith, "Constructive Trusts in the Law of Theft" [1977] Crim. Law Rev. 395. Nor was any attempt made to explain whether, and if so why, the profits of bribery were treated differently from the gains from other acquisitive wrongdoing, such as libel, passing off, and so on: (Birks, "Personal Restitution in Equity" [1988] L.M.C.L.Q. 128, cf. [1993] L.M.C.L.Q. 30). In the law school these questions have been the stuff of the *Lister* v. *Stubbs* debate for a decade and more. There cannot but be some regret that, when the right facts finally arrived in court, they were not addressed.

[68] For an extreme example, see P. Birks (ed.) *Examining the Law Syllabus: Beyond the Core* (Oxford, 1993) 3; cf. (1993) 6 *SPTL Reporter* 3; John Mortimer, Q.C., *Law Student* (October 1993) 9.

large come to the law through a law school, that they should either have
a law degree or, if coming with a degree in some other subject, should
have spent at least two years in the academic study of the law. This
renunciation will undermine the foundations of our legal science. Those
who have not studied the law seriously will not encourage others to do
so. That was Dicey's theorem, no less true today than it was a century
ago.

3.1. The Conversion Cohort

Both the Law Society, which represents solicitors, and the Council of
Legal Education, which is responsible for the educational qualifications
of barristers, have decided that a law degree shall not be required. Anyone who has a degree, in any subject, may proceed to the vocational
phase of legal education, which lasts one further year and is heavily
committed to the teaching of the practical skills which a lawyer needs,
provided only that he or she has taken a one-year course in law. We
tend to call that the conversion route, because the one-year course is
deemed to convert into a lawyer the graduate in, say, history or biology
or sociology.

The Ormrod Committee thought that that conversion should take two
years. It also thought of it as a route for a small number of people. No
other inference is possible from the language of the report, which spoke
of the law degree as the normal vehicle. The professions have cut the
requirement to a single year and have at the same time thrown the
conversion route open to very large numbers. For this academic year,
1993–4, there were almost 5,000 applicants from graduates in other
fields wishing to go through the one-year conversion course, and almost
3,000 of them have begun their course. There would have been even
more applicants but for a filter unworthy of admiration: conversion is
open only to the rich, since the one-year course attracts no public funding.

The numbers converting have to be seen against a gloomy background in which law graduates are finding it difficult to get jobs. Taking barristers and solicitors together, the legal profession is thought
likely to have at most 4,500 jobs to offer in 1995 when the people now
converting finish their vocational year.

3.2. The QD Cohort

QD stands for 'Qualifying Degree'. It is through a qualifying degree that
the majority of entrants reach the vocational phase of legal education.

Again taking barristers and solicitors together despite the fact that their segregation begins at this point, there are approximately 7,000 places on the vocational phase, of whom about 5,000 may be expected to have come through a qualifying degree. These candidates will all have studied sufficient law in the course leading to their first degree at the university. They therefore come directly into the vocational course, with no need of conversion.

What do the professions regard as sufficient? They have just agreed a new announcement on this subject, which they want to take effect in 1995. Under the proposed rules the aspiring lawyer must have studied law for at least one and a half years during his degree course in order to be able to proceed to the vocational year. In those eighteen months the candidate must have studied land law, trusts, contract, tort, crime, constitutional law and European law. Each of those seven subjects must have occupied at least one ninth of the one and a half years. The assumption is that a degree will always consist, taken as a whole, in eighteen one-semester modules, three modules taken in each semester for each of three years. Hence, law must be studied for nine modules. If the minimum time is spent on each of the seven named subjects, there are two spare modules for extra subjects. Beyond the nine modules (one and a half years' study) there is no requirement for any further study of the law. Many students will, of course, opt for more law, but there is no requirement that they do so.

The people who regard law as a product to be marketed on the cheap have won a great victory, or will have won it when this minimalist programme is put into operation.[69] There is nowhere in the civilized world where so little legal education is required of a future practitioner. It is a programme promoted by people who have no notion of legal science or the public interest. It is a programme designed around the minimum investment which will get a certain set of fortunate people earning. I was myself present at an occasion when the Secretary-General of the Law Society spoke to us on the subject.[70] His view was that the requirement of one and a half years' legal study was more than enough. He thought that one year would probably be enough. He said

[69] The new proposals, superficially similar to the present regime, are in fact fundamentally different, in that the present regime stipulates core subjects within a law degree, what is necessary not what is sufficient. The present scheme is published at [1991] 3 *SPTL Reporter* 24; cf. [1993] 7 *SPTL Reporter* 14–15.

[70] Law Society's Academic Consultative Committee, Law Society's Hall, 113 Chancery Lane, Tuesday, 16th June 1992.

that the universities should accept that all that was needed was an "absolute minimum." That is what is being brought about. It is a minimalist, anti-intellectual victory. If Dicey's theorem was right, it will damage our law. It will certainly make us a laughing stock in Europe.

It is important not to exaggerate. Of those going into the vocational phase of legal education, which lasts one further year and is heavily oriented towards practical skills, it will perhaps not be more than 33% who will have followed the conversion route with its single year of academic study of law. Of the remaining 66% it is impossible to say how many will have studied no more than the nine required modules (1.5 years' study). We might conveniently, and optimistically,[71] guess that it will not be more than the 16% which will leave 50% of entrants still with a full law degree. Let us therefore assume, tentatively, that one potential practitioner out of two will have studied law seriously. A similar proposition in medicine would set alarm bells ringing. The one-year doctor will never be. Here in the Netherlands the same must be true of the one-year lawyer.

The minimalist argument has a long history. It can be read in Cicero's *De Oratore*. In that discourse one side claims with easy eloquence that all an advocate needs is native wit and personal skills, while the other points out, laboriously, that there is matter in the law and that lawyers who are all show and no substance cost their clients dear. Nothing is more disgraceful, says Crassus, who takes this latter line, than to hold yourself out to defend a client's interests only to wreck his hopes because the technicalities of learning in the law have been beneath your notice.[72] Such people should be condemned for lazy arrogance:[73]

Quod tamen os est illius patroni, qui ad eas causas sine ulla scientia iuris audet accedere (What a nerve a barrister has who dares to involve himself in such cases without any learning in the law)![74]

It might have been thought, however, that the clever amateur had had his day, killed off by embittered litigants, by the massive complexity of modern law, by the arguments of those who have seen the necessity of law schools in the universities and by the practice, responding to those arguments, of every jurisdiction in the developed world. We hear

[71] Mixed degrees including law have never hitherto involved large numbers. Modularization, which implies the possibility of many more "pick and mix" degrees is likely to increase the numbers.
[72] *De Oratore*, 1.27. 169.   [73] *Ibid.*, 1.138.173–4.   [74] *Ibid.*, 1.38.175.

continually of a return to Victorian values, but the earlier parts of this paper have shown that the great Victorians renounced amateurism. They saw that the wilderness of single instances could not be studied, and could not be comprehended, without a scientific legal education.

Let us review some of the dangers in reversing the tide that flowed from Dicey, Pollock and Anson to the great expansion of law schools since the Second World War.

3.3. Professional Status and Remuneration

A legal profession which opts for a contemptuous attitude to its education and training must go into decline. Its public esteem must fall, and with the esteem also the business and remuneration. Its business must be thrown open. The physician will not be displaced by the paramedic, but, if legal work takes no more than paralegal learning, then paralegal ancillaries must be allowed to do it and at paralegal rates. The Bar must reckon on surrendering its independent existence. This process is already underway, as the Bar cedes work to solicitors and the solicitors cede theirs to licensed conveyancers, licensed debt-collectors, marital mediators, and so on. There is no point in going to counsel who have no special learning on which to draw.

In the world of international trade and finance, our professionals, if they think that there is nothing to the law, must expect gradually to lose their competitive edge. The seven obligatory subjects do not include any company law and/or corporate finance; they touch on commerce only in the one module on contract. A smidgin of this vast body of legal learning, essential to the creation of the nation's wealth as well as to the competitive position of our lawyers in international markets, will rub off in the vocational year. The emphasis there will be on practical skills, sharp-end negotiation and bedside manner—hollow externalities when the substance of the law is neglected.

3.4. Fraud on the Public

The fate of the legal professionals themselves is not in itself of much concern. Nor is there any need to labour the potential harm to the country's law schools which, declared unnecessary by the professions, must suffer in their battle for resources. There will be more worrying damage, direct and indirect, to the people who need legal services. No less than the corporate client, the private individual goes to a lawyer for expert advice, often at times of personal crisis. Relations with employers and relations with spouses frequently threaten a client's life-chances. Neither employment law nor family law figures among the seven required modules, and none will be necessarily encountered in the path through the vocational year. Human rights make life bearable. They secured a late toehold in the minimalist programme, attracting all of two weeks' attention in the public law module.

Those who suffer the miseries of divorce believe, as the sick believe of doctors, that they will receive caring, resourceful advice from the lawyers whom they consult. Their confidence is without foundation. Individuals and communities at the wrong end of the exercise of governmental power—compulsory purchase, school closure, refusal of licences, oppressive application of planning controls—must be similarly disabused. They will not find much comfort in knowing that administrative law has formed perhaps one quarter of one module of their lawyer's training, one twenty-fourth part of one year's study. The most deprived members of our society are caught up in the welfare system. Social security does not appear.

3.5. Law in Modern Society

The indirect damage to the public is, if anything, more worrying. Dicey's programme was essential to respect for the courts and the rule of law. *Nam, ut eleganter Celsus definit, ius est ars boni et aequi. Cuius merito quis nos sacerdotes appellet.*[75] The lawyer to whom you turn should understand more than the simple technicalities of your trouble, the forms to fill up and the offices in which to make inquiries. A society which is plural, democratic and heavily regulated looks to the law for its equilibrium. Moral consensus having fragmented with monolithic religion, and regulated dynamism having displaced stasis, the law has become the instrument of balance between competing interests. It is the law, with less and less help from other social structures, which must assure the most diverse groups of the security and value of their essential interests. And it is the law, criminal and civil, which has to constrain, even in some cases reverse, every kind of power, of government over citizens, majorities over minorities, rich over poor, parents over children, men over women, and so on.

Lawyers cannot be merely one more self-interested group whose

---

[75] D. I.I pr.-I (Ulpian, libro primo institutionum).

power has to be curbed. They must be the guardians of the law, and repositories of knowledge and understanding of its workings. If, for example, the system of criminal justice falls into disrepute, all lawyers share the responsibility for diagnosis and cure. The same applies on countless fronts, from the humdrum working of the housing market or the procedures for inheritance to the constitutional propriety of government action and the protection of human rights. The questions have become more difficult: When should a life-support machine be turned off?[76] What are the best interests of children in family breakdown?[77] In what circumstances should a person of low intelligence be sterilised?[78] When do changing perceptions of social relations effect a change in the law, as for example in the law of rape?[79] Paralegals trained efficiently to dispatch excessive caseloads and clock up untold chargeable hours cannot discharge this deeper responsibility of the profession for knowledge, informed vigilance and secular wisdom.

Criminal law provides a currently painful example. We are in the midst of troubles of our criminal law and its administration. At this very point the minimalists are busy cutting down to one module the quantum of criminal law required to be learned. They cannot even be brought to address the questions whether more lawyers should know more criminology and penology, or what should be done about the general ignorance of criminal procedure. There is no room for such questions even to be asked in or of the minimalist programme. Many would find a satisfactory answer in the optional end of a law degree. But nothing is more obstinately resisted by the minimalists in power than the reinstatement of the Ormrod commitment to the LL.B. Anti-intellectual prejudice combines neatly with commitment to low-cost, high-speed production.

3.6. Comparative Law and the Common Law in Europe

Another matter of contemporary concern evokes a similar absence of response. The English lawyer of the next century will increasingly need to know something of the private law of other European countries and something of the constitutional arrangements in those countries. One

---

[76] *Airedale N.H.S. Trust* v. *Bland* [1993] 2 W.L.R. 316.
[77] Children Act, 1989, section 1 and sections 8–12. Cf. *Re R* (a minor) (Residence: Religion); *Re W* (a minor) (Residence Order) [1993] 2 F.L.R. 625.
[78] *Re F* (Mental Patient: Sterilization).
[79] *Reg.* v. *R.* (Rape: Marital Exception) [1992] 1 A.C. 599.

module of the law of the European Union will not suffice. With legal history and legal philosophy, comparative law provides the foundations of systematic analysis, but no power on earth could in the current climate persuade the Law Society of England and Wales of the importance of attending to these foundations.

On the private law side knowledge of the law of other European jurisdictions has obvious and immediate utility in dealings with them. But it will also streamline our own progress. Dicey regretted the waste of time entailed by want of systematic legal education.[80] There is no point in being flummoxed by soluble problems. Professor Markesinis and Mr. Deakin have recently shown that the muddles of our law of tort, especially in relation to liability for pure economic loss, have been aggravated and prolonged by reluctance to look at other systems.[81] Similar observations might be made of our law of restitution for unjust enrichment. It is not a question of borrowing but of accelerating analysis. The comparative method makes the real problems stand out from local distractions.

On the public law side we not only need to know more of the constitutions of our European partners but also, at a higher level of abstraction, we must learn more of federalism. The minimalist programme has no place or patience for these important tasks. Indeed the insular mentality has somehow turned "federalism" into a synonym for "centralization" and, having acquired that visceral certainty, feels no need to find time to study the devolved constitutions of Germany or Switzerland.[82]

There is a deeper question. The common law has much to offer in the European Union. Uncodified, pragmatic and adaptable it can fairly claim some superiorities over its more doctrinaire continental cousins.[83] Will it make the methodological contribution of which it is capable? When the common law neglects system and analysis, its powers of reason weaken. It becomes a game played with a handful of unscientifically selected cases. A single year of low-grade juristic training then seems

[80]   Above, text to n. 32.
[81]   B.S. Markesinis and S. Deakin, "The Random Element in their Lordships' Infallible Judgment," (1992) 55 M.L.R. 619, esp. 620, 645. Cf. also B.S. Markesinis, "Judge, Jurist and the Study and Use of Foreign Law," (1993) 109 L.Q.R. 622.
[82]   This curious blindness is discussed, too charitably perhaps, by Raoul van Caenegem, "Historical and Modern Confrontations between the Continental and Comparative Law," in B. de Witte and C. Forder (eds.), *The Common Law of Europe and the Future of Legal Education* (Deventer, 1992), 621, 621–4.
[83]   H. Kötz, "The Role of the Judge in the Court-Room," (1987) *Tydskrif* v. *S.-A. Reg.* 35, 41–2.

to be no handicap; any amateur can join in. This is the common law at its worst, and if it is played that way every continental lawyer will see through it. English law will become a little local peculiarity, a Louisiana in Europe. If the professions continue to encourage one-year and one-and-a-half year lawyers, that is what will happen.

The real future ought to be brighter. The common law as uncodified case-law, flexible but structured by rational analysis, can exercise a vivifying influence on the jurisprudence of Europe, in both substance and method. The condition is that it be taken no less seriously than the lawyers of the continent take their law. That requires the professions to shake off their minimalism and commit themselves to the programme which Dicey urged in 1883 and Lord Goff commended in 1983. The common law must not be a party game played with random groups of cases. Its magic lies in achieving responsiveness to change without sacrificing structured rationality and hence predictability. That balance depends, absolutely, on an interpretative partnership between the courts and the law schools in the universities. We ought not to be concealing but bringing out into the open the changes brought about by a century of extra-judicial juristic science. Law schools have become part of the interpretative process. The age of the textbook and periodical has made them law-making institutions of the common law.

On the educational front, however, the minimalist counter-revolution has been winning all the victories. Law schools must suffer, since if the professions do not believe in the necessity of serious legal education the government most definitely will not. In the short term there is more trouble ahead. It may be that the hostile climate will for a while deter good lawyers from dedicating their lives to the academic study of law. Nevertheless, when the destructive mood passes, the longer term future cannot but consist in a return to the Dicey-Ormrod project. What we actually need are stronger law schools and deeper legal education.

4. CONCLUSION

Dicey's inaugural lecture as Vinerian Professor provided a starting point. Contract was taken to illustrate the university's modern responsibility for the literature of the law, and the choice of illustration might be said to have focused on the quite exceptional contribution of Professor Treitel, the present holder of Dicey's chair. It is not to be forgotten that the first Vinerian Professor was Blackstone, not only the first Vinerian but the very first professor of the common law. His inaugural lecture was given 25th October, 1758. I will conclude by drawing on some passages from it. Blackstone was already fighting the battle which Dicey took up. The Ormrod Committee, two centuries later, seemed to mark the final victory, though matters have turned out differently.

The first passage is chosen because the minimalists never tire of pointing to the fact that some of our greatest modern judges did not read law at universities—Lord Diplock did not, Sir Thomas Bingham, M.R., did not—as though this would justify a return to the amateurism that the great Victorian jurists urged us to abandon. In 1758 Blackstone already had an answer. Referring to direct immersion in practice, he said:

A few instances of particular persons, (men of excellent learning and unblemished integrity) who, in spite of this method of education, have shone in the foremost ranks of the bar, have afforded some kind of sanction to this illiberal path to the profession, and biassed many parents, of short-sighted judgment in its favour; not considering that there are some geniuses, formed to overcome all disadvantages, and that from such particular instances no general rules can be formed.[84]

It is of course true that "some geniuses, formed to overcome all disadvantages" can still become great lawyers by following the kind of legal education which Dicey thought obsolete in 1883. That fact makes no argument for winding the clock back. A few lines later Blackstone sums up the deficiencies of the lawyer who is pushed hastily into practice to pick his law up as he goes:

If practice be the whole that he is taught, practice must also be the whole he will ever know: if he be uninstructed in the elements and first principles upon which the rule of practice is founded, the least variation from established precedents will totally distract and bewilder him: *ita lex scripta est* is the utmost his knowledge will arrive at; he must never aspire to form, and seldom expect to comprehend, any arguments drawn *a priori*, from the spirit of the laws and the natural foundations of justice.[85]

That passage should carry one's thoughts back to the responsibilities which lawyers as a group bear as guardians of the law and of justice according to law. Those responsibilities entail a level of understanding which cannot be reached if legal education is treated simply as the

[84] W. Blackstone, "On the Study of the Law," 1 *Commentaries on the Laws of England* 32.
[85] *Ibid.*

preparation for a trade, judged by the learner's readiness to make money for himself and his seniors.

Finally, since Christmas is approaching, and in the hope that the winter will not deepen, I will set out a passage which affirms the importance and the difficulty of the study of law, both liberal education and essential equipment for professional practice. The inevitability of adjudication, and the requirement of justice that like cases be adjudicated alike, oblige interpretative legal science to achieve a consistency and stability not incumbent on moral philosophers. Nobody who perceives the intense intellectual difficulty of that task can ever enlist in the cause of the minimalists. To all of whom I would, if I could, send by way of Christmas greeting these few lines from the first Vinerian Professor:

But that a science, which distinguishes the criterions of right and wrong; which teaches to establish the one, and prevent, punish or redress the other; which employs in its theory the noblest faculties of the soul, and exerts in its practice the cardinal virtues of the heart; a science which is universal in its use and extent, accommodated to each individual, yet comprehending the whole community; that a science like this should ever have been deemed unnecessary to be studied in an university, is a matter of astonishment and concern. Surely, if it were not before an object of academical knowledge, it was high time to make it one: and to those who can doubt the propriety of its reception among us, (if any such there be) we may return an answer in their own way, that ethics are confessedly a branch of academical learning; and Aristotle himself has said, speaking of the laws of his own country, that jurisprudence, or the knowledge of those laws, is the principal and most perfect branch of ethics.[86]

---

[86] *Ibid.*, 27.

9

The Anglo-American Jury System as Seen by an Outsider (Who Is a Former Insider)

*Professor Stephen Goldstein**

I. INTRODUCTION

In the title of this lecture I have referred obviously to myself, an Israeli law professor for the last seventeen and a half years who was born, grew up, and educated in the United States, and, indeed served as an American lawyer and law professor for fourteen years prior to immigrating to Israel.

In my view my American experience has given me a knowledge of the Anglo-American (or at least the American) jury that is difficult to be achieved by pure outsiders. On the other hand, my Israeli experience has given me an outsider's perspective which, I hope, allows me to understand aspects of the system that would not be so clear to the pure insider.

Moreover, an Israeli perspective in this regard may be even of more interest than would be a Dutch, or other continental perspective. For the Israeli procedural system has the important characteristic, from the perspective of a comparative proceduralist, that it is based, at least in theory, on Anglo-American, i.e., common law procedure, yet has never employed a jury, either in civil or criminal litigation. Thus, it provides the comparative proceduralist with almost a laboratory study of effects of the use (or lack thereof) of the Anglo-American jury on a procedural system.

In the short compass of this lecture, I cannot present a comprehensive analysis of the Anglo-American jury, including its desirability in civil and criminal litigation. And, indeed, I will not attempt to do so. Rather, after a brief survey of the history of the jury and its current use,

* This text represents a somewhat expanded version of a lecture given in the University of Leiden on 4 March 1994 at the invitation of the Institute of Anglo-American law.

I will concentrate on the issue stated above, i.e., the effect of the use (or lack thereof) of an Anglo-American jury on a procedural system. I cannot resist, however, closing this lecture without commenting on the major political problems confronting the use of juries in criminal cases today, particularly in the United States, and thus will close with this discussion.

2. A BRIEF SURVEY OF THE HISTORY AND CURRENT USE OF THE ANGLO-AMERICAN JURY

As is well known, a jury is a group of lay people, chosen at random, who perform most important functions in Anglo-American litigation. Without going into detail as to the historical controversies surrounding the origin of this peculiar institution, I would emphasize the most curious and important fact that the jury was transformed during the Middle Ages in England from a group of neighbours who decided according to their personal knowledge of the case to neutral deciders who enter the proceedings as a tabula rasa and must decide solely on the basis of what is presented to them during the judicial proceedings. Thus, inter alia, juries are ad hoc bodies with no collective memories. Moreover, they do not give reasons for their decisions.

These characteristics of the jury, I would suggest, are the source of many systemic features of common law (as distinguished from civil law or continental) procedure.[1] Moreover they also help to explain certain developments in Anglo-American substantive law. Indeed, in my view, one cannot really understand the Anglo-American legal systems without appreciating the enormous influence of the jury on those legal systems.

Thus far, I have discussed Anglo-American law and the Anglo-American jury as if England and the United States and their use of juries represent one system. And, indeed, this assumption is true as to many matters that I will discuss in this lecture.

However, we should not neglect the important differences between England and the United States in terms of the jury.

While England is the mother country of the jury and, indeed, the jury

---

[1] For a general discussion of the systemic features of common law and civil law procedural systems, see S. Goldstein, "On Comparing and Unifying Civil Procedural Systems", in *Butterworth Lectures 1994* (London, 1994).

is still very significant in England in criminal cases, it has virtually disappeared there in civil cases.[2] The present stronghold of the civil jury is the United States.[3]

Moreover, as I have discussed at length elsewhere, the continued extraordinary adherence to the jury—particularly to the civil jury—in the United States is clearly a result of the uniquely American view of adjudication, i.e., that it is an integral part of the democratic politic process.[4]

The jury represents that process in that its members, laymen selected at random from the community, are deemed to represent the political-legal ideology of that community as contrasted with professional judges, even though the latter are, in the United States, themselves generally also chosen by the democratic-political process.

This is made very clear by the history of the American civil jury.

Whereas the decline of the use of the civil jury in England began in the nineteenth century as part of the reform attack on English procedure led by such eminent thinkers as Jeremy Bentham, it was precisely in that era that in the United States the jury was in its heyday of popularity and influence.

Indeed, "while there seems to be no difference between English and American law on the point today, for the first 40 years of the Republic the settled rule in both the state and federal courts in America was that jurors were the judges of the law as well as of the fact, and juries were

---

[2] See *Ward* v. *Ward* [1966] 1 Q.B. 273; *H.* v. *Ministry of Defence* [1991] 2 W.L.R. 1992 (C.A.).

[3] Z. Stalev and H.M. Morales, "Roles of Lay Participants in Litigation", in *Role and Organization of Judges and Lawyers in Contemporary Societies (International Association for Procedural Law, IX of World Congress Procedural Law, Coimbra-Lisbon 1991)* at 305, 322. For further discussion of the controversy in the United States as to the continuing use of the civil jury, see e.g., H. Kalven, "The Dignity of the Civil Jury", 50 *Virginia L. Rev.* 1055 (1964) and sources cited therein. See also T.B. Smith, "Civil Jury Trial: A Scottish Assessment, 50 *Virginia L. Rev.* 1076 (1964); B. Kaplan, "Trial by Jury", in *Talks on American Law*, (H.J. Berman ed.) (Rev. ed.) (1972), at 51 ff.

[4] S. Goldstein, "Contrasting Views of Adjudication: an American-Israeli Comparison", in *Gedachtnisschrift fur Peter Arens*, D. Leopold, W. Luke, Sh. Yoshino, eds., (Munchen, 1993), 169. In this article I presented the thesis that in the United States adjudication is not viewed as a professional institution, but rather as an integral part of the democratic-political process. This view of adjudication in the United States is reflected not only in its use of the jury, but also in other aspects of the system including the popular election or political appointment of judges and the American attitude to criticism of the judiciary. This is in marked contrast not only to Israel but also to continental Europe, and, to a lesser but still significant degree, to England.

instructed that they had the right to substitute their own view of the law for the court's".[5] (emphasis in the original).

That this situation was a result, at least in part of the populist demand for popular control of adjudication, there is no doubt.

As stated by Prof. Paul Carrington: In many parts of the early United States, there was a widely shared mistrust of professional lawyers and of judges drawn from that profession. Mistrust of officials in general and professional judges in particular was a feature of the Jacksonian politics of the first half of the nineteenth century which was reflected in provisions for the election of judges and the reaffirmation of the importance of jury trial as a means of deprofessionalizing the exercise of judicial power. These political impulses were magnified in the populism of the late nineteenth century.[6]

This view is confirmed by the contemporaneous utterance of that most astute nineteenth century observer of American society and government, de Tocqueville: The institution of the jury . . . places the real direction of society in the hands of the governed . . . and not in that of the government . . . [It] invests the people, or that class of citizens, with the direction of society . . . The jury system as it is understood in America appears to me to be as direct and as extreme a consequence of the sovereignty of the people as universal suffrage. They are two instruments of equal power, which contribute to the supremacy of the majority.[7]

And, indeed, the extraordinary continuation in the United States today of the jury, including the civil jury, despite very persuasive arguments against such continuation can, in our view, only be explained by the

---

[5] J.D. Gordon, "Juries as Judges of the Law: the American Experience", 108 *The Law Quarterly Review* 272 (1992). See also, M.D. Howe, "Juries as Judges of Criminal Law", 52 *Harv. L. Rev.* 582 (1939); A Scheflin and J. Van Dyke, "Jury Nullification: The Contours of a Controversy", 43 (4) *Law and Contemporary Problems* 51, 54–59, 79–85 (1980).

[6] P. Carrington, "Trial by Jury", in *Encyclopedia of the American Constitution* (L.W. Levy, ed.) 1913, 1914–1915 (1968). As noted by Prof. Carrington, the historic American antipathy to professional participants in the adjudication practice applies not only to judges but also to attorneys and, indeed, may explain, at least in part the origins of the traditional American rule against awarding attorneys' fees to victorious litigants. See J. Leubrdorf, "Toward a History of the American Rule of Attorney Fee Recovery", 47 *J. Law and Contemporary Problems* 9 (1981): A.L. Goodhart, "Costs", 38 *Yale L.J.* 849, 873 (1929). For recent advocacy of increased civil jury power based, inter alia, on the historic democratic-political role of the civil jury, see R.G. Johnson, "Jury Subornation through Judicial Control", 43 *Law and Contemporary Problems* 24 (1980).

[7] Alexis de Tocqueville, *Democracy in America*, 282–283 (Phillips Bradley ed., 1945).

fact that the use of the jury is seen as an integral part of the democratic-political nature of adjudication.[8]

As noted above, the current use of juries in the United States, particularly in civil litigation, has been a matter of controversy for some time. Yet, this use is still quite prevalent.

I would disagree with those scholars that have concluded that "as an empirical matter, jury trials [in the United States] are relatively infrequent",[9] and would contend that the data they present support the opposite conclusion. Indeed, their statistics do show quite accurately that in the United States completed trials are infrequent. Thus, they report that in the federal system, in 1986, trials were completed in 17% of criminal cases (6,966 out of 41,490 cases filed in 1986) and in only 5% of civil cases (13,276 out of 254,828 filed).[10] Yet of the small percentages of trials completed in the federal system in 1986, a jury was used in 55% of the criminal cases and in 39% of the civil cases.[11] This, in my view, is by no means "infrequent".

3. ATTRIBUTES OF THE JURY AND ITS INFLUENCE ON THE ANGLO-AMERICAN LEGAL SYSTEMS

3.1. The Common Law Trial

A "trial", i.e., a clearly defined formal proceeding in which all the facts are adduced before the decision maker and at the end of which he renders his decisions only on the basis of what has been produced and learned in this proceeding is unique to common law procedure. The existence of this trial dictates that all that precedes it is pre-trial, the primary purpose of which is preparation for the great event, the happening, the trial.

This contrasts clearly with the Continental model of a continuing process of exchange of written matter, punctuated when necessary by short proof-taking hearings, with no central, dramatic proof-taking event.

---

[8] Compare A. Scheflin & J. Van Dyke, supra n. 5, particularly at 95–96, 113. See also J. Van Dyke, "The Jury as a Political Institution", 16 *Cath. L. Rev.* 224 (1970); A. Scheflin, "Jury Nullification: The Right to Say No", 45 So. *Cal. L. Rev.* 168 (1972); M.A. Dawson, "Popular Sovereignty, Double Jeopardy and the Dual Sovereignty Doctrine", 102 *Yale L.J.* 281 (1992).

[9] R.W. Cover, O.M. Fiss, J. Resnick, *Procedure* (New York, (1988)), 1190.

[10] *Ibid.*   [11] *Ibid.*

What is the explanation for this difference? The Continental method would seem to need no explanation, for it represents the normal decision-making process. However, the Anglo-American trial is extraordinary. It needs explanation. In my view, the explanation for this is the use—or at least historic use—of the jury in the common law procedure.

The connection between the jury and the common law trial has been recognized by a number of scholars.[12] However, the literature as a whole has not given sufficient emphasis to the fact that the common law trial, as we know it, is a direct result of the use of the jury. Without the common law jury, there would be no common law trial.

A jury is not a group of public officials present in their offices on a daily basis to whom information can be provided on an ongoing basis over an extended period of time. Rather it is a body of people otherwise occupied who must be convened specially for the purpose of receiving the information on which they will base their decision.

Moreover, the equality of the members of the jury means that all must receive the same information in the same manner. Thus the exclusive nature of the information process that takes place in the presence of the jurors.

Once this is established, it follows quite naturally, if not inexorably, that this information be provided, as far as possible, orally rather than in writing. The jury is a collective body both in its information reception and its decision-making process. Listening is typical collective activity. Reading, however, is typically a solitary one.

Moreover, until recently it could not be assumed that jurors could read and, even now, there may be substantial differences among the members of a jury as to reading ability.

Other typical aspects of a common law trial, such as detailed rules of common law evidence which emphasize the admissibility of, rather than the prohibitive weight of, evidence, as against the Continental freedom of proof, also must be attributed, in great part at least, to the common law jury.

Of course, as we have mentioned above, civil juries are almost extinct today in England. Yet this does not affect our conclusion that they are the direct cause of the existence of the civil common law trial in England even today. For the important fact is that civil juries were used

[12] See, e.g., J.A. Jolowicz, "Fact-Finding: A Comparative Perspective", in the *Option of Litigation in Europe* (D.L.C. Miller and P.R. Beaumont, ed.) Law U.K. *Comparative Law Series,*, Vol. 14; B. Kaplan, "Civil Procedure—Reflections on the Comparison of Systems", 9 *Buffalo Law Rev.* 409 (1959).

in England when the features of the common law trial crystallized. Moreover, juries are most important still in England in criminal matters and the similarity of civil and criminal adjudication in common law jurisdictions also has helped to perpetuate the effects of the civil jury well after the time of its prevalence.

Another typical aspect of a common law trial is its concentrated and continuous nature. This aspect of a common law trial is also clearly a result of the jury. It is quite impractical, if not completely impossible, to reconvene a jury of laymen for a number of short hearings held over an extended period of time.

Indeed its concentrated and continuous nature is generally viewed as such an integral part of a common law trial that scholars often refer to the common law continuous trial as one concept; as if the term trial itself necessarily implied its concentrated and continuous nature. However, a closer comparative analysis shows that this is not necessarily so.

In order to explain this we must return to the concept of a common law "trial". The essence of such a trial is the presentation of all factual information (and, incidentally generally also legal matters) in an oral open session before the decider (judge or jury) whose decision is then based on such information.

All other parts of the process (pre-trial or post-trial) are extra-trial, i.e., they do not serve as significant sources of the information provided to the decider and their primary importance in terms of the decision on the merits of the action is in the assistance they provide to the efficient functioning of the trial itself.

This situation is diametrically opposed to the Continental system, pursuant to which there is no division between extra-trial and trial, rather the entire process, from the first document, serves to provide information to the decider and there is really no difference in this respect between the information provided by various documents served and that provided by an occasional oral hearing, whether for testimonial or argumentation purposes. All of the process is aimed at accumulating one integrated file which will serve as the basis for the decision on the matter.

Thus, in the Continental model there is no trial at all. It is, in my view, misleading therefore to refer to the sporadic oral hearings that may occur in Continental civil litigation as "piecemeal trials";[13] they

---

[13] Compare M.R. Damaska, *The Faces of Justice and State Authority* (New Haven, 1986), 51–53.

are not "trials" at all for they lack the fundamental aspect of a trial, exclusivity (or almost so—there is no perfect model) of the oral hearing as a means of providing information to the adjudicator.

And, indeed, despite various attempts to give exclusivity to the hearings by adopting the principle of "orality", the systemic nature of the Continental process has rejected these attempts.

Thus, while the classic common law trial is, indeed continuous, the terms "trial" and "continuous trial" are not synonymous.

Moreover, the continuity of a trial seems to be even more directly attributable to the jury than is the trial itself. This fact is, perhaps, more obvious to an Israeli jurist than it would be to an American, Englishman or Dutchman. Israel is a testing case of a nominally common law jurisdiction in terms of its procedure that has never used a jury, neither civil nor criminal.

English rules of procedures and evidence were introduced into Mandatory Palestine and, in essence, continue in force in Israel until this day. The result is the use of a trial, both in civil and criminal procedure. However, this trial is not continuous, but is piece-meal. The trial consists of short sessions spread over a period of weeks, months or even years. Yet it is true trial in the meaning I have ascribed to trial; it is the exclusive means of providing factual information to the adjudicator. Nothing of substance relating to the decision on the merits occurs in the interims between the piece-meal trial sessions.

The lack of concentration of the trial also leads to the fact that trial judges often delay delivering their opinions for months (even years) after the last segment of the piece-meal trial.

This situation exists in spite of clear provisions both in the Rules of Civil Procedure and the Criminal Procedure Law that require a continuous trial and the delivery of the opinion within a short time of such a trial. This, I would submit, suggests that in the absence of the compulsion created by the use of a jury, at least historically, there will not be a concentrated continuous trial, even if there is a trial.

This tendency against concentrated continuous hearings may also explain, at least in part, why the attempt to impose concentrated oral hearings (not trials) in Germany and Italy have, in practice, failed.

Indeed, I know of no system of adjudication in which there are concentrated trials or hearings, in which such a system does not currently use, or has not historically used, juries.

One can only speculate as to the reason for this. I would suggest two: (1) first and foremost, interests of the lawyers, particularly when there is no specialized litigation bar, in terms of the undesirability of devoting an extended segment of time exclusively to one's client; (2) secondarily, interests of courts in terms of the problems created in a continuous trial system by last minute settlements.[14]

I would note, in passing herein, that the concurrence of a concentrated continuous trial and a specialized litigation bar raises an interesting cause and effect problem. Is a specialized bar a necessary condition of, or the result of, a continuous trial?

3.4. A Judicial Decider that Does Not Give Reasons for its Decisions

No less significant than the influence of the jury on the Anglo-American continuous trial is the fact that it does not give reasons for its decisions. As such it is virtually unique among judicial decision makers. Indeed, the clear tendency today is to require even administrative decision makers to give reasons for their decisions.

There are a number of very good reasons for requiring decisions makers, and perhaps, particularly judicial decision makers to give reasons for their decisions. First, is the improved quality of the decision itself. Every decision maker can attest to the fact that there are decisions that seem correct, until the decider has to put them in written, reasoned form; then they "do not write". This requires him to rethink the decision itself.

The second reason is for the satisfaction of the litigants, particularly the losing party. This may be seen both as an aspect of justice, i.e., the losing party is entitled to know why he has lost and, perhaps, also as a matter of efficiency, i.e., the losing party is more likely to accept his loss it he is given persuasive reasons for the decision. While the latter basis obviously is a function of the persuasiveness of the reasons and all of us can point to judicial decisions in which the reasons were far from persuasive, the former basis would seem to hold in all cases.

The third reason concerns review of the decisions, both internal review through the judicial appellate process and external review by the press, public, etc. It is obvious that a decision without reasons is much more difficult, if not impossible, to review than a reasoned one.

[14] Compare the discussion of the Royal Commission on Criminal Justice as to "cracked" trials, Report (London, 1993), at 103, 110–114.

Indeed, the Israeli Supreme Court has stated expressly that the need for effective appellate review requires trial court judges to write detailed, reasoned decisions, in which they must meticulously review each piece of evidence.[15]

In contrast, jury decisions are, in fact and in law, not subject to appellate review.[16] This is in contrast even to decisions of judges presiding in jury trial cases, which decisions are subject to appellate review even when they concern judicial interaction with the jury such as occur in jury instructions, motions for directed verdicts, judgments n.o.v., and new trials.

Lastly, it may be suggested that reasoned judicial decisions enhance the educational value of judicial decisions. While this may, in general, be of lesser importance as to trial court judgments than as to appellate decisions, it does have some significance even as to the former.

Given these very persuasive reasons for requiring judicial deciders to give reasoned decisions, the obvious question is what justification, if any, is there for exempting the jury from this requirement.

Explanations, as distinguished from justifications, can be found in the historic development of the jury described above, including the problem of literacy among jurors.

And, indeed, even today with presumably literate jurors, the problem of an ad hoc collegial body of twelve lay people writing a reasoned decision would be most formidable. Anyone who has experienced the problem of having a large collegial body draft any document can attest to the problems involved. On the other hand, those problems could be overcome substantially, if not eliminated completely, by such devices as the jury adapting alternative versions presented by the parties or the judge, or by the delegation of the drafting of the decision to the jury foreman, if the system wanted to require some form of reasoned decisions by juries.

And, indeed, where they are used, grand juries do "prepare" indictments and reports.

The fact that those devices have not been attempted as to trial juries suggests that the basis for not requiring such juries to give reasons is not only these historical and technical ones.

I would suggest that the justification for juries not giving reasons for their decisions is to be found in the source of their authority. While part

---

[15] See *Jutari* v. *State of Israel*, 44(2) P.D. 573 (1990).

[16] Compare the Seventh Amendment of the Constitution of the United States.

of the judicial apparatus, the source of jury authority is quite different than that of judges; they are not public officials acting pursuant to a hierarchical governmental structure.

Rather the jury, selected by random from the total citizenry, represent directly that citizenry. Thus their authority comes from this direct representation status. As suggested by de Tocqueville, the jury is seen as a microcosm of the people, with its authority stemming, therefore, from the sovereignty of the people.[17]

The legislature which is decreed to represent more directly the sovereignty of the people than do the executive and judiciary is not subject to a requirement of reasoned decisions. It would seem that this should also be true, therefore, of juries, and, indeed, the situation of juries in this regard may be a fortiori from that of legislatures.

The jury may be seen as a "mini-legislature" also in terms of its law making function related to its exemption from the obligation of reasoned decisions. That is, by not having to give reasons, the jury is allowed, if not encouraged, to deviate from the law. Whether historically this is an intended or unintended result of the fact that juries are not required to give reasons, and, indeed, are prohibited from doing so, I am not sure.

On either assumption, it is a most important aspect of the Anglo-American jury. One aspect of reasoned decision making which we have not yet expressly mentioned is that the requirement of giving reasons is aimed also at requiring the decision maker not to deviate from accepted decision making criteria, and, related to that, to allow his decision to be reversed on appeal if he does so deviate. In judicial decision making these criteria include the legal rules that apply to the given case. Thus, in being required to give reasons for his decision, a judge is thereby limited in his ability to deviate from the applicable legal norm. Moreover, if he does so, he can be reversed on appeal.

On the other hand, an "oracular" decision maker that gives no reasons for his decision has much greater flexibility in this regard. Moreover, in the absence of reasons for his decision it is most difficult to say he was wrong and, thus, reverse him on appeal.

The archetype "oracular" decision maker is the Anglo-American jury. And, indeed, the history of the civil jury, at least in the United States

---

[17] Supra n. 7, and accompanying text. For a contemporary comparable statement as to the criminal jury in England, see Lord Devlin, "The Conscience of the Jury", 107 *The Law Quarterly Review* 398, 402–403 (1991).

where it is still used extensively, contains numerous examples of jury exploitation of its flexibility derived from its oracular nature.[18]

Thus, for example, juries have reacted to what seems to be an undesirable legal rule by modifying it on a fairly consistent basis. An example of this is the common law rule of contributory negligence, which, through jury decisions has been moved toward the doctrine of comparative negligence.[19] Another example concerns the amelioration of the American rule pursuant to which a winning plaintiff is generally not awarded attorneys fees.[20]

An extensive discussion of whether such a situation is desirable would go beyond the confines of this lecture. Such discussion would, of course, have to deal with questions as to whether the jury amelioration of a given legal rule was desirable or not as to the merits of the rule and its amelioration. Even more fundamentally, however, the discussion would have to include the question of whether this jury amelioration, even if desirable as to a given defective legal rule, might not have prevented de jure changes in the law that would have been necessitated by its stricter application.[21] Such, indeed, may have been the effect of jury amelioration of the negligence requirement in traffic accident cases in preventing the enactment of other ways of dealing with this class of accidents.

No less significant, is the flexibility that is given to an oracular jury to do "justice" or "aequitas" in a given case by, for example, reaching a compromise verdict.

In general legal rules do not allow a decision maker to compromise

---

[18] As distinguished from jury nullification in criminal cases, i.e., jury acquittals of criminal defendants despite their obvious guilt of the crime charged, which I will discuss at the close of this lecture, civil juries are not completely free to deviate from the law. Rather they are controlled somewhat by the judge through such devices, mentioned above in the text, as directed verdicts, judgments n.o.v. and new trials, as well as the use of special verdicts. These devices, however, prevent only the most extreme jury deviation from the law and still leave great leeway for jury discretion as described in the text. For a discussion of these devices of limited jury control, see R.G. Johnston, "Jury Subornation through Judicial Control", 43 (4) *Law and Contemporary Problems* 24 (1980) 2nd sources cited therein.

[19] See R. Lempert, "A Jury for Japan?" 40 *American J. of Comp. Law* 37, 60; H. Kalvan, supra n. 3, at 1072.

[20] H. Kalvan, supra n. 3, at 1068–1071; H. Kalven. "The Jury, The Law and Personal Injury Damage Award", 19 *Ohio St. L.J.* 188, 163, 176 (1958). For a general discussion of the effect of juries on American tort law, see also B. Markesinis, "Bridging Legal Cultures", 27 *Israel L. Rev.* 363, 379–380 (1993).

[21] See B. Markesinis, supra n. 20; H. Kalven, supra n. 3, at 1071, R. Lampert, supra p. 19, at 58–63.

between liability and damages; each issue is to be decided independently and absolutely.[22] On the other hand, it is commonplace that juries do so.[23]

The possibility of jury compromise between liability and damages in civil cases is obvious, since the jury typically determines both issues. This is less true, however, in criminal cases, since, with the noticeable exception of the death penalty in the United States,[24] generally the jury determines only guilt or innocence with the judge then determining the sentence. However, even when this is the case, there may still be room for jury compromise, since the jury may, in an appropriate case, reach a compromise by convicting only on a lesser offence than the maximum offence charged, despite the fact that the defendant, if guilty at all, is guilty of the greater offence.

From the perspective of an Israeli jurist, the difference between judges and juries in reaching compromise decisions, particularly in civil cases, is very marked.

This is so since in Israel not only have juries never been used, but Israel is at the opposite extreme from oracular judicial decision makers.

Judging in Israel is viewed as a highly professional matter. Even more to the point herein, as mentioned above, Israeli procedure emphasizes greatly the rendering of reasoned decisions, particularly at the trial level, in which the judge must meticulously review each piece of evidence,

---

[22] In a most intriguing article, written almost thirty years ago, Prof. John E. Coons indeed advocated compromises being made expressly by judges in cases of doubt, either factual or policy, as to the correct result in a case. J.E. Coons, "Approaches to Court Imposed Compromise—The Uses of Doubt and Reason," 58 *Northwestern Univ. L. Rev.* 750 (1964). See also, S. Goldstein, "Equity in Civil Procedure—Introduction," to be published in *Acquitas and Equity: Equity in Civil Law and Mixed Jurisdictions* (A.M. Rabello, ed.) (Jerusalem, 1994), which discusses, inter alia, a relatively new and most curious provision of Israeli law that allows a judge, with the consent of the parties, "to adjudicate by way of compromise.".

[23] For a most interesting recent discussion related to this point, see W.M. Landes, "Sequential versus Unitary Trials: An Economic Analysis", 22 *Journal of Legal Studies* 99, 120–121 (1993).

[24] This exception, itself, demonstrates the role of jury as that of the people exercising their collective conscience. This most delicate issue, i.e., life or death, is not determined, as are other sentences, by a judge, but rather by the people themselves, as reflected in the jury. On the other hand, such a determination as to life or death by an unruly, populist body that does not give reasons for its decision raises serious questions of arbitrariness, inconsistency, or, perhaps, even racial prejudices, as will be discussed infra, in the section on jury nullification. The Supreme Court of the United States has dealt with these issues and upheld standardless jury determinations of the death penalty, over the dissent of Justices Douglas, Brennan and Marshall, see *McGautha* v. *Calif.* 402 U.S. 350 (1971).

as well as the legal rules he employs and their application to the facts he has found.[25]

This is in sharp contrast to the decisions of an oracular jury and prevents, virtually completely, an Israeli judge from reaching a compromise decision. On the other hand, compromise decisions, rather than zero-sum adjudication, may often be, or at least seem to be, the better way to resolve a dispute.

The historic inability of the Israeli judge to reach such compromise decisions on his own may explain, at least in part, the very strong tendency of Israeli judges to try to induce the parties themselves to reach compromise settlements rather than compelling them to adjudicate on a zero-sum basis.[26]

The Israeli emphasis on the writing of very detailed opinions by trial judges not only contrasts completely with decisions of oracular juries it is also different at least in degree, from the practices prevailing in England and the United States. This may also be a function of the fact that, unlike England and the United States, Israel nominally employs common law procedure but has never utilized the jury.

In England and the United States it would seem that the non-reasoned decisions of juries have had a spillover effect also on cases that are tried by judges without juries. Thus, in those systems, in contrast to Israel, there is much less emphasis on trial courts writing detailed, written decisions.

In some jurisdictions trial courts do not write reasoned decisions at all. In others such written opinions are quite conclusory and almost perfunctory, particularly when compared with their Israeli counterparts.

Moreover, in England and the United States appellate courts intervene far less in trial court factual determinations than they do in Israel.

While I cannot prove a clear cause and effect relationship between those differences between Israel, on the one hand, and England and the United States, on the other, and the lack of the use of a jury in Israel, my sense is that there is, indeed, a connection between them.

Finally, I should note that in addition to the very significant and dramatic effects on Anglo-American procedure produced by the existence of an oracular judicial decider, as described above, there may be others, less dramatic, but still significant.

---

[25] For a general discussion of the Israeli system of professional adjudicators as contrasted, inter alia, with the American jury, see S. Goldstein, supra n. 4.

[26] See, S. Goldstein, "Reflections on the Possibilities and Problems of the Judicial Process", 7 (1985–1986) *Tel Aviv Studies in Law* 50, 68–76.

An example is again found in the difference between Israel, and England and the United States. This time as to an aspect of common law res judicata, in particular issue preclusion (or collateral estoppel as it is sometimes termed). Under the general common law rule, subject to a number of other conditions, an issue once determined by a court is binding against a party to that litigation in future litigation.

Israeli law, however, has limited this rule by providing that it does not apply if the first decision is not "positive", which, in this context means, a definitive statement such as "the defendant was negligent", or "the defendant was not negligent", as contrasted with a judicial determination in favour of the defendant since "the plaintiff has failed to prove that the defendant was negligent."[27]

In criticizing this Israeli rule that distinguishes between positive determinations and failure of proof, scholars have pointed out that this rule is not found in England, from which Israel has inherited the general common law rules of res judicata, nor in the United States.[28] Without commenting, either on the relevance of the uniqueness of the Israeli rule to the question of its desirability, or on the desirability of the rule itself, it is clear to me that these commentators have missed the crucial point that the Israeli rule, based as it is not on the ultimate decision in the case but rather on its reasoning, i.e., the difference between a decision in favour of the defendant since he was not negligent and one in his favour since the plaintiff failed to prove the defendant's negligence, is dependent on the fact that Israeli trial court judges write detailed opinions making such distinctions.

Clearly, such a rule could not have developed in common law jurisdictions such as the United States that use oracular juries in civil litigation nor in England that did use such juries when its rules of res judicata crystallized and in which, as mentioned above, even today trial court judges write much less detailed opinions than their Israeli counterparts.

3.3. An Ad Hoc Judicial Decider with no Collective Memory

As discussed above, juries are ad hoc bodies that come together for a given case and are to decide the matters presented to them only on the basis of what is presented to them in open court. Moreover, decisions

---

[27] See, N. Zaltzman, *Res Judicata in Civil Proceedings* (Tel-Aviv, 1991) 186–192 (Hebrew).

[28] *Ibid.* and sources cited herein.

of previous juries do not have the status of precedents and juries are not informed of them.

The effects of such a situation are illustrated well by English cases refusing to use juries as to the assessment of damages in personal injury cases.[29] As discussed above, the use of civil juries in England is today quite rare. Juries are employed, as of right, only in cases of charges of fraud against the party who requests the use of a jury and as to claims in respect of libel, slander, malicious prosecution or false imprisonment.

However, there is discretionary power in the court to allow the use of juries in other civil cases. In the 1966 personal injury action, *Ward* v. *James*, Lord Devlin explained why juries should not be allowed to assess damages in personal injury cases. He stated that damages for pain and suffering and loss of the amenities of life in personal injury cases could never be truly compensatory and that conventional scales of awards had evolved. The unsuitability of juries for determining such awards stemmed from the practical difficulty of informing them of the conventional scales or of the judge giving them sufficient guidance to enable them to make an appropriate award without usurping their function. On the other hand justice plainly required consistency of approach. He expressed his conclusion in the following terms.

The result of all is this: We have come in recent years to realise that the award of damages in personal injury cases is basically a conventional figure derived from experience and from awards in comparable cases. Yet the jury are not allowed to know what that conventional figure is. The judge knows it, but the jury do not. This is a most material consideration which a judge must bear in mind when deciding whether or not to order trial by jury. So important is it that the judge ought not, in a personal injury case, to order trial by jury save in exceptional circumstances. Even when the issue of liability is one fit to be tried by a jury, nevertheless he might think it fit to order that the damages be assessed by a judge alone.[30]

In a 1991 decision of the Court of Appeal, the then Master of the Rolls, Lord Donaldson of Lymington, adopted this reasoning of Lord Devlin and reversed a decision of the Queens Bench that had granted the plaintiff's request for a jury trial on the assessment of damages (the defendant having admitted liability) on the grounds that the plaintiff

---

[29] See *Ward* v. *James* [1966] 1 Q.B. 273; [1965] 2 W.L.R. 455; [1965] 1 All E.R. 563, (C.A.); *Hodges* v. *Harland and Wolff Ltd.* [1965] 1 W.L.R. 523; *H.* v. *Ministry of Defence* [1991] 2 W.L.R. 1192 (C.A.).

[30] *Ward* v. *James*, supra n. 29, [1986] 1 Q.B., at 303.

had suffered a unique injury, i.e., amputation of a major part of his penis.[31]

In rejecting the uniqueness of this injury as grounds for a jury trial, the Master of the Rolls stated:

Mr. Sedley submits that the feature of this claim which makes it so exceptional is that the plaintiff's injuries involve a loss of personal esteem and a change in the way in which he will be regarded by those whom he meets in a social context. This, he submits, is something which a jury is better able to evaluate than a judge. The difficulty about this submission is that, whilst the plaintiff's injuries are indeed most unusual and very distressing, the same could be said of some other cases involving mutilation or indeed gross scarring of visible parts of the body. Furthermore, whilst in no way seeking to belittle the loss which the plaintiff has suffered, we are far from convinced that his damages for pain and suffering would have been less if, for example, he had been left a quadriplegic. Whilst the scale of conventional awards may give no direct guidance on what damages should be awarded to him, the requirement of justice that there be consistency of approach demands that any award to him should be made against the background of and be compatible with that scale. This is not something which a jury is as likely to achieve as a judge.[32]

Later in his opinion he refers to the unattractiveness of requiring a jury to perform an almost impossible task, namely to award a sum of damages which justly compensates the plaintiff having regard to a scale of conventional awards of which they are unaware.[33]

Unattractive or not, this is precisely the typical task of civil juries in the United States who regularly determine damages in personal injury actions, with all the attendant problems of inconsistency described above by the English courts.[34]

3.4. Lay v. Professional Deciders

The main obvious difference between juries and judges is that the former are laymen. Thus, it may seem strange that I am addressing this attribute of the jury only towards the end of this lecture.

Of course, without expressly emphasising this issue, it has formed part of our previous discussion. Thus, the inclination of juries to deviate from the law, as allowed them by the fact that they do not give reasoned decisions, is a function, at least in part, of the fact that they are

---

[31] *H.* v. *Ministry of Defence*, supra n. 29.   [32] *Id.*, at 1197–1198.
[33] *Id.*, at 1198.   [34] See B. Markesinis, supra n. 20, at 380.

laymen who may bring to the adjudication a different view of justice than does the professional judge.

Similarly, the problem discussed in the immediately preceding section concerning the assessment of damages for personal injuries stems also, in part, from the fact that the individual jurors are laymen and thus not part of the professional club of lawyers and judges who know the conventional scale of damages.

Yet I have refrained from dealing expressly with the lay status of jurors until this point and, indeed, will deal with it now only briefly precisely because this attribute of jurors is so well known and so well discussed. My primary object in this lecture is to explore less well known attributes of juries and the influence of such attributes on Anglo-American law in general and procedure in particular.

In terms of the general effect of jury versus judge determination of cases, the major 1960s, empirical study in this area, conducted by Zeisel, Kalven, and others, showed that American judges and juries would agree as to the result in 80% of criminal cases and 79% of personal injury civil cases. In the 20% of cases in which the jury would disagree in criminal cases, the disagreement is generally due to the jury being more lenient to the criminal defendant than would be the judge. On the other hand, in the 21% disagreement between judge and jury in personal injury cases, the study found, somewhat surprisingly, no jury tendency either in favour of plaintiffs or defendants.[35]

Alongside this empirical data, it has been noted, correctly in my view, that professional judges may "err on the side of thinking that all men are as logical as they are: juries tend to make better allowances for the muddle-headedness and blundering of simple people."[36]

It has also been suggested that professional judges may "place more emphasis on niceties of knowledge or specific intent than a practical juror ever would."[37]

This difference between lay and professional deciders is again very apparent to an Israeli jurist. As I have mentioned a number of times, in Israel the great emphasis on professionalism in the judiciary has led to an extreme emphasis on the writing of reasoned decisions, particularly at the trial level, in which the judge must meticulously review each piece of evidence.

---

[35] For an excellent summary of the above data, see H. Kalven, supra n. 3, at 1063–1066. For more recent discussion of this and other data, see R. Lempert, supra n. 19, at 54–58.

[36] B. Kaplan, supra n. 3, at 58–59.   [37] J.D. Gordon, supra n. 5, at 278.

The necessity to write such detailed trial court opinions may promote the exaggeration of the tendency of professional judges noted above: to attribute to people excessive rationality and to overemphasize technicalities in analysing actions of ordinary people. Moreover, in dissecting this evidence in such a manner, the judge is necessarily influenced by the fact that his long factual opinion may be examined further under the microscope of appellate judges who themselves are extremely professional.

In short, under such circumstances the extremely professional judge may unduly focus on the trees at the expense of the forest. An example of such a situation may have been the recent, highly published trial court acquittal (popularly known as the Shomrat case), which was subsequently reversed on appeal, of a group of six older teenage boys on charges of having repeatedly raped, during one week, a 14 year old girl. The acquittal was based on the grounds that there was a reasonable doubt as to whether the girl had consented.[38]

The problem of the superprofessional dissection of evidence in Israel may be even further exacerbated when the professional judge at the first instance sits alone and thus lacks the possibility of collegial discussion which occurs with the jury or with multi-judge panels.

In terms of collegiality, in Israel trial judges have always sat alone in civil cases, no matter how significant the matter. Until 1989, a panel of three judges sat in all criminal cases in which the maximum penalty was ten years or more imprisonment. However, in that year, the law was changed so as to provide that almost all criminal trials, including those for rape, generally be held before a single judge. This change, of course, was not made on the grounds that in such cases one judge is better than three, but rather because of a felt need for optimal use of the available judicial personnel.

And, thus one judge sat in the Shomrat case. In a most interesting response to this case, Judge Hannah Avnor, a retired District Court judge, has suggested that all rape cases be tried before three judges, one of whom is a woman.[39] Her argument about three judges, as against one is the familiar one of the value of collegial discussion among decision

---

[38] Compare J.D. Gordon, supra n. 5, at 278, who notes that juries may not only acquit in cases where a professional judge would convict, but "practical" jurors may also convict in cases where professional judges who may "place more emphasis on niceties of knowledge or specific intent" would acquit. See also, G. Simson, "Jury Nullification in the American System: A Skeptical View", 54 *Tex. L. Rev.* 488, 516–520 (1976).

[39] Ha'aretz, 18.11.92, p. B1.

makers.[40] Her argument that one of the three be a woman is rather unique in Israel, as it is based on the view that a women judge can better understand the reactions of a woman rape victim than can her male colleagues.

A discussion of the question of whether or not special efforts should be made to have professional judges be representatives of all sectors of the population, including women and minority groups, is not within the parameters of this lecture.

Yet I would note herein, that even if, in general, the judiciary as a whole is representative of all sectors of the population, that would not mean that a single judge in a given case would be so. Nor would even a panel of three necessarily be so. On the other hand, the jury because of its method of selection and the large number of its members, if properly selected, may be representative of all sectors of the population.

4. JURY NULLIFICATION

We have already discussed the power of the jury to deviate from the law as to civil litigation. In criminal litigation, the unique power of the jury to acquit despite absolutely clear and unequivocal evidence of the accused's guilt is referred to by the special term, jury nullification. This power is, indeed, unique since, in contrast to the civil area[41] there is no power whatsoever in the presiding judge to prevent or overturn any jury verdict in favour of the defendant. Thus the jury does, indeed, have the power to nullify the law in favour of the accused in the case before it.

There has been extensive debate in the literature and the courts as to whether the jury should be explicitly informed of its nullification power.[42] The proponents of informing the jury are in favour of rather extensive use of the jury's nullification authority as part of the Anglo-American criminal process.

The opponents of so informing the jury see its nullification power as

[40] Compare T.B. Smith, supra n. 3, at 1087–1092 who argues that if the civil jury is abolished in Scotland, as he thinks it should be, the important collegiality aspect of jury trial in terms of fact finding be retained either through the use of judicial panels or through that of law assessors sitting with judges. See also H. Kalven, supra n. 3, at 1067 who stresses the collective recall of evidence of a collegial jury as distinguished from an individual lay decider.

[41] See supra n. 18.

[42] See generally, A. Scheflin and J. van Dyke, supra n. 5 and sources cited therein.

precisely that: a power as contrasted with a legitimate authority or right. They wish to limit the use of jury nullification to those extreme cases in which the conscience of the jury compels it to act in violation of its legal duty. They want the jury to feel it is doing something legally wrong when it acquits an accused despite the fact that he is clearly guilty.

While the majority of Anglo-American jurisdictions have sided with the power view of jury nullification and do not instruct the jury as to this power, the fact remains that juries have such power and do, indeed, use it.

As will be discussed later in this lecture, the desirability of the continued existence of this power remains virtually unquestioned in the United States.

While it has been questioned in England,[43] and, indeed, the recent Report of the Royal Commission on Criminal Justice does recommend restricting somewhat an accused's right to trial by jury,[44] neither the Royal Commission nor any other public body in England has recommended abolishing jury nullification in cases tried by a jury.

In defending jury nullification, Lord Devlin has noted that a criminal jury exhibits "the element of popularity that is appropriate in a democracy."[45]

[The jury] lets the workings of conscience into the system. Judges are sworn to uphold the law; the jury is not. Sooner or later in life a man may be confronted with a struggle between what the law demands and what conscience urges. It is not a struggle that is peculiar to the jury box.

This is the situation which gives the jury its peculiar place in our Constitution. It gives it what is tantamount to a democratic veto on law enforcement.

It is true that the law is made by Parliament which is a democratic body. But the function of Parliament in modern times is to approve, reject or modify the plans of the Executive. Members of Parliament are made of the same stuff as jurors. But they operate at planning headquarters behind the lines. Juries are in the front line. They see the impact of the law on its subjects and they have to decide when to use its weapons. They exercise the discretion of the man on the spot. This is as far as military analogy can be pushed. Put into constitutional terms, the jury is invested with a dispensing power to be used when their respect for law is overridden by the conviction that to punish would be unjust.[46]

---

[43] See Lord Devlin, "The Conscience of the Jury", 10 *Law Quarterly Rev.* 328, 399–400 (1991).

[44] Royal Commission on Criminal Justice, supra n. 14, at 85–89.

[45] Supra n. 43, at 402.   [46] *Id.*, at 403.

As with jury deviation from the law in civil litigation, jury nullification in criminal litigation is of two types:

(1) jury reaction to what seems to be an undesirable legal rule, by refusing to apply it on a fairly consistent basis; and

(2) doing "justice" in an individual case, i.e., not convicting a clearly guilty person on the basis of the unique characteristics of the case before it.

Historic English examples of the first cited by Lord Devlin include cases in which mandatory death penalties applied to relatively petty offences, bigamy cases, "statutory rape" cases involving relatively mature girls and boys of the same age, and dangerous driving cases that carried mandatory jail sentences.[47]

It should be pointed out that in some of these situations jury nullification resulted not in absolute acquittals, but rather in convictions of lesser offences than the maximum offence charged.

I would note further that in many of these cases, such consistent jury nullification eventually resulted in amendment of the formal law.

A new and fascinating phenomenon in the United States may be providing us with a current example of this use of jury nullification. I am referring to jury decisions in favour of wives who, having been habitually abused by their husbands, eventually turn on these husbands and kill or maim them. These jury verdicts may reflect a growing societal appreciation, influenced by the feminist movement, that the legal defences of self defence and temporary insanity, as historically defined, are not adequate in such cases and need redefinition.

The second type of jury nullification concerns the jury dispensation power in order to do justice in a given case. This power may be defined as refusing to convict where there is no public interest in such a conviction in the particular case involved, despite the fact that the accused did, indeed, commit the serious crime with which he is charged.

Such jury power, as thus defined, would conflict with the principle of "legality" found in some European continental countries. In the common law world, however, it raises no such problem. This is so since in common law jurisdictions, discretionary power not to employ the full

---

[47] Supra n. 43, at 403–404. A different, but related phenomenon occurred in the United States in the 1970's when juries, at times, refused to convict anti-Vietnam War protesters for violating various criminal laws in the course of their protests. This jury nullification was based not on the juries' disapproval of these criminal laws themselves, but rather reflected their view of the Vietnam War and civil disobedience in opposition to it.

criminal process against those who have committed even serious crimes is well recognized.

The question arises, therefore, in Anglo-American law, not whether such power should exist, but rather who should have such discretionary power. Lord Devlin argues that the unique status of the jury as an ad hoc body makes it appropriate to put such power in its hands. In his words: "The power that puts the jury above the law can never safely be entrusted to a single person or to an institution, no matter how great or how good. For it is an absolute power and, given time, absolute power corrupts absolutely. But jurors are anonymous characters who meet upon a random and unexpected summons to a single task (or perhaps a few), whose accomplishment is their dissolution. Power lies beneath their feet but they tread on it so swiftly that they are not burnt."[48]

While Lord Devlin's argument as to the unique suitability of the jury for this discretionary power is quite persuasive, it must be recognized that, in general, in common law jurisdictions such discretionary power is not limited to the jury. In the United States, for example, such discretionary power is recognized also in the police and the prosecutorial authorities.[49] Indeed, all participants in the criminal process, except for the judge, are imbued with such power.

This discretionary power in police and prosecutors may be, at least in part, a spillover from such jury power; for example, prosecutors may be reluctant to prosecute if they have grave doubts that a jury will convict. However, it also reflects another element in Anglo-American criminal process: the dispute resolution function of such process. I have discussed this matter at some length elsewhere and thus will not do so herein.[50]

This brings us to the final point as to jury nullification: the very disturbing phenomenon today in the United States of juries apparently motivated by racial prejudice in their refusing to convict apparently guilty defendants.

The most notorious case was the California State Court acquittal of the four white police officers who were accused of beating a black man, Rodney King; a beating that was well documented by a video film. Yet

---

[48] Supra n. 43, at 405. See also, J. Gobert, "The Judge Presides but the Jury Decides Where Justice Lies", *The Independent*, 5.7.91, p. 19.

[49] England also recognizes prosecutorial discretion not to continue with criminal proceedings if it is not in the public interest to do so. See, The Royal Commission on Criminal Justice, supra n. 14, at 74–78.

[50] See, S. Goldstein, supra n. 1.

this is just one of many and, indeed, others include juries dominated by blacks who refused to convict members of their race for very serious crimes against whites, including Jews.

Some of the literature has recognized this problem as a serious one. Thus in his very perceptive 1976 article, Prof. Gary Simson argued that an invitation to jurors to vote their conscience is inevitably an invitation to greater parochiation in jury decision-making. "Local biases . . . are legitimated and activated. . . ."[51] Moreover, such local biases may, at times, "in effect immunize criminal acts visited upon members of society's discrete and insular minorities. . . ."[52]

In the Rodney King case, itself, the effect of the apparently racially motivated jury acquittals in the State Court was ameliorated somewhat by a later conviction of the white police offers in a Federal Court for a federal crime based on the same event.

This was possible due to United States Supreme Court case law that allows a defendant acquitted by a jury in a State Court as to a State crime, to be tried later in a Federal Court for a federal crime based on the same incident as the State offence for which he was acquitted.[53]

Yet this is clearly not a solution to the problem of racially motivated jury acquittals. First, a second trial on a federal offence of a defendant acquitted by a jury in a first trial for a State offence based on the same facts is problematic, to say the least, in a system committed to the finality of jury acquittals[54] and even more so to the fundamental constitutional right of a criminal defendant not to be twice put in jeopardy of life or limb for the same offence.[55]

And, indeed, the problem of double jeopardy in this situation proved a true dilemma for the justices of the Supreme Court who believed strongly in a defendant's right against double jeopardy and the finality

---

[51] G. Simson, supra n. 38, at 514.   [52] *Ibid.*

[53] See *Abbate* v. *the United States*, 359 U.S. 187 (1959); *Bartkus* v. *Illinois*, 359 U.S. 121 (1959); *Heath* v. *Alabama*, 474 U.S. 82 (1985). Indeed, these cases not only allow a federal conviction after a State acquittal but also a State conviction after a federal acquittal and, indeed, a conviction in a second State after an acquittal in the first State. Moreover, this jurisprudence applies also if in the first case the defendant was convicted, thus allowing multiple convictions for the same factual event. The doctrinal basis for this extraordinary avoidance of the right of an accused not to "be subject for the same offence to be put in jeopardy of life or limb" (the Fifth Amendment to the Federal Constitution) is that an integral element of an "offence" is the identity of the sovereign offended, and that for this purpose the federal government and each State are separate sovereigns. Thus despite the fact that the factual elements of the offence may be virtually identical, the "offences" are not the same since the sovereign involved is different.

[54] See M.A. Dawson, supra n. 8.

[55] *Ibid.* See also the discussion, supra n. 53.

of jury acquittals, yet were deeply troubled by the possibility of perverse jury acquittals on racial or other clearly improper grounds.[56]

Secondly, as distinguished with State law which generally determines criminal offences in the American federal system, federal criminal law is interstitial and consists of relatively few offences. Thus, the California police officers could be tried for a federal offence in the Rodney King case since they were, indeed, police officers.[57] However, generally, private citizens would not be committing a federal offence by causing grievous bodily harm to, or, indeed, by murdering other private citizens.

Lastly, while it may be that a jury in a federal criminal trial may feel a greater sense of national, rather than parochial identity, particularly after a well-publicized State acquittal on apparently racial grounds, it must be emphasized that also Federal juries are popular deciders drawn from the local population[58] and may, indeed, also act out of racial prejudice.

Thus, the possibility of a later federal trial is not an answer to the problem of a State court jury acquitting a defendant on racial grounds.

Despite that fact, most American commentators who have written about jury nullification do not seem to view the possibility of jury nullification on racial prejudice grounds as a basic flaw in the system and, therefore, a serious challenge to the continuing correctness of the

---

[56] See the dissents of Chief Justice Warren and Justices Black and Douglas in the Abbata and Bartkus cases, supra n. 53. Compare also the fact that Justice Brennan joined Justice Marshall in dissenting in the Heath case, supra n. 53, despite the fact that he was the author of the opinion of the Court in the Abbata case (but not the companion Bartkus case.) Justice Marshall, who was not on the Court at the time of the Abbata and Bartkus cases, indicates in his dissent in the Heath case that he would, as does Justice Brennan, accept a later federal conviction after a State acquittal but not visa versa and not a later State conviction after an acquittal in another State. As such both he and Justice Brennan, despite their strong views of the rights of criminal defendants which should include protection against double jeopardy, found the problem of the Rodney King type situation too compelling to ignore and thus, in this type of situation would sacrifice a defendant's rights against double jeopardy to that of ameliorating the effect of State jury racially motivated acquittals by allowing later federal trials for the same incident.

[57] Thus they were convicted of violating 18 U.S.C. Sec. 242 which makes it an offence for a person acting "under color of law (i.e., in an official capacity) to wilfully deprive someone of any rights protected by the Federal Constitution or law or to different punishments, pains, or penalties on account, inter alia, of the race of the victim. Indeed this provision is most apposite to the Rodney King case since it was originally adopted by the Congress after the American Civil War to allow for federal prosecution of State and local officials who violated the rights of the newly freed Blacks.

[58] Territorial jurisdictional differences between a federal district in a State and the various State courts of the State may affect somewhat the area from which a jury is drawn and thus its composition.

doctrine of jury nullification. Rather they tend to regard it as merely "noise" in an otherwise most admirable system; or at most, the price that American society must pay for the continued use of the jury as an important aspect of adjudication being part of the democratic-political process.[59]

Indeed, even the notorious acquittal in the Rodney King case which produced, inter alia, very serious rioting in Los Angeles, did not prompt American legal commentators to challenge the continuing validity of jury nullification. Rather the response concerned such peripheral issues as the mistake in transferring the venue of the case.[60]

In my view, this American refusal to face the true implications of the recent spate of racially motivated acquittals can be explained only by the fact that, as I have previously mentioned, Americans are passionately devoted to the absolute power of the criminal jury as part of their general view that adjudication is not predominantly a professional activity but rather a populist one which is an integral part of the political-democratic process.

It may very well be that one reason that the United States has been able to adhere to such a view of adjudication is the fact that traditionally the United States has not been a highly politicized society.

To an Israeli observer this is quite obvious. For Israel is, indeed, a most highly politicized society. Thus, for example, very many elements of the society are organized along, or heavily influenced by, political movements or parties. This is true as to the organization of the labour unions, sick funds and student unions in the University, as well as to various forms of collective or cooperative settlements. It was once true even as to primary and secondary education, as to which there are still significant remnants of this situation.[61] In a less serious vein, even sports clubs in Israel have been connected historically to political movements or parties.

In this highly politicized environment that exists in Israel, it is accepted that State conducted adjudication, rather uniquely, should not be a part of the political process. Rather it should be apolitical and

---

[59] See, A. Scheflin and J. van Dyke, supra n. 5, at 93–96. See also the dissenting opinion of Bazelon, J. in *United States* v. *Dougherty*, 473 F. 2d. 1113, 1142–1143.

[60] For a very clear expression of such a view, see M.A. Dawson, supra n. 8, at 302–303, i.e., the postscript to the Note appended after the Rodney King case acquittal.

[61] See, S. Goldstein, "Israel", in *Comparative School Law* (I.R. Birch and I. Richler, eds., Pergamon Press, Oxford, 1990), 275 ff; S. Goldstein, "The Teaching of Religion in Government Funded Schools in Israel", 26 *Israel L. Rev.* 36 (1992).

professional. This system is not only desirable for Israel, it is absolutely essential.

Yet the United States traditionally has been an apoliticized society not only in contrast to Israel, but also in contrast to the countries of continental Europe and even, albeit to a lesser degree, in contrast to England.

And, as I have stated it may very well be that it is just this apolitical society that has allowed the United States to afford a judicial structure which is highly political.

On the other hand, it may be that the United States is now becoming a more politicized society, particularly in so far as minority groups are gaining more political power. Such a situation may mean that the United States may not be able to afford indefinitely a democratic-political judiciary, including a highly politicized jury system. The recent spate of very controversial jury acquittals, and the popular reaction to them, may, indeed, signal the beginning of such a situation.

10

Immigration Law and Practice in the United Kingdom

*by the Rt. Hon. Sir Iain Glidewell**

It was a great honour to be asked to deliver this year's Clifford Chance lecture. I accepted the invitation with alacrity, but if I had known how distinguished and learned an audience I should be addressing, I might have paused to consider whether I could give a talk fitting the reputation of this great and eminent university, and of the academic prowess of Dutch lawyers. But, if I had hesitated longer, I should still have accepted. I say that because it was Professor Basil Markesinis who invited me.

I have come to know Professor Markesinis since he was elected a Master of the Bench of Gray's Inn some four years ago, and to admire the energy and enthusiasm which he devotes to any enterprise in which he is engaged. One reason why I accepted this invitation was my desire to visit the Institute of Anglo-American Law, which is so much his creation and his major cause. The other was that if Basil Markesinis asks you to do something, it is impossible to refuse.

I. INTRODUCTION

Great Britain is an island. It follows that immigration control, when a Government seeks to apply it, is relatively easy compared with control of immigration across a land frontier. The occasional small boat or aircraft cannot be stopped from bringing in a few passengers to some relatively deserted spot, but a ship or an aircraft carrying hundreds of passengers can only dock at a relatively limited number of ports or land at a major airport. Thus the control of major immigration is physically not too difficult.

* The text of a lecture delivered at the University of Leiden on 2 December 1994.

My purpose in this talk is to examine the ways in which, in the last half century, the United Kingdom Government has used its powers, originally derived from the royal prerogative and more recently derived from Statute, to control entry into the United Kingdom of persons coming from abroad. The growth and evolution of immigration law and practice illustrates continuing change in the Government's attitude towards immigrants, presumably in response to what the Government of the day perceives as being in the public interest, or as representing the wishes of the public, ie its voters.

Any discussion of immigration law and practice must include also some account of the law of nationality. The two are inevitably interlinked. It is therefore with our nationality law that I start.

2. BRITISH NATIONALITY ACT 1948

Before this Act, all those who owed allegiance to the Crown—by reason of birth in a country recognising the King as King or Emperor—were British subjects, and those not born in the UK were also commonwealth citizens. Since 1922 the position of the Irish has been and remains anomalous. For present purposes, however, they can be treated as if they were British subjects born in the UK.

Before 1948 all British subjects had, at common law, the right of abode in the UK. Thus they were not subject to any immigration control on entry into the country. Put broadly, to an Immigration Officer at Southampton in 1947, passengers could be divided into two categories—British subjects, whether they came from the old or the new countries of the commonwealth, and aliens.

It should be noted that not all other commonwealth countries applied the same principles to each other's subjects. Thus for example in both Australia and Canada from the mid-nineteenth century there were controls on the entry of workers from Hong Kong and India. The mechanism by which such control was exercised in those countries was adopted in part by the UK Government for the control of immigration from the commonwealth when the power to exercise such control was later created by Statute.

The Act of 1948 for the first time broadly divided British subjects into two categories:

(i) Citizens of the United Kingdom and Colonies (CUKCs); and
(ii) Citizens of the independent Commonwealth Countries.

Normally, when a former colony became independent, persons born in that country became citizens of the newly independent State and ceased to be CUKCs. However, citizenship of the United Kingdom and Colonies could be acquired not merely by birth in the United Kingdom or Colonies, but by descent from a father so born. So it followed that as most of the former colonies in the commonwealth gained their independence, many of their citizens were entitled to dual nationality—the nationality of the newly independent country and citizenship of the UK and colonies. Certainly there was nothing to prevent this in UK legislation, though a few of the newly independent states did not allow dual nationality. I shall refer later to the effect of the right to such dual nationality on the right of abode in the UK.

There was also an intermediate category of persons who, when the countries in which they lived became independent, did not acquire citizenship of those countries, but were not entitled to citizenship of the UK and colonies. This applied for instance to many Indians living in East Africa, where there was a substantial community of people, mostly shop-keepers and businessmen, of recent Indian descent.

Presumably at that time our Parliament was trying to enact legislation, in the flush of the post-Second World War enthusiasm for the universal rights of man, which recognised the status of the newly independent countries but made realistic distinctions.

What nobody appears to have anticipated was that within a relatively short time, there were going to be many thousands of would-be immigrants, who were entitled to enter the UK because they held citizenship of the UK and colonies, but were not the relatively well-to-do who had travelled in the past, but the relatively poor. Obviously what brought them to the UK was the prospect of work—West Indians who came to work on London transport, Pakistanis to work in the woollen mills of West Yorkshire, Indians to work in the factories of Slough and West London. Initially they came to fill vacancies in the more menial jobs which the native born British were increasingly unwilling to do. But as such immigrants continued to come, and settled, and were joined by their families then increasingly they came to be seen by many who were living near them as a threat. In this way they were following the pattern of their predecessors, the Jews from Eastern Europe who moved into London and a few other large cities at about the turn of the century.

I interpolate that most immigrants from the West Indies and the Indian Sub-continent settled in our large cities, and despite the passage of time they and their families are still there. In an average small

English country town there will probably be several Chinese restaurants or take-away food shops, some of the newsagents' and chemists' shops may well be staffed by Indians, but otherwise black or brown faces will be rare. On the other hand, in some parts of our major cities the opposite is true. In the infant class of a primary school close to Gray's Inn there are this year three children of Caucasian descent. In Whitechapel, immediately east of the City of London, a substantial Bangladeshi community has taken over the garment district which was settled similarly by Jews from Eastern Europe a century ago.

3. THE BEGINNING OF CONTROL OF IMMIGRATION FROM THE COMMONWEALTH

Commonwealth citizens were first made subject to immigration control to the UK by the Commonwealth Immigrants' Act 1962. This Act imposed immigration control on most British subjects, whether they were citizens of the UK and colonies or citizens of an independent commonwealth country. The major groups who were not subjected by the Act to immigration control were persons born in the United Kingdom, and holders of UK passports who lived in another commonwealth country but were entitled to such passports because their fathers or grandfathers had been born in the UK. There were other exceptions which were not sufficiently important to alter the general pattern. I should however mention one special category of UK passport holders —the Kenyan Asians to whom I have already referred. At the time when the 1962 Act was brought into force it was known that they might not be accorded Kenyan nationality by the legislation of that country when it became independent. For that reason the Kenyan Independence Act of the UK Parliament made specific provision under which this group were entitled to UK passports.

After 1962, the combined effect of the Nationality Act of 1964 and the Commonwealth Immigrants' Act of 1968 had the effect of giving the right to claim or resume UK citizenship to those with at least one parent or grandparent born in the UK, but to impose immigration control on others, even if they were holders of UK passports. This immediately drew a distinction between the unfortunate East African Asians, who were thus subjected to immigration control and only became entitled to enter the UK with leave, and many white residents in east and central Africa, who were often second or third generation immigrants into those countries from the UK, and thus could resume UK citizenship by virtue of descent from a UK born parent or grandparent.

These Acts were succeeded and replaced by the Immigration Act 1971, which is still the principal Statute governing the control of immigration into the UK. Unlike the earlier Acts, it is concerned with the control of immigration of people of all nationalities, whether from member states of the commonwealth or from other foreign countries. However its major impact has been and continues to be on immigration from the countries of the commonwealth, or former commonwealth states such as Pakistan.

4. CONTROL OF IMMIGRATION UNDER THE 1971 ACT

A person who enters another country may do so with the wish and intention of staying there permanently, or of staying only temporarily before returning to his country of residence (throughout this talk the masculine is intended to include the feminine). There is no problem about the person who visits another country, genuinely intending to leave after a short time. Most states—certainly the UK—welcome visitors who come as tourists or to transact business. Students, if not so actively welcomed by Governments, are at least tolerated. The problem is thought to be with those who arrive wishing to stay indefinitely, and if possible to settle. Such a person will probably want to get a job which might otherwise be taken by an existing resident, to make use of the resources of the health and social services, to occupy a house in an area where inexpensive housing is scarce. Thus inevitably immigration control is principally directed at those arriving for settlement, but it must also deal with the person who says that he is only coming for a short stay, but actually wishes to remain indefinitely if possible. Obviously obtaining leave to enter another country as a visitor or a student is seen as a way of surmounting the first hurdle which needs to be overcome in order to become a permanent resident ie physical presence in the UK.

This has inevitably meant that, whatever its intentions, the impact of our immigration control over commonwealth immigrants has varied according to race, by which I really mean skin colour. Visitors from the old commonwealth, ie the countries with predominantly white populations, normally want to return home after a time. Young Australians and New Zealanders often come to the UK to spend six months or a year before returning home to join the world of jobs and families and mortgages. But return home they usually do. Of course, some people from India or black Africa genuinely want to come for a temporary period—to study and perhaps to qualify in medicine or law or economics. But many who arrive from the Indian Subcontinent or Africa or the West Indies do so wishing to stay, to make a new life and achieve a better standard of living than that which is open to them at home. It is noticeable that there are very few permanent immigrants from Malaysia or Singapore, because the standard of living there is so high. Hong Kong is of course a special case.

The 1971 Act starts with a statement of general principles. It reads as follows:

1(1) All those who are in this Act expressed to have the right of abode in the UK shall be free to live in, and to come and go into and from, the UK without let or hindrance except such as may be required under and in accordance with this Act to enable their right to be established or as may be otherwise lawfully imposed on any person.

(2) Those not having that right may live, work and settle in the UK by permission and subject to such regulation and control of their entry into, stay in and departure from the UK as is imposed by this Act; and indefinite leave to enter or remain in the United Kingdom shall, . . . be treated as having been given under this Act to those in the UK at its coming into force, if they are then settled there. . . .

Sub-section (3) provides that journeys within what is called "the common travel area", ie the UK together with the Republic of Ireland, the Channel Islands and the Isle of Man, are not subject to control under the Act. This is the provision which exempts citizens of Ireland from UK immigration control in most respects.

Section 3 of the Act as originally enacted provided that persons who were not entitled to the right of abode in the UK should be subject to immigration control ie should not enter the UK unless given leave to do so in accordance with the Act. If leave is given, to enter or to remain in the UK, it may be for a limited or an indefinite period. Leave to enter for a limited period may be, and normally will be, subject to conditions restricting or prohibiting obtaining employment. The entrant may also be required to register with the police.

These provisions raise two broad questions:

(i) Who has the "right of abode" in the UK so as to be free of immigration control? and

(ii) Who, though not having such right of abode, was nevertheless to be regarded as "settled" in the UK when the Act came into force on 1 January 1973?

5. THE RIGHT OF ABODE

The four main categories of persons who were described in section 2 of the 1971 Act as having the right of abode in the UK were:

(i) Citizens of the UK and colonies who had been born in the UK (including the Channel Islands and the Isle of Man);

(ii) Citizens of the United Kingdom and colonies not born in the UK but born of a parent born in the UK, or with at least one grandparent born in the UK;

(iii) Citizens of the UK and colonies who had at any time been settled in the UK and had at that time been ordinarily resident there for at least five years; and

(iv) Women who were themselves commonwealth citizens and married to men falling into any one of the first four categories.

To this list were added several other categories of less effect, e.g. those who acquired citizenship by adoption, naturalisation or registration.

I have already commented that those who came into the second category would particularly include people whose parents or grandparents had emigrated eg to east or central Africa in the early years of this century.

6. SETTLEMENT

The effect of the 1971 Act as originally enacted was that a person was settled in the UK when the Act came into force if he was ordinarily resident in the UK and had indefinite leave to remain. Such leave was and is given eg to those who establish themselves in self-employment or in business, initially with the benefit of a work permit.

A person with indefinite leave to remain in the UK has many advantages over one who only has limited leave. Thus there is no restriction on such a person taking, or changing, employment. However, he remains subject to immigration control, and under the Act his indefinite leave to remain lapses if he leaves the UK, even for a short period.

Moreover, unlike a person with the right of abode, he may be deported if he commits a serious criminal offence, or if for other reasons his presence in the UK is thought to be "not conducive to the public good".

The apparent hardship caused by the fact that a person with indefinite leave to remain in the UK who leaves for a short period of time and has no right to return without leave is ameliorated by a provision of the Immigration Rules. (I shall refer to these Rules later). This is known colloquially as the "returning residents" rule. It provides that if such a person returns to the UK after a period overseas, and satisfies the Immigration Officer that before he left he had indefinite leave to remain in the UK, that he has been out of the UK for no longer than two years and that he now seeks to re-enter for settlement, he is to be granted leave to re-enter with another indefinite leave to remain. However, the provisions of the rule can create problems in some cases. Thus suppose a person with indefinite leave to remain in the UK obtains a job in the Middle East on a four years' contract. After 18 months he comes back to the UK for a month's leave. He will be given leave to enter, but probably only as if he were a visitor, ie for a limited period. Thus at the end of his contract he will have been out of the UK for more than two years, and cannot claim that he had indefinite leave to remain when he last left the country. In most cases such a person would again be given indefinite leave to remain without any difficulty, but it is not guaranteed; there have been cases of people who have fallen into this trap.

7. THE BRITISH NATIONALITY ACT 1981

This Act made major changes in two important respects. Firstly, it had a major impact upon those who were already citizens of the UK and Colonies when the Act came into effect on 1 January 1983. At that date, a person who was already a citizen of the UK and Colonies, and had the right of abode in the UK under the pre-existing law, became a British citizen—a status which in terms had not existed under the 1948 Act. Other existing citizens of the UK and Colonies, who did not have the right of abode, were divided into two new categories of citizenship, British Dependent Territories citizens (ie citizens of the remaining colonies, particularly Hong Kong) and British Overseas' Citizens. Persons in both categories, if they have lived in the UK for at least five years with unlimited leave to remain, are entitled to register as British citizens. Otherwise they are not entitled to such citizenship. Thus for the first time citizenship is effectively equated with the right of abode, a concept which as I have said derives not from any previous nationality law, but from the law governing immigration.

Moreover, having defined citizenship by reference to the right of abode, the Act proceeds to define the right of abode by reference to citizenship. It achieves this by substituting a new section 2 for the former section of the 1971 Act, which provides that a person is to have the right of abode in the United Kingdom if either he is a British citizen or he is a commonwealth citizen who had the right of abode in the UK immediately before the 1981 Act came into force. Such persons are to be treated as if they were British citizens. I have already said that those who came within this last category were mostly persons whose parents or grandparents had immigrated to one of the colonies in the early years of this century eg to east or central Africa.

The other major changes made by the British Nationality Act 1981 were in regard to the acquisition of citizenship at birth. As I hope I have made clear, until the 1 January 1983 a child born in the UK became a citizen of the UK and Colonies by virtue of the 1948 Act and immediately acquired the right of abode in the UK by virtue of the 1971 Act. This was so whatever the citizenship of his parents. Under the 1981 Act, this is no longer the case. By section 1(1) of the Act:

"A person born in the UK after commencement shall be a British citizen if at the time of birth his father or mother is:

(a) a British citizen; or
(b) settled in the UK."

The restriction this imposes upon the acquisition of British citizenship is, however, to some extent ameliorated by a following provision, that if a person born in the UK who is not a British citizen spends at least the first 10 years of his life in the UK, and does not stay out of the UK for more than 90 days in any one of those first 10 years, he is then entitled to be registered as a British citizen.

In another respect, however, the 1981 Act widens the ambit of citizenship. Under the 1948 Act, citizenship of the UK and Colonies was acquired by a person born out of the UK but whose father had been born in the UK. Since the 1981 Act, the more restricted category of British citizenship can be acquired by descent if either his father or his mother was born in the UK. There are also special provisions for the children of British citizens born out of the UK at a time when their parents are abroad because of service in the armed forces or in a community institution.

8. THE EUROPEAN COMMUNITIES ACT 1971

Since the accession of the UK to the Treaty of Rome in 1972, the provisions of that Treaty—Articles 48, 52 and 60—providing for free movement within the Community for persons crossing a national frontier in order to obtain or take up employment, or to establish themselves in business or self-employment, have been applied in the UK. A national of a member state of the European Community is entitled to be admitted to the UK to take or seek employment, to set up in business, to become self-employed or otherwise to exercise the right of establishment as provided in Community law. Moreover members of his family are also entitled to be admitted to join him. The only condition on family members is that if eg a spouse is not herself a Community national, she must obtain entry clearance before joining her husband. A Community national coming for these purposes, and members of his family, may only be refused admission if their exclusion is "conducive to the public good on the grounds of public policy, public security or public health." This provision would eg entitle the immigration authorities to refuse entry to a person suspected of terrorist activities, even if he had obtained a job in the UK.

The normal procedure is that leave is granted in the first place for a temporary period of six months without formality. Thereafter, if the Community national wishes to stay in the UK, he must apply for a resident's permit. If, when he makes that application, he has obtained a job or has established himself in business or is self-employed, he and his family will be granted a permit. If the employment is for a fixed term, the permit will be for the duration of the job. In every other case it will normally be for five years. After four of those five years have passed, the Community national will be entitled to apply to have his resident's permit endorsed to show that he and his family have permission to remain in the UK indefinitely.

It follows that nationals of other EEC countries who have taken advantage of these provisions in our immigration law are in much the same position as—indeed in some ways in a better position than—citizens of the British Dependent Territories who are settled in the UK.

9. THE IMMIGRATION RULES

Under section 3(2) of the Immigration Act 1971 the Home Secretary is required to lay before Parliament statements of rules laid down by him "as to the practice to be followed in the administration of this Act for regulating the entry into and stay in the UK of" persons subject to immigration control. This power has been continually exercised since the Act came into force. Indeed, the earliest rules were made in 1966 under earlier legislation. Parliament has the power to disapprove rules laid before it by negative resolution, and it has occasionally used this power to stop the Home Secretary from making a change in the rules. Apart however from taking this drastic step, it must be doubtful how far Parliament considers the detailed provisions of the rules. The Immigration Rules are amended from time to time, and every few years a completely new set of rules, incorporating all recent amendments and sometimes some additional amendments is put before Parliament. The most recent version of the rules came into effect on 1 October 1994. They run to 395 paragraphs on 79 pages of type.

The Immigration Rules are a most unusual form of legislation. In one sense they are no more than rules drawn up by the Home Secretary for the instruction or guidance of his officials, particularly Immigration Officers, when making decisions in the course of immigration control. However the Act requires that if on an appeal to him (to which I shall refer later) an Adjudicator considers that the decision against which the appeal is brought is not made in accordance with the Immigration Rules, he shall allow the appeal. The rules are not binding on the courts, and occasionally the High Court has determined that a particular rule is outside the powers of the Act, and has struck it down. However normally the courts in immigration cases are much concerned to enquire whether the Home Office officials have complied with the terms of the relevant Immigration Rules, and have played a major part in deciding the proper interpretation of some of the rules. As an example of the effect of the rules, the provisions to which I have referred above relating to the entry into the UK of nationals of other EC countries for the purposes of employment etc were all until 1 October 1994 contained in the Immigration Rules. (They are now contained in a separate Order.)

10. VISAS AND ENTRY CLEARANCE

The Immigration Rules require that nationals of many countries who wish to enter the UK, for whatever purpose, must first obtain a visa or entry clearance from the appropriate British Consulate or High Commission before arriving at the UK port or airport. A person from one of those countries who arrives without the appropriate visa or entry clearance will normally be refused entry on that ground alone.

The list of countries to which this provision applies is contained in an Appendix to the Immigration Rules. The list is altered from time to time, as the political situation in various parts of the world changes. At present it includes much of Africa, virtually all of the Far East, most of the Middle East (but not Israel), but not any country in North America or on the mainland of South America (Haiti is on the list). Poland was deleted from the list when the communist regimes fell, but Romania and the member states of the former Soviet Union are still on it.

Moreover, nationals of all countries not on the list in the Appendix, other than those in the EC Community, must obtain an entry clearance before arriving if they seek to enter the UK for settlement for the purposes of business or self-employment, or for marriage to a person in the UK, or as the spouse of a person already settled in the UK.

The list of countries whose nationals all require entry clearance includes a number of major countries in the British Commonwealth, including Bangladesh, India, Pakistan, Ghana, Nigeria, and Uganda. The process of obtaining entry clearance in such a country normally requires, especially for a wife seeking to join her husband in the UK, an interview with an official at the relevant High Commission. The whole process can take a considerable period of time—two or three years is not unusual. There are complaints that this period of delay is being used as a form of immigration control in itself, but it is equally explicable by the inability of the staff in those countries to cope with the volume of applications for entry clearance.

II. DEPORTATION

Deportation is the process by which persons other than British citizens may be removed from the UK, and required not to re-enter, compulsorily. A British citizen cannot be deported.

The grounds on which a person who is not a British citizen may be liable to deportation from the UK are:

(a) if he has leave to enter the UK but remain only for a limited period, and has overstayed the condition imposing that time limit;

(b) if the Home Secretary "deems his deportation to be conducive to the public good";

(c) if he is convicted of a criminal offence punishable with imprisonment and at the time of conviction the court recommends that he be deported; and

(d) if he is a member of the family of a person who is deported for any of the first three reasons.

The procedure for deportation, except in cases in which the court has made a recommendation, requires that the Home Office shall first serve or attempt to serve on the person concerned a notice that the Home Secretary has decided to deport him. The intended deportee then has a right to give notice of appeal against the decision to deport within 14 days of receiving the notice. The rules, however, provide that a notice may be sent by registered post to a person's last known address, and it not infrequently happens that intended deportees, particularly overstayers, have long ago left the last address known to the Home Office. Thus frequently such a person does not receive the notice of intended deportation, and does not exercise his right of appeal. Nevertheless once valid steps have been taken to seek to serve the notice, the Home Secretary is entitled after the 14 days have expired to sign the order for deportation. If or when the deportee is arrested, the order can then be put into effect.

Attempts are sometimes made by persons who have over-stayed their leave to be in the UK, and may have remained many years before being detected by the Home Office, to challenge a deportation order by Judicial Review. However, such challenges rarely succeed.

12. ILLEGAL ENTRY

Section 24 of the 1971 Act relates to offences against Immigration control. The section provides, amongst other matters, that it is a criminal offence if a person knowingly enters the UK in breach of a deportation order, or without leave, or if he over-stays after being given leave to enter for a limited period only. I have already said that in the last of these situations he may be deported. The process of deportation does not however apply to a person who enters without obtaining leave. Nevertheless such a person is not only guilty of an offence, but may be removed from the UK as an illegal entrant.

Obviously a person who simply evades immigration control when he enters the UK—in the jargon, "comes across the beach"—is an illegal entrant. But the meaning of the phrase has been much extended as a result of decisions of the courts. In the case of *Zamir* in 1979 the House of Lords decided that if a person has obtained leave to enter by deception, the deception vitiates the leave, and he has thus entered without leave and is an illegal entrant. This clearly applies in the case of somebody who has come in using a passport which he knows is forged or is not his, ie he is using a false name as well. But it has been extended to cover the case of somebody who simply presents false travel documents, without making any statement about them. Moreover, a decision that somebody is an illegal entrant may be made many years after he has entered the UK. Thus for instance somebody may denounce another person as being an illegal entrant when he has lived in the UK for many years.

For this reason at one stage the Government gave an amnesty to illegal entrants in 1974, which covered most of those who had entered illegally before 1973 and who claimed the amnesty. However this amnesty has not been renewed.

The possible harshness of this interpretation of who is an illegal entrant stemmed in part from the fact that there is no statutory right of appeal against a decision by the Home Office that a person is an illegal entrant. The only means of challenge open is by way of Judicial Review. But as is well known, this is a procedure for challenging the way in which the decision has been made, not the correctness of the decision itself. Thus at the time when *Zamir* was decided, it was held by the court that if there was material upon which the Home Office could properly decide that an entrant had used deception when originally entering the UK, the decision that he was an illegal entrant was one which could not be challenged or quashed by the courts.

The logic of these decisions, and their apparent harshness, were mitigated by the later decision of the House of Lords in *Khawaja* in 1984. In that case the House of Lords laid down the following principles. The question whether a person is an illegal entrant because he practised deception when he entered the UK is a question of fact, upon which the courts must rule. It is not enough for the courts to say that there was material upon which the Home Office officials could properly conclude as they did. If such a person produces evidence of leave to enter—usually a stamp in his passport—then the burden of proving that leave was obtained by deception falls on the Immigration Service. Proof of deception is to be established on the normal balance of probabilities concept, but the courts must have regard to the seriousness of a finding that a person is an illegal entrant upon him and probably his family. The decision in *Khawaja* no doubt achieved a broad measure of justice, but it did breach what was otherwise the logical application of the normal principles of Judicial Review, that the court is not concerned with the rightness of the decision itself. Moreover, it imposed on the court of first instance the duty of applying a fairly flexible approach to the question whether the Home Office had proved to a sufficiently high standard that the entrant had obtained leave to enter by deception. The courts have shouldered this burden without any apparent problem.

I have the impression that cases of illegal entry alleged to be by deception are declining in number. If this is the case, it is probably because DNA profiling will now go a long way towards establishing family relationships, or at least proving that they do not exist. Thus if S seeks to enter the United Kingdom claiming that he is the teenage son of F, a DNA profile will readily establish if he is not. This of course is a procedure which was not available until a few years ago.

13. THE APPEAL SYSTEM

Until 1969 there was no statutory right to appeal against any decision of an official of the Home Office in relation to immigration matters. However, on the recommendation of a committee appointed to consider the matter, a statutory system of appeals was instituted in 1969, and was thereafter incorporated into the 1971 Act.

It is not every decision which may be the subject of an appeal under the Act, and there are qualifications and limitations upon the right to appeal where it is given. Put broadly, however, there was under the 1971 Act a right to appeal against decisions in the following categories:

(i) against refusal either of leave to enter or of an entry clearance;
(ii) against a refusal to extend the period of a limited leave to remain in the UK, or against the imposition of conditions on the grant of leave;
(iii) against decisions to deport (to which I have already referred);
(iv) against the validity of directions to remove a person as an illegal entrant, but not against the decision on the facts that the person entered illegally;
(v) against removal to a particular country in the case of an illegal entrant.

The effectiveness of this right to appeal was however restricted by the condition that in some circumstances the appeal might not be entered while the appellant was in the United Kingdom. Thus an appeal against the refusal of entry clearance could only be made while the applicant was outside the UK, and an appeal against a refusal of leave to enter would not be entertained in a case where the applicant was not equipped with an entry clearance until he had left the UK. The right of appeal is however particularly useful to those who have applied for but been refused an extension of a limited leave to enter, and against notice of intention to deport.

Where an appeal lies under the Act, the appellant body has two tiers. The lower tier is to an Adjudicator from a panel of Adjudicators appointed by the Lord Chancellor. The Adjudicators sit to hear appeals in many of the major cities in the UK. An Adjudicator must allow an appeal to him if he considers that the decision against which the appeal lies was not in accordance with the law or with the relevant immigration rules, or where the decision involved the exercise of a discretion by the Home Secretary or an officer, that the discretion should have been exercised differently. This obviously gives Adjudicators fairly wide powers, which in my view they normally exercise extremely carefully and sensibly. They inevitably gain a good deal of knowledge of the problems with which they may be expected to meet, together no doubt with a fair amount of cynicism about some of the stories they are likely to be told.

The upper appellant tier is the Immigration Appeal Tribunal, which sits only in London. Any party to an appeal to an Adjudicator may appeal further to the IAT, but only with leave. Thus if the Tribunal considers that an Adjudicator's decision depended purely upon his findings of fact, having heard the witnesses, or upon an exercise of discretion which was in the circumstances open to him, the Tribunal will normally refuse leave for a further appeal.

However, there has been ever since the 1971 Act a constant flow of appeals from Adjudicators to the IAT, which has resulted in some important decisions in immigration law.

14. JUDICIAL REVIEW

There was under the 1971 Act, and indeed until recently, no right of appeal from the Adjudicator/IAT appellant system to the ordinary courts.

Moreover as I have said there are important areas of decision making under the Immigration Act on which no appeal lies to the Adjudicator, or in which an appeal may only be exercised when the applicant has left the UK.

For these reasons, from the early 1970's onwards dissatisfied applicants for entry sought to overturn the decisions made by the Home Office or its officers, or by Adjudicators of the IAT after an appeal, by means of what is now known as Judicial Review. As I have said earlier, Judicial Review is a remedy which lies only in a case where the procedure followed in arriving at a decision has in some way or other not been proper, or the decision making authority has not acted in accordance with the law. It does not provide a remedy by way of a review of findings of fact or of an exercise of discretion. Such a remedy is of course precisely what most would-be immigrants want, and it is what they try to achieve, by means of Judicial Review. Sometimes they succeed—the court will decide that the Home Office, or less frequently an Adjudicator, has not interpreted a particular paragraph in the Immigration Rules correctly, and will then remit the matter for reconsideration in the light of the proper interpretation. This may result in a decision which benefits the applicant. But in many cases the procedure by way of Judicial Review is really inappropriate for the purpose.

Nevertheless from the 1970's onwards the number of applications for Judicial Review in immigration matters has grown steadily. In 1993 immigration matters were 23 per cent of the total number of applications made for Judicial Review to the High Court.

The requirement that a person who is refused leave to enter the UK and who is not in possession of an entry clearance cannot appeal against the refusal until he has left the UK, is sometimes sought to be circumvented by Judicial Review. If, before he is actually sent back whence he came, the intended immigrant can obtain the help of a Member of Parliament (often the member for a constituency in which one of his friends or relations lives) he may succeed in being allowed to remain in the United Kingdom temporarily pending the hearing of an application for Judicial Review. Sometimes he will be detained in custody, sometimes he will be granted bail during this period. Since the list of applications for Judicial Review is now so long that very often many months will have passed before his application is heard, it often transpires that somebody who has been refused leave to enter for, say, three months, has actually achieved residence in the UK for several times that period before a decision is finally made against him. This is clearly absurd. However, any suggestion that it might be better to give a right of appeal while a person is still in the UK has so far not persuaded Government to change this particular provision.

In one way the flood of Judicial Review applications in immigration cases has played a major part in the development of British administrative law. As is well known, administrative law in the British Isles is largely the creation of the Judges and academic writers. In particular, the ideas stem from a series of great decisions of the courts, starting in the 1960's. However the readiness of courts to develop the law in this way would have been to no avail if there had not been appropriate procedures by which the matters could be heard in the courts themselves. It was the invention of the remedy now known as Judicial Review, and the setting up in 1981 by rules of court of new procedures for dealing with applications, which enabled the courts to make the decisions which have expanded the law since the early 1980's. Those changes came about because of the flood of immigration cases which was clogging the procedure before then. So while the judiciary frequently complain about the number of immigration cases, it is perhaps right to say that in some ways they have been beneficial to the development of the law.

15. ASYLUM

In recent years the Immigration Authorities have been faced with many more people than was previously the case claiming asylum in the UK. The Immigration Rules deal with such claims. They provide that where a person seeks, or may be eligible for, asylum in the UK, his case is to be referred by the Immigration Officer to the Home Office for decision. The rules continue:

The Home Office will then consider the case in accordance with the provisions of the Convention and Protocol relating to the status of refugees. Asylum will not be refused if the only country to which the person could be removed is one to which he is unwilling to go owing to a well-founded fear of being persecuted for reasons of race, religion, nationality, membership of a particular social group or political opinion.

The last sentence is of course taken directly from the Convention.

Until, 26 July 1993 the only method by which a person who was refused asylum could challenge the decision was by way of an application for Judicial Review. However, on that date the Asylum and Immigration Appeals Act 1993 came into force. The Act contains a Code of Procedure for dealing with applicants for asylum. In particular, it provides that such a person is not to be removed from the United Kingdom until his claim has been finally determined.

The Act provides for the first time a right of appeal against a decision that a person is not entitled to asylum. The appeal is to a Special Adjudicator, one of a group dealing as rapidly as possible with such appeals. The Adjudicator has to decide whether the removal of the claimant from the United Kingdom would be contrary to the UK's obligations under the Convention. The Adjudicator must first consider whether the person's claim to asylum is "without foundation". The normal basis for so deciding is that the claimant has arrived in the UK, not directly from the country in which he fears persecution, but via a "safe third country". This is of course not infrequently the case with a person who has come from a former colonial territory of France or the Netherlands. The only question for the Adjudicator in such a case is whether the intermediate country itself provides a procedure for determining a claim to asylum under the Convention. If it does, then the claimant will be removed to that country without further consideration of his claim to asylum in the UK.

Where however a claimant has arrived directly from the country in which he fears persecution, his claim to asylum must be determined on its merits. An appeal lies under the normal provisions of the 1971 Act against the Adjudicator's decision to the Immigration Appeal Tribunal. The 1993 Act then gives a further right of appeal, on a point of law only, from a decision of the IAT in relation to an asylum claim to the Court of Appeal (or Court of Session in Scotland). The appeal can be brought only with the leave of the IAT or of the Court of Appeal itself. This is a novel and beneficial provision, which in my view could with advantage be extended to other appeals to the IAT in relation to other types of decision in immigration cases.

Under these provisions, the Court of Appeal has recently considered the case of a claimant for asylum who was with good reasons suspected of being implicated in what could properly be regarded as terrorist offences in the country from which he came, and in which he claimed to fear persecution if he returned. The court decided that in such cases the asylum provisions of the Convention do not apply. The applicant has been granted leave to appeal to the House of Lords.

The 1993 Act also contains a provision which restricts rights of appeal in cases other than those of claimants for asylum. A person who seeks to enter the United Kingdom as a visitor, or as a student without having been accepted for a particular course or intending to follow a course of less than six months duration is now not entitled to appeal against refusal of an entry clearance nor against refusal of leave to enter unless he has an entry clearance. This provision however does not affect nationals of other European Community States exercising the freedom of movement to which I have referred above. No doubt this restriction will soon result in a number of challenges in the courts by way of applications for Judicial Review.

It was a claim to asylum which led to a recent decision of the House of Lords which is perhaps the most important in the field of constitutional law in the last few decades. *M* was a citizen of Zaire who came to the UK seeking political asylum. His claim was rejected by the Home Secretary, and an application for leave to move for Judicial Review was refused. He was notified that he would be removed to Zaire via Paris on the evening of 1 May 1991. On that day solicitors acting for him applied again for leave to move for Judicial Review on what was said to be fresh grounds. A High Court Judge indicated that he wished the applicant's departure to be postponed until the following day, and understood that counsel for the Home Office had given an undertaking to that effect. This was however a misunderstanding. On the evening of 1 May the Judge was informed that *M* had been put on a flight to Paris and thence onwards to Zaire. The Judge made an immediate Order requiring the Home Secretary to take all possible steps to secure *M's* return to the jurisdiction of the English courts.

The Home Secretary was advised by his legal advisers that the courts had no jurisdiction to make a mandatory Order of this kind against him. This advice was based in large part upon an earlier decision of the House of Lords, the first *Factortame* case. *M's* solicitors then started proceedings claiming a declaration that the Home Secretary was in contempt of court in not obeying the Judge's Order. There were thus two questions:

(i) did the court have power to make a mandatory Order of the kind which the Judge had made against a Minister of the Crown and

(ii) could the Home Secretary as a Minister of the Crown be held to be in contempt of court?

In a speech delivered by Lord Woolf, with which all the other members of the House of Lords agreed, the House decided that, though such orders cannot be made against the Crown itself, both a mandatory order requiring such steps as those which the Judge had required and a finding of contempt of court can be made by a court against a Minister of the Crown acting in his official capacity. Lord Templeman, in his short speech agreeing with Lord Woolf, said:

The argument that there is no power to enforce the law by injunction or contempt proceedings against a Minister in his official capacity would, if upheld, establish the proposition that the executive obey the law as a matter of grace and not as a matter of necessity, a proposition which would reverse the result of the Civil War.

I do not myself think that this overstates the importance of the decision, which is the culmination of the history of judicial decisions in the last 30 years by which the courts have increasingly exercised jurisdiction to decide whether Ministers and Government officials have or have not exceeded their powers or acted without regard to the limits of those powers. It is interesting that a decision should be made in relation to a claim for asylum, when as I have said it was the spate of immigration cases 20 or more years ago which played a major part in the extension of Judicial Review. It is also not without interest that at an earlier stage of his career Lord Woolf was standing junior counsel for the Government in all matters of administrative law, including of course immigration.

16. CONCLUSION

Since our Immigration law is statutory its content, and the changes in both the legislation and the rules, are properly the province of politicians, not of Judges. The problems associated with immigration, and perhaps especially in claims to asylum, arouse strong emotions in the intending immigrant. The temptation to resort to deceit in order to obtain leave to enter must sometimes be strong. Some sections of the public, and of the media, have from time to time expressed strong opposition against what is thought to be too large an influx of immigrants.

It is the task of all who are concerned in the administration and oversight of immigration control—immigration officers, adjudicators and tribunal members, and ultimately the Judges—to try to make decisions without regard to the emotions aroused, which admit those who have a genuine claim to admission and only reject those who have not.

Of course in this process mistakes are inevitably made. Nevertheless I believe that our procedures for appeal and Judicial Review are effective in checking abuses, and that, if a regime of tight immigration control is necessary, we operate the system with as much fairness and humanity as can reasonably be expected.

II

Should There Be Rules of Procedure?

Samuel Issacharoff [*][1]

In the American federal system, the term "procedure" refers to two separate bodies of law. The first is the constitutional command of due process, applied to all levels of state actors by the Fifth and Fourteenth Amendments to the Constitution, that restricts the actions of government that impinge upon life, liberty or property. The contours of this system of procedure are primarily defined by judicial caselaw giving specific form to the open-textured commands of the Constitution. The second system refers to the internal operating commands of the federal courts, since 1938 embodied in the Federal Rules of Civil Procedure. These Federal Rules aim at approximating the ideals of a procedural system: the costless transmission from substantive law into judicial decisions. Unlike the constitutional framework, the Federal Rules take as their point of departure a rather detailed series of commands that propose to govern all circumstances that might present themselves in the judicial system, regardless of the merits of the controversy. The rules attempt to be not only specific in their commands, but all-encompassing in their operation—what is termed the "trans-substantive" sweep of the Rules in the legal jargon.[2]

The divide between the broad outline of constitutional due process and the trans-substantive specificity of the Federal Rules in turn reflects a divide between two forms of regulation, that of "standards" versus

[*] This paper was prepared for a presentation at the Institute for Anglo-American Law at the University of Leiden on 3 February 1995. I am deeply appreciative of the hospitality and comments extended by Professor Basil Markesinis and the students and faculty of that University.

[1] This paper is an outgrowth of the work I have undertaken with Professor George Loewenstein over the course of several years. I am grateful for the research assistance of Jon Dyck.

[2] Linda S. Mullenix, "Civil Procedure Rulemaking Reform: The Counter-Reformation in Procedural Justice", 77 *Minn. L. Rev.* 375, 439 (1992).

"rules." As formulated by Professor H.L.A. Hart, all systems of regulation must, of necessity,

[C]ompromise between two social needs: the need for certain rules which can, over great areas of conduct, safely be applied by private individuals to themselves without fresh official guidance or weighing up of social issues, and the need to leave open, for later settlement by an informed, official choice, issues which can only be properly appreciated and settled when they arise in a concrete case.[3]

Standards are a broad gauge form of regulation, ones that outline the general commands to be obeyed without specifying the precise application in any given fact situation. As such, standards are generally easier to formulate, but yield greater uncertainty in their exact requirements. In an economic sense, it may be said that standards defer the cost of factual inquiry to the moment of application, and then require that parties bear the burden of figuring how the standards are to be implemented.

In general, we may assume with confidence that standards are best utilized either when there will be relatively few actual applications of the regulations, such as to provide relatively little pay off for a greater initial investment, or when the applications are likely to be so factually specific as to make the development of more specific rules hopelessly either over- or underinclusive. By contrast, rules attempt to govern with specific commands for all fact situations that fall within their sway. Rules focus decision-making power in the hands of the initial drafters of a regulation as opposed to the final arbiter of their application.[4] Rules therefore require greater initial investment in devising the precise commands, but create less uncertainty in their operation and therefore require far less expenditure of resources once they are in place. As Professor Schauer explains, "[i]nstead of allowing decision-makers to scrutinize a large, complex, and variable array of factors, rules substitute decision based on a smaller number of easily identified, easily applied, and easily externally checked factors."[5] While standards risk costly uncertainty as to how they should apply, rules risk rigidity that creates inefficiencies through misapplication. With the increasing complexity

---

[3] H.L.A. Hart, *The Concept of Law* 127 (1993).

[4] Frederick Schauer, *Playing by the Rules: A Philosophical Examination of Rule-Based Decision-Making in Law and Life* 161 (1991). Professor Schauer describes the process of deciding on the level of specificity in commands as a tool "for the *allocation of power*." *Id.*, at 159.

[5] Schauer, *supra* note 4, at 152.

of matters now brought before the national judiciaries, it may be that, as Adrian Zuckerman notes, the search for global process regardless of the nature of the dispute, is a romantic notion that is simply unaffordable.[6]

At the constitutional level, the American law of procedure has moved decisively in the direction of standards.[7] Since the breakthrough case of *Matthews* v. *Eldredge*,[8] the Supreme Court has increasingly abandoned attempts at setting categorical rules of constitutional procedure in favor of fact-based balances between competing private interests, the interest of the state, and the systemic risk of error from inadequate process.[9] Recent Supreme court cases involving pre-judgment deprivations and civil forfeiture illustrate the use of procedural standards to mediate the tension between individual rights and the need for effective judicial process.[10]

On the other hand, the Federal Rules of Civil Procedure, perhaps

---

[6] A.A.S. Zuckerman, "Quality and Economy in Civil Procedure: The Case for Commuting Correct Judgments for Timely Judgments", 14 Oxford J. of Leg. Studies 353 (1994).

[7] An example of the broad, standards-like language often used by the Supreme Court is that "[D]ue process is flexible and calls for such procedural protection as the particular situation demands." *Schweiker* v. *McClure*, 456 U.S. 188, 200 (1982) (quoting *Morrissey* v. *Brewer*, 408 U.S. 471, 481 (1972)). As two scholars have pointed out, "The Supreme Court has continued to adhere to its long-standing position that the content of due process is extremely flexible, and not susceptible to precise definition." Martin H. Redish and Lawrence C. Marshall, "Adjudicatory Independence and the Values of Procedural Due Process", 95 Yale L.J. 455, 456 (1986). Justice Harlan proclaimed that "Due process has not been reduced to any formula; its content cannot be determined by reference to any code. The best that can be said is that through the course of this court's decisions it has represented the balance which our Nation, built upon postulated of respect for liberty of the individual, has struck between that liberty and the demands of organized society . . . "*Poe* v. *Ullman*, 367 U.S. 497, 542–43 (1961) (Harlan, J., dissenting). As noted by another commentator, the standard developed in *Matthews* v. *Eldridge* "says *how* to think about due process; it does not say *what* to think about it." Mark Andrews, "Aristotle and Mr. Eldridge: A Development of the Calculus in *Matthews* v. *Eldridge*", 20 Gonz. L. Rev. 343, 346 (1984/85). He went on to describe the *Matthews* standard as "broad enough to include the factors which are necessary and sufficient to settle questions presented to a court, and flexible enough to include pertinent social goals and public purposes which arise as constitutional law evolves." *Id.*, at 343. Other commentators, however, describe the *Matthews* test in less edifying terms, and see the rather open-endedness of the standard as its fundamental weakness rather than its strength. *See generally* Jerry L. Mashaw, *The Supreme Court's Due Process Calculus for Administrative Adjudication in* Matthews v. Eldridge: *Three Factors in Search of a Theory of Value* (1976) (arguing that the calculus developed in *Matthews* focused too heavily on technique and not enough on questions of value).

[8] 424 U.S. 319 (1976).   [9] 424 U.S. at 355.

[10] *See Connecticut* v. *Doehr*, 501 U.S. 1 (1991) and *U.S.* v. *James Daniel Good Real Property*, 114 S.Ct. 492 (1993), both of which are discussed at length in the following pages.

burdened by nomenclature, hesitate uneasily at the brink between rules and standards. Although the command of the Rules often devolve into standards-like formulations of treating all matters arising out of the same "transaction or occurrence" in like fashion,[11] there are still notable tendencies to devise sweeping rules that should categorically apply. The central part of this paper will address just such an example of a mistaken impulse to create procedural reforms too sweeping in their command and too likely to undermine the systemic efficiencies that should be a prerequisite for regulation. The example is drawn from the overhaul of the Rules governing the production of information in the pretrial phase of litigation. The alteration of the Rules to move from a process of party-controlled discovery of information, to rule-mandated disclosure of predetermined categories of information is, I shall argue, a prime example of the misapplication of Rules to a situation where factual nuances doom efforts at such all-encompassing regulation.

I. CONSTITUTIONAL STANDARDS

The American Constitution guarantees the security of life, liberty and property from state deprivation absent due process of law.[12] Central to the constitutional order of due process must be the right of security in one's home from either arbitrary deprivation of ownership or uninvited entry. Yet, any state must reserve to itself the right to breach the sanctity of the home when, for example, executing a search warrant or securing the payment of taxes. What then does it mean to have a due process protection that is necessarily less than absolute?[13] Two recent

---

[11] The phrase "transaction or occurrence" is used throughout the Federal Rules, and appears in either the text or notes of Fed. R. Civ. P. 7, 8, 10, 13, 14, 15, 18, 20, 21, 26, 42, 54, 56, and 59.

[12] U.S. Const. amends. V, XIV.

[13] It should be noted that there has been considerable debate among legal scholars about the meaning of the Constitution's due process provisions, particularly regarding the level of "substantive" protection it affords and the extent to which the courts have the constitutional authority to define the standard. Professors Redish and Marshall, for example, argue that the Supreme Court has a duty to establish a baseline, and that "[a]lthough a certain degree of situational flexibility is both necessary and advisable, it should come into play only after the establishment [by the Court] of a solid, value-oriented floor serving as the necessary 'ground' for procedural due process." Redish and Marshall, *supra* note 7, at 456. Contrast that to the positivist approach of Judge Easterbrook, who argues that an examination of the text of the Constitution and framers' intent make it clear that "there is no sound argument that this is a legitimate power or function of the Court," Frank H. Easterbrook, "Substance and Due Process", 1982 Sup. Ct. Rev. 85, 125,

Supreme Court cases develop the principle of due process while eluci-
dating the underlying evolution of a standards-based constitutional
conception of procedure; one in the context of state-initiated legal action, the other in private disputes *sub judice.*

1.1. Civil Forfeiture

The first case, *U.S.* v. *James Daniel Good Real Property*,[14] involves the
forfeiture of property following a criminal conviction. In 1985, James
Daniel Good was found in possession of substantial quantities of mari-
juana and various drug paraphernalia, and was duly convicted.[15] More
than four years later, the federal government brought an *in rem* action
for the forfeiture of the house and four acre site on which the drugs had
been found.[16] Under the federal forfeiture statute,[17] if the government
could establish probable cause to believe that real property had been
used in furtherance of a specified list of crimes, the government could
obtain an order allowing a seizure of the property in an *ex parte* proceeding. The government seized the property without notice and then
proceeded to prosecute its claim for formal title to pass from Good to
the United States.[18]

The question before the Supreme Court was simply whether the *ex
parte* seizure of Good's home satisfied due process. As Chief Justice
Rehnquist argued strongly in dissent, there is a long tradition of civil
forfeiture in American law.[19] The perceived wisdom was that "summary proceedings to secure prompt performance of pecuniary obligations to the government have been consistently sustained."[20] The reigning

a position championed by Judge Bork and Justice Rehnquist, among others. Redish and
Marshall (and many others) strongly criticize this approach, claiming that the positivists
"fail to establish that the framers intended so narrow and technical a construction of the
clause," Redish and Marshall, at 459, and that "even apart from questions about the
framers' intent, the structure and purpose of both the Bill of Rights and Fourteenth
Amendment militate against the positivists' conclusion." *Id.*, at 467. To find otherwise,
they argue, would make the clause a "meaningless exercise," *Id.*, and would "effectively
make the guarantee a rubber stamp for all legislative enactments." *Id.*, at 456. For another
discussion (and criticism) of the positivist approach to due process, *see generally* Richard
B. Saphire, "Specifying Due Process Values: Toward a More Responsive Approach to
Procedural Fairness", 127 Penn. L. Rev. 111 (1978) (arguing that a highly positivist
approach ignores the relationship between standards of due process and basic human
dignity, and that institutional constraints arguments justifying judicial "inaction" are not
convincing).

[14] 114 S.Ct. 492 (1993).   [15] 114 S.Ct. at 497.   [16] *Id.*
[17] Title 21 U.S.C. § 881(a)(7).   [18] 114 S.Ct. at 498.
[19] *Id.*, at 509.   [20] *Phillips* v. *Commissioner*, 283 U.S. 589, 595 (1931).

theory in governmental forfeiture cases was that "[w]here only property rights are involved, mere postponement of the judicial enquiry is not a denial of due process, if the opportunity given for the ultimate judicial determination of the liability is adequate."[21] Indeed, the issue had seemed settled by a 1974 Supreme Court case, *Calero-Toledo* v. *Pearson Yacht Leasing Co.*,[22] upholding the seizure of a yacht used in drug transport under a Puerto Rico variant of the federal forfeiture law.

In *Good*, however, the Court refused to adopt a *per se* rule of any sort governing the *ex parte* seizure of goods subject to forfeiture. While recognizing that the right to prior notice and the opportunity for a hearing are central to any constitutional conception of due process,[23] the Court was also attentive to exigencies in the exercise of state authority. Thus the propriety of the yacht seizure in *Calero-Toledo* turned not on a blanket exception for forfeiture cases from the general constraints of due process, but on the particular circumstance which, on balance, made the seizure compelling. In *Good*, the Court revisited *Calero-Toledo* to find it critical that a yacht was the "sort [of property] that could be removed to another jurisdiction, destroyed, or concealed, if advance warning of confiscation were given."[24]

The seizure of real property in *Good* was instead analyzed according to the standards set forth in *Matthews*:

The *Matthews* analysis requires us to consider the private interest affected by the official action; the risk of an erroneous deprivation of that interest through the procedures used, as well as the probable value of additional safeguards; and the Government's interest, including the administrative burden that additional procedural requirements would impose.[25]

Under this analysis, the seizure of a home produces a significant deprivation, unjustified by any governmental exigency. Unlike the yacht in *Calero-Toledo* which could presumably be spirited away, "real property cannot abscond, the court's jurisdiction can be preserved without prior seizure."[26] The combination of the lack of exigency, the importance of one's homestead, and the necessarily escalated risk of error in *ex parte* proceedings rendered the seizure unconstitutional.

The Court abjured any categorical rules either sanctifying the right to process before seizure or insulating historic forfeiture procedures from constitutional balancing. Much to the chagrin of the three dissenters, *Good* confirms the sweeping direction in favor of standards as the

---

[21] *Id.*, at 596–97.   [22] 416 U.S. 663 (1974).   [23] 114 S.Ct., at 500.
[24] 114 S.Ct., at 500, *quoting Calero-Toledo*, 416 U.S., at 679.
[25] 114 S.Ct., at 501.   [26] 114 S.Ct., at 503.

benchmark of constitutional proceduralism under "the notion that the *Matthews* balancing test constitutes a 'one-size-fits-all' formula for deciding every due process claim that comes before the Court."[27]

1.2. Securing a Potential Judgment

The expansive use of constitutional due process standards in *Good* confirms the general trend most visible in the Court's handling of pre-judgment attachments two years prior. In the 1991 case of *Connecticut v. Doehr*,[28] the Supreme Court examined the validity of a statute allow-ing the prejudgment attachment of real estate. The case involved an attachment on the home of Brian Doehr to secure a potential civil assault and battery claim arising out of a bar room brawl.[29] The suit did not involve in any way Doehr's home.[30] The statute did not require the plaintiff to post a bond to insure payment of damages defendant might suffer in the event of an unsuccessful claim or wrongful attachment, did not require a showing of "extraordinary circumstances," and did not provide defendant with prior notice or a pre-attachment hearing.[31] The statute only required a plaintiff to sign an affidavit (in this case, five one-sentence paragraphs) and, without any further proof, the Superior Court found "probable cause to sustain the validity of the plaintiff's claim."[32] Only after the property had been attached (and before he had been served with a complaint in the assault case) did Doehr receive notice of the attachment.[33]

The Supreme Court once again employed a *Matthews*-type standard in declaring the constitutional infirmity of the Connecticut statute. The Court articulated the *Matthews* three-part inquiry and stated that "[h]ere the inquiry is similar but the focus is different."[34] While the first two parts of the test were the same—consideration of the defendant's pri-vate interest that would be affected by the state's action as well as the risk of erroneous deprivation of that interest and the probable value of additional safeguards—the focus of the third part shifted from the gov-ernment's interest to the plaintiff's interest in the property.[35] The Court emphasized that the defendant had a significant property interest at stake and that there was a high risk of erroneous deprivation.[36] The Court pointed out that a judge "could make no reasonable assessment concerning the likelihood of an action's success based upon these one-sided, self-serving, and conclusory statements" (and nothing more), and

---

[27] 114 S.Ct., at 507 (Rehnquist, C.J., dissenting).   [28] 501 U.S. 1 (1991).
[29] *Id.*, at 7.   [30] *Id.*, at 5.   [31] *Id.*, at 4.   [32] *Id.*, at 7.
[33] *Id.*   [34] *Id.*, at 10.   [35] *Id.*, at 11.   [36] *Id.*, at 11–13.

that the plaintiff's interest was relatively minimal, as he had no existing interest in the property prior to the attachment.[37] The government's interest was dismissed as being no greater than the plaintiff's, which in this case was "de minimis."[38] Thus, while refusing to say that any *particular* form of process is due in *all* prejudgment attachment cases, the Court found that the statute lacked adequate due process protections, and that it did not properly address the balancing of the various interests involved.[39]

As with *Good*, the Court's opinion in *Doehr* represented a revisiting of pre-judgment seizure law in light to an expansive application of *Matthews*. Under a series of cases in the 1970's authored by Justice White, the Court had attempted to define the precise contours of what process would substitute for a hearing in cases of a prejudgment seizure.[40] Under this "checklist" approach, certain indicia of reliability—such as a detailed affidavit, a bond, and the participation of a judicial officer in authorizing the seizure—would establish the constitutionality of the seizure. Although Justice White tried to revive portions of this approach in *Doehr*, a majority of the Court rejected any *per se* approaches to constitutionality or unconstitutionality of a privately-initiated prejudgment seizure. Instead, the indicia of reliability from the pre-*Matthews* caselaw were incorporated into a constitutional balancing standard as evidence of the ease with which decisional accuracy could be improved.

2. PROCEDURES FOR PROVIDING INFORMATION

I wish to now turn to a radically different approach taken in the context of the Federal Rules of Civil Procedure. I should first add a caution for

---

[37] 501 U.S. 1 (1991), at 14.   [38] *Id.*, at 16.

[39] A similar form of balancing has been utilized by the Court in other areas of the law as well. In the realm of personal jurisdiction, whether or not jurisdiction will exist over an out-of-state defendant revolves around whether it is "fair and reasonable" under the circumstances. The Court developed a *Matthews*-type test which weighs the burden on the defendant, the plaintiff's interest in the forum, the states interest in adjudicating the particular type of conduct, and overall systemic efficiency. See *Asahi Metal Industry Co.* v. *Superior Ct. of California, Solano County*, 480 U.S. 102 (1987). For further discussion of the Court's tendency to use balancing tests in assessing constitutional issues see T. Alexander Aleinikoff, "Constitutional Law in the Age of Balancing", 96 Yale, L.J. 943 (1987).

[40] *See Fuentes* v. *Shevin*, 407 U.S. 67 (1972) (White, J., dissenting); *Mitchell* v. *W.T. Grant Co.*, 416 U.S. 600 (1974); and *North Georgia Finishing, Inc.* v. *Di-Chem, Inc.*, 419 U.S. 601 (1975).

those unfamiliar with the role of the Federal Rules. The Rules were adopted in 1938 to govern practice in the federal courts through two major innovations. First, the Rules were intended to simplify and make less technical the practices of lawyering that had held sway under common law forms of pleading and various forms of highly-technical code pleading. No longer would it be fatal to a plaintiff's case, for example, if the claim of replevin turned out to be trover because of changed factual circumstances. Second, the Rules combined the practices of courts of law and equity so as to render a uniform system of administering federal law. The combination of uniformity and streamlined procedure gave rise to a strong commitment to "trans-substantivity"—the idea that the Rules should be all encompassing in their sweep, regardless of the merits or size of the dispute.

Nowhere is the limitation on the aspiration for trans-substantivity more apparent than in the costs associated with the production of information. Under the American rule of cost allocation, each party to litigation is expected to bear the entirety of its costs in the case.[41] This creates a situation rife with the possibility of strategic imposition of costs in the pretrial discovery process. In discovery, each party may seek information from the opposing side pursuant to a variety of approved mechanisms. Because the cost of complying with requests for information generally substantially exceeds that of making the request, there is a significant risk of using discovery as a strategic ploy to impose burdens and costs on the opposing side. This is a classic form of what economists term a "moral hazard" in which parties are not forced to internalize the full costs of their conduct.[42]

While the risks of strategic misuse of discovery are exaggerated under the American rule, they would apply as well under the British rule of cost-shifting to the losing side. Even under the British rule, once

---

[41] There are exceptions where statutes expressly direct that the prevailing party may recover its costs from a losing party, as with various civil rights statutes and the antitrust laws. *See, e.g.,* the fee shifting provisions in 42 U.S.C. § 1988 (Civil Rights Attorney's Fee Awards Act of 1976); 29 U.S.C. §§ 206–207 (1976) (in an employee's claim against employer in suit involving minimum wage, maximum hours, and sex discrimination); 28 U.S.C. § 2412(d)(1)(A) (Supp. IV 1980) (in certain non-tort civil actions); 5 U.S.C. § 504(a)(1) (Supp. IV 1980) (in certain administrative proceedings against the federal government). These provisions, however, remain the decided exception.

[42] The classic moral hazard occurs whenever a party is able to obtain insurance that will relieve it of the consequences of conduct, particularly risk seeking conduct. *See generally The New Palgrave: A Dictionary of Economics* 549 (John Eatwell *et al.* eds., 1987); Richard Posner, *Economic Analysis of Law* 376–77 (3d ed., 1986) (discussing moral hazards involved in bankruptcy).

parties are in litigation, they are responsible for their costs only if they lose. If a party has a fifty percent chance of prevailing, for instance, then the discounted expected cost of each additional amount spent on discovery is only half the actual amount. In other words, if a party has a 50–50 chance of prevailing, then that party has only a one-in-two chance of paying for its own costs. While the moral hazard is not as great as under the American rule, it exists nonetheless.

The concern over "discovery abuse" as a result of unrestrained potential escalation of information costs prompted a categorical revision of discovery in 1993. I will now turn to the adoption of a sweeping mandatory disclosure regime in order to contrast its procedural wellsprings with the flexible standards for gauging procedure that is found in the constitutional context.

2.1. Mandatory Disclosure

The adoption of mandatory disclosure under amended Rule 26 of the Federal Rules of Civil Procedure inaugurated a sweeping regime of reform aimed at curtailing litigation costs. Despite widespread (indeed almost complete) opposition,[43] and without benefit of any systematic review of the trial efforts in pilot jurisdictions,[44] the amended procedures that went into effect on December 1, 1993 mark a significant alteration of the litigation process.[45] Almost immediately following the initiation of a law suit, and without any formal requests, the new procedural rules require each party to provide the other with large categories of information.

The central target of the reforms are the costs associated with

[43] *See* Griffin B. Bell, Chilton Davis Varner & Hugh Q. Gottschalk, "Automatic Disclosure in Discovery—The Rush to Reform", 27 Georgia L. Rev. 1, 29 nn. 110 & 111 (1992) (recounting near universal opposition to mandatory disclosure when proposal was first presented by Rules Advisory Committee).

[44] *See* Communication from the Chief Justice of the United States, Amendments to the Federal Rules of Civil Procedure and Forms, H.R. Doc. 74, 103d Cong., 1st Sess. 108 (1993) (Scalia, J. dissenting) [hereinafter Supreme Court Transmittal]; Linda S. Mullenix, "Hope Over Experience: Mandatory Informal Discovery and the Politics of Rulemaking", 69 North Carolina L. Rev. 795, 814–19, 828–30 (1991) (reviewing mixed early experiences in pilot districts and proposals for systematic study of discovery costs and reform proposals); Carl Tobias, "In Defense of Experimentation with Automatic Disclosure", 27 Georgia L. Rev. 665, 668–69 (1993) (advising against adoption of mandatory disclosure prior to significant experimentation).

[45] For an oversight of the curious history leading to the amendment of Rule 26 to provide for mandatory disclosure, *see* Carl Tobias, "Improving the 1988 and 1990 Judicial Improvements Act", 46 Stan. L. Rev. 1589, 1611–14 (1994).

discovery.[46] Since an estimated 95 percent of cases in the federal system are resolved either through settlement or otherwise prior to trial, the likeliest sources of excessive expense are those incurred prior to trial, and the costliest element of pretrial practice is discovery.[47] Thus, discovery reform is a prime target for curtailing the costs of adjudication.[48] The disclosure requirement is intended to reduce the costs of discovery by eliminating the need for formal requests which had, prior to the reform, preceded all exchanges of information. As expressed by the Rules Advisory Committee, "a major purpose of the revision is to accelerate the exchange of information about the case and to eliminate the paper work involved in requesting such information."[49] Proponents of disclosure also claim that it is likely to limit discovery abuse[50] by fostering a less combative style of litigation in general and discovery in particular.[51]

The primary practical alterations under the new rule are two-fold. First, the amended rule eliminates the need for filing formal discovery requests for the information that is now covered under mandatory

---

[46] *See Agenda for Civil Justice Reform in America, A Report for the President's Council on Competitiveness* (August 1991) (Report of Commission Chaired by Vice President Dan Quayle); Bell, *et al.*, *supra* note 43, at 2 n. 3 (summarizing concerns over discovery costs).

[47] *See* Marc Galanter & Mia Cahill, "'Most Cases Settle': Judicial Promotion and Regulation of Settlements", 46 Stan. L. Rev. 1339, 1387 (1994) (repeating 95 percent figure for pre-trial resolution of disputes and observing that component of those cases resolved by settlement is increasing).

[48] *See* Linda S. Mullenix, "Discovery in Disarray: The Pervasive Myth of Pervasive Discovery Abuse and the Consequences for Unfounded Rulemaking", 46 Stan. L. Rev. 1393, 1395 (1994).

[49] Proposed Amendments to the Federal Rules of Civil Procedure and Forms, Advisory Committee Notes, 146 F.R.D. 535, 628 (1992).

[50] The concept of "discovery abuse" is itself quite complicated. In general, there is far greater cost in complying with a discovery request than in making the discovery request. As a result, there is a strong temptation to inflict harm on one's adversary by seeking additional information for which the adversary will have to incur the cost. This creates the conditions for a moral hazards problem in which a party is absolved of the cost consequences of its conduct. Thus, some commentators have tried to define abusive discovery requests in terms of the relative costs imposed compared to the benefits obtained from additional information. *See* Robert D. Cooter & Daniel L. Rubinfeld, "An Economic Model of Legal Discovery", 23 J. of Legal Stud. 435, 450 (1994) (defining abusive discovery as that "whose compliance costs more than the expected increase in value to the requesting party's claim"). On the other hand, discovery as a part of litigation produces public benefits in terms of deterring wrongful conduct that may reach beyond the immediate costs to the parties, thereby justifying a more generous discovery regime. *See* Bruce Hay, "Civil Discovery: Its Effects and Optimal Scope", 23 J. Legal Stud. 481, 506–10 (1994) (comparing privately versus socially desirable levels of discovery).

[51] For a dramatic challenge to the empirical bases of claims of discovery abuse as part of a generalized litigation explosion, *see* Mullenix, *supra* note 48, at 1397–1418.

disclosure.[52] The categories of information subject to mandatory disclosure are quite broad. At the outset of litigation each side is responsible for identifying the names of all individuals with relevant information and the content of the information they possess,[53] copies or descriptions of all documents bearing on the subject of litigation,[54] a computation of all damages suffered,[55] and copies of all insurance agreements that may underwrite all or part of an eventual judgment.[56] While there is no evidence that the costs associated with filing the largely boilerplate requests for such information is a particularly significant source of litigation expenditures, the reform presumably does mildly reduce the costs of requesting the early information necessary for litigation to advance.

Second, the new rule advances the time in which discovery information must be produced and, consequently, accelerates the costs associated with the early stages of litigation. All disclosures are to be made within 10 days of a preliminary conference of the parties,[57] which is now required to be held "as soon as practicable" after the commencement of the litigation.[58] A failure to disclose witnesses or information available to a party at the opening salvoes of litigation may result in the preclusion of the use of such witnesses or information at trial.[59] The threat of evidence preclusion will almost inevitably push litigants to advance the production of information beyond what would have occurred prior to the reform.[60]

In assessing the effect of mandatory disclosure, and specifically its success in terms of reducing litigation costs, it is necessary to examine its impact on the timing and prevalence of case settlement. The importance of settlement in federal litigation cannot be gainsaid. Somewhere on the order of 95 percent of the cases filed in federal court terminate prior to trial, a large portion through settlement.[61] In addition, the most extensive surveys of litigation practices estimate that half the cases

---

52 *See* Fed. R. Civ. P. 26 (Amended Dec. 1993).

53 Fed. R. Civ. P. 26(a)(1)(A).   54 Fed. R. Civ. P. 26(a)(1)(B).

55 Fed. R. Civ. P. 26(a)(1)(C).   56 Fed. R. Civ. P. 26(a)(1)(D).

57 Fed. R. Civ. P. 26(a)(1).   58 Fed. R. Civ. P. 26(f).

59 Fed. R. Civ. P. 37(c) ("A party that without substantial justification fails to disclose information . . . shall not, unless such failure is harmless, be permitted to use as evidence at a trial, at a hearing, or on a motion any witness or information not so disclosed.").

60 For a discussion of the incentives on parties to produce favorable information in order to favorably alter the settlement demands of their adversaries, *see* Steven Shavell, "Sharing of Information Prior to Settlement or Litigation", 20 Bell J. of Econ. 183 (1989).

61 This same figure appears to hold in state court litigation. *See* Edward F. Sherman, "A Process Model and Agenda for Civil Justice Reform in the States", 46 Stan. L. Rev. 1553, 1583 (1994).

filed in the federal court system conclude without any discovery at all.[62] Another quarter are resolved with only token discovery.[63] This leaves only 25 percent of cases filed in which there is any significant discovery at all—of which only a fraction falls into the "abusive" or "exorbitantly expensive" category. Other, more informal, estimates, suggest that two-thirds to three-quarters of cases are resolved without extensive discovery.[64] The net effect of mandatory disclosure on litigation costs will depend not only on its impact on discovery costs when discovery occurs, but also on the rate of settlement prior to discovery; any effect of mandatory disclosure on rates of settlement prior to discovery will have a major impact on such costs.

The main effect of mandatory disclosure is to bifurcate what has been conventionally a single period of bargaining prior to discovery into two smaller bargaining periods, one preceding and the other following the mandatory disclosure of information. Were parties able to reason perfectly, there should be no effect to dividing bargaining periods into incremental units since the aggregate cost of the pretrial period would remain constant. However, there is little reason to believe that parties will be so perfectly calculating as to resist the temptation to escalate if the incremental costs are diminished or even eliminated. Since the main incentive for settling at any stage of the process is the cost associated with proceeding to the next, the bifurcation of discovery costs introduced by mandatory disclosure is likely to affect the prevalence and timing of settlement and hence the litigation costs incurred by the two parties.

The basic question raised by bifurcation of costs is whether two settlement periods, each with weaker incentives for settlement, are more likely to produce settlement and control costs than one settlement period with a commensurately larger settlement zone.[65] There are three distinct scenarios that may be considered:

---

[62] David M. Trubek *et al.*, "The Costs of Ordinary Litigation", 31 UCLA L. Rev. 72, 90 (1983); Paul R. Connolly, Edith A. Holleman & Michael J. Kuhlman, *Judicial Controls and the Civil Litigative Process: Discovery* (1978). The same pattern holds in state court litigation. Keilitz, Hanson & Daley, "Is Civil Discovery in State Trial Courts out of Control?", 17 State Ct. J. 8, 10 (1993) (finding that over 40 percent of cases in trial courts of four states settled with no formal discovery).

[63] *Id.*

[64] *See* Bell, *supra* note 43, at 41 (quoting Judge Barefoot Sanders criticizing mandatory disclosure because it is "likely to burden all because of the vices of a few . . ."). *See generally*, Mullenix, *supra* note 48, at 1432–42 (summarizing conclusions from various social science studies of discovery behavior).

[65] The formal analysis of settlement based on cost-avoidance does not take account of the short duration of the settlement period prior to mandatory disclosure, and thus

Strike suits: In general, frontloading litigation costs should serve a gatekeeping function to litigation. To the extent that litigants expect initial expenditures to be high they should be deterred from the decision to enter the litigation process. Most simply, an elevated filing fee will deter litigants with claims falling below the level of the filing fee from commencing suit. However, mandatory disclosure imposes costs asymmetrically. In federal court litigation it is fair to assume that the overwhelming share of early disclosure costs will be borne by the defendant. This is based on the general rule of thumb that, in litigation, information concerning liability is generally in the hands of defendant, while information concerning damages is likely to be held by plaintiffs.[66]

The focus of mandatory disclosure on information that will likely lead to sources of potential liability results in an elevation of early cost to the defendant. Since the decision to file suit in the hands of the plaintiff, there is consequently no gatekeeping function served by the early costs associated with mandatory disclosure. The effect is not, however, limited to imposing at an earlier stage the costs that would ultimately be incurred by the defendant were the case to be fully litigated.

By imposing costs almost exclusively on the defendant, and by providing sanctions for lackluster provision of information, the new statute greatly increases the attractiveness of strike suits. Strike suits are suits in which the expected value to plaintiff is zero or negative as a result of a low probability of success combined with the anticipated costs of litigation, but where the settlement value, defined as the mid-point of the settlement zone, is greater than zero.[67] In such circumstances, the

probably overstates the likelihood that the parties will settle during this period. Mandatory disclosure significantly compresses the initial period in which the parties may bargain. Because of the short time frame for producing information that must be disclosed, and the severe sanctions for its non-disclosure, the process of information production must begin almost immediately, unless there is quick agreement that the case will indeed be settled.

[66] This is in part a reflection of the many forms of civil cases in the federal courts in which liability turns on the state of mind of defendants in claims involving, e.g., securities fraud, civil rights violations, antitrust conspiracy, etc.

[67] This can be expressed as the conjunction of two conditions: First, the expected value to the plaintiff of a trial award is zero or negative because of the low probability of victory and the likely costs of pursuing the matter to trial. Second, the suit may nonetheless be viable for the plaintiff because of the threat to force the defendant to expend costs in excess of a possible settlement. Under such circumstances, if the plaintiff can credibly threaten to proceed to trial or to inflict costs on the defendent, the defendant is likely to settle as the cheaper alternative to either expending resources on litigation or confronting some measure of uncertainty on a likely trial outcome. Thus, strike suits are likely to be successful when the defendant's early litigation costs are high and when the

sole incentive for bringing suit is the expectation of a negotiated wealth transfer. Strike suits are encouraged by mandatory disclosure because it is possible for the potential initiator of a strike suit to credibly threaten to force a potential defendant to incur disclosure costs, even in the relative absence of a strong legal case. The threat is credible because if the defendant fails to comply or discloses information in a cursory fashion, the resulting preclusion of evidence might strengthen the plaintiff's hand, turning a nonexistent or weak case into a strong one. To avoid incurring such disclosure costs, the potential defendant may be willing to pay the plaintiff to avoid proceeding with suit. Note that this option is much less viable in the absence of mandatory disclosure, since initial discovery costs are more evenly distributed between the two parties; discovery has a downside potential for both parties.

Psychological factors: The second negative potential consequence of the asymmetry of disclosure costs is that serious plaintiffs—those not engaged in strike suits—may view such disclosure as costless to themselves. In fact, after the defendant has incurred the costs of mandatory disclosure, the defendant will be in the beneficial position for settlement negotiations since the defendant will have already borne a greater proportion of its discovery costs than the plaintiff. At this point, the prospect of non-settlement has less drastic consequences in terms of cost expenditures for the defendant than the plaintiff. In other words, the plaintiff should expect to negotiate a smaller settlement—the difference being approximately half of the defendant's disclosure costs—after such disclosure has taken place. If the assessment of mandatory disclosure were limited to an economic analysis, this anticipated shift would create an equivalent incentive for both the plaintiff and defendant to negotiate in good faith prior to mandatory disclosure.

However, economic models typically exaggerate the rationality of actors in litigation. Research in psychology points to significant limitations in people's abilities to process and store information.[68] Of special

defendant is pessimistic concerning the likely outcome of an adjudicated settlement. *See* David Rosenberg & Steven Shavell, "A Model in Which Suits are Brought for the Nuisance Value", 5 Int'l Rev. L. & Econ. 3 (1985) (developing the asymmetric cost theory of nuisance suits); Lucian Bebchuck, "Suing Solely to Extract a Settlement Offer", 17 J. Legal Stud. 437 (1988) (describing asymmetric information situation in which a plaintiff that can mask a nuisance suit and present a credible threat of going to trial is capable of extracting settlement value in excess of expected value); Avery Katz, "The Effect of Frivolous Lawsuits on the Settlement of Litigation", 10 Int'l Rev. of L. & Econ. 3 (1990).

[68] H.A. Simon, "A Behavioral Model of Rational Choice", 69 Q.J. of Econ. 99–118 (1955).

relevance to legal disputes is the finding that people do not "solve" economic games in the manner prescribed by economics. Economic analyses of multistage bargaining (of which legal disputes are an example) assume that players solve the game by a process of "backward induction."[69] Backward induction implies that people base their bargaining in the final settlement bargaining phase on an analysis of what they expect would happen if they went to trial, their bargaining in the penultimate phase on what they expect to be the outcome of the final phase, and so on.[70] Contrary to this view, empirical research on behavior in games has found that people actually proceed in a more myopic fashion, "looking ahead" at most by a single stage; they do not make use of information about later phases of bargaining even when such information is costless to acquire.[71]

The failure to "look ahead" implies that plaintiffs may fail to anticipate or take account of the effect of mandatory disclosure on the settlement zone. Mandatory disclosure will appear to the serious plaintiff *and* to the strike suit plaintiff alike as a free good, a chance to obtain costless information about potential weaknesses in the defendant's case. If plaintiffs ignore this negative consequence of disclosure (that extensive disclosure will ultimately decrease the post-discovery settlement value), they will be less likely to negotiate in good faith at the outset, and much more likely to delay serious negotiations until following disclosure. In other words, limited rationality may create the illusion that it is costless to require the other side to disclose information. If this is the case, then parties will be less likely to settle prior to mandatory disclosure, thereby increasing costs that result from mandatory disclosure.

Escalation: Another basic assumption of economic models is that people treat costs they incurred in the past as "sunk"—i.e., as irrelevant to subsequent decision making. Decision makers are assumed to decide between options solely on the basis of prospective costs and benefits. However, psychological research on "escalating commitment" suggests that people who have incurred costs in the past are more likely to continue to invest in an enterprise even when prospective expected

---

[69] *See* Eric Rasmusen, *Games & Information: An Introduction to Game Theory* 88 (1989); Richard Seltan, "The Chain Store Paradox", 9 Theory & Deduction 127, (1978).
[70] *Id.*
[71] Colin Camerer, E. Johnson, T. Rymon & S. Sen, "Cognition and Framing in Sequential Bargaining for Gains and Losses", in *Contributions to Game Theory* (K. Binmore, A. Kirman & P. Tani, eds., Cambridge: MIT Press, 1994).

returns fall below those offered by other options.[72] Applied to bargaining in multistage games, this tendency to "throw good money after bad"[73] suggests that people who have incurred costs in early stages of a game are likely to be more intransigent in later stages than would be predicted by a narrow economic analysis.[74]

The most common explanation for escalating commitment attributes it to decreasing sensitivity to losses as losses mount. For example, the psychological difference between losing nothing and losing $100 is much greater than the difference between losing $1,000 and losing $1,100.[75] Since the main incentive for settling at any point in a dispute is the threat of future losses, if one or more of the parties becomes desensitized to losses (as a result of having incurred prior losses) then they will have less incentive to settle the dispute. Mandatory disclosure, by leading to an early outlay by defendants, may decrease their subsequent willingness to settle.

2.2. Strategic Incentives

In addition to the strategic misincentives created by mandatory disclosure, there are a number of what may be termed structural problems raised by the amended discovery procedures. First, as many commentators have pointed out, there is an inherent vagueness to the command that names of witnesses and identification of documents with information "relevant"[76] to the case be produced.[77] In light of the liberal standards

[72] *See* Barry Shaw, "The Escalation of Commitment to a Course of Action", 6 Acad. Mgmt. Rev. 577 (1981) (describing how bankers throw good money after bad into the same failing investments).

[73] Donald L. Langevoort, "Where Were the Lawyers? A Behavioral Inquiry into Lawyer's Responsibility for Client Fraud", 46 Vand. L. Rev. 75, 103 (1993).

[74] *See* Thomas Gilovich, "Biased Evaluation and Persistence in Gambling", 44 J. Pers. & Soc. Psych. 1110 (1983) (describing the phenomenon of gamblers playing too long); Hersh Shefrin and Meir Stetman, "The Disposition to Sell Winners Early and Ride Losers too Long: Theory and Evidence", 40 J. Fin. 777 (1985); and Irving L. Janis & Leon Mann, *Decision Making: A Psychological Analysis of Conflict, Choice, and Commitment* 280 (Free Press, 1977) (attempting to explain why nations continue to fight wars long after any apparent usefulness).

[75] *See* D. Kahneman & A. Tversky, "Prospect Theory: An Analysis of Decision Under Risk", 47 Econometrica 363 (1979).

[76] This is the language of amended Rule 26(a).

[77] This was one of the primary arguments raised by opponents of mandatory disclosure prior to the amendment of Rule 24. *See, e.g.*, Jeffrey J. Mayer, "Prescribing Cooperation: The Mandatory Pretrial Disclosure Requirement of Proposed Rules 26 and 37 of the Federal Rules of Civil Procedure", 12 Rev. Litig. 77, 112–16 (1992).

of notice pleading,[78] reaffirmed only last year by the Supreme Court,[79] it is by no means self-evident what the full scope of disclosure should be. Opponents of mandatory disclosure have pointed to the vague claims in products liability cases, for example, where the complaint would state only that a defendant "had caused a defective product to be placed in the stream of commerce."[80]

Under such circumstances, the search for "relevant" information or documents could be open-ended.[81] To the extent that the attorney for a producing defendant narrows the request to that which is truly relevant to the issue of liability, for example, the information to be disclosed is not simply an abstract category of documents, but one that has been filtered by the producing attorney. In effect, the disclosure rule allows a plaintiff to secure not simply information responsive to a request of the plaintiff's formulation, but information with "value added by the litigation lawyer" of the opposing side.[82] This creates two significant concerns. First, by treating the information to be disclosed as if it were a prepackaged good, the mandatory disclosure rule ignores the costs associated with production—and all the attendant problems already discussed. The inescapable bottom line is that "information is simply not free."[83] Second, at the point of forcing the disclosing attorney to create a value-added package, the disclosure rule inevitably threatens to

---

[78] *See* Fed. Rule Civ. Pro. 8; *Conley* v. *Gibson*, 355 U.S. 41 (1957).

[79] *Leatherman* v. *Tarrant County*, 113 S.Ct. 1160 (1993).

[80] *See* Bell, *supra* note 43, at 42.

[81] This problem led to a wonderful parody of an attorney's presumably required letter to a client under the new discovery rules:

We will need to schedule a meeting with you at the earliest possible opportunity to review all facts tending to support the plaintiff's charges for relief. I will immediately provide this information to the plaintiff's attorney. If the plaintiff has failed to pursue any appropriate claims against your company, we should gather together and pass on to plaintiff's counsel all facts which he would want to know in order to amend his complaint and pursue such additional theories against your company.

If you or your employees are aware of any fact which might support a claim for punitive damages, please organize that information in a format that will be easily understandable to plaintiff's counsel. Although no theories supporting punitive damages have been raised, the plaintiff's attorney would surely be interested in learning any such facts and would undoubtedly be anxious to amend the complaint to include such a prayer for relief. It is our obligation to exercise our best efforts to collect any appropriate data which the plaintiff's attorney would want and I am sure punitive damages would be high on his list. Bruno, "The Disclosure Rule is a Mistake", Maricopa Lawyer, Aug. 1992, at 6, *quoted* in R. Marcus, M. Redish & E. Sherman, *Civil Procedure* (1994 Supplement), at 69–70.

[82] Bruce H. Kobayashi *et al.*, *The Process of Procedural Reform: Centralized Uniformity Versus Local Experimentation*, at 8 (unpublished manuscript on file with author).

[83] *Id.*, at 11.

commandeer the work-product exception carefully protected by the Supreme Court in *Hickman* v. *Taylor*[84] and subsequently incorporated into Rule 26(b)(3).

The confrontation with the work-product privilege is somewhat alleviated by the final language of Rule 26(a)(1) which requires mandatory disclosure only as to those facts set forth with particularity.[85] Even where such specificity is met, however, it is unlikely that parties seeking the information will be satisfied to accept only the proffered disclosure. Since the determination of what should be disclosed is made by the party providing information, mandatory disclosure provides a source of newly contested litigation. There are three reasons for this. First, the looseness of both the initial pleading and disclosure standards will undoubtedly require ample discovery to test the sufficiency of the information produced at the automatic disclosure stage. The new rule then provides an incentive for an aggressive second round of discovery to determine whether information that should have been disclosed was instead withheld.[86] Second, since the amended Rule carries with it a generous preclusion of evidence sanction, there is a strong incentive for parties to engage in escalated discovery to expose omissions in production that can be used to strategic advantage at trial. Third, the amended rule could then easily lead to a new round of motions practices identified by Justice Scalia,[87] in which the quality of the automatically disclosed information is tested under the potential preclusion sanction.

In response to this problem, there is an impulse to diminish the open-textured quality of mandatory disclosure by specifying the exact information that needs to be produced at the beginning of each case.[88] To the

---

[84] 329 U.S. 495 (1947). See also *id.*, at 516 (Jackson, J., concurring) ("But a common law trial is and always should be an adversary proceeding. Discovery was hardly intended to enable a learned profession to perform its functions without wits or on wits borrowed from the adversary.")

[85] *But see*, Mayer, "Prescribing Cooperation: The Mandatory Pretrial Disclosure Requirement of Proposed Rules 26 and 37 of the Federal Rules of Civil Procedure", 12 Rev. of Lit. 77, 114 (1992) (arguing that restricting the scope of disclosure in this fashion saps the disclosure rule of any vitality).

[86] *See, e.g.*, *Scheetz* v. *Bridgestone/Firestone, Inc.*, 152 F.R.D. 628 (D. Mont. 1993) (challenging sufficiency of mandatory disclosure under local Montana variant of new Rule 26).

[87] Supreme Court Transmittal, *supra* note 44, at 107.

[88] This more limited form of disclosure is reflected in the final version of amended Rule 26 which specifies certain confined categories of information subject to mandatory disclosure. Specifically, the disclosure obligation extends to materials "relevant to disputed facts alleged with particularity in the pleadings." Fed. R. Civ. P. 26(a)(1)(C). This corresponds to the Advisory Committee's desire to focus mandatory disclosure on "certain basic information" in the possession of each party. *See* Fed. R. Civ. P. 26 advisory committee note, *reprinted* in 113 S.Ct. *orders* 609, 701–02.

extent that this is accomplished, however, mandatory disclosure begins to resemble a prearranged series of interrogatories that must be answered at the beginning of each lawsuit.[89] At this point, some justification must be given for taking the request for information out of the hands of litigants, who can cheaply tailor them to the particular needs of individual cases. If these interrogatories are truly of such obvious and universal need in litigation, they are most likely already part of the standard discovery repertoire of any modestly experienced attorney. It is therefore unclear, in the first instance, that requiring production in the form of mandatory disclosure, rather than through service of a standard set of interrogatories and requests for production of documents, entails any significant cost savings at all.[90] Moreover, there is absolutely no evidence that mandatory disclosure will reduce expenses in the "mega"-cases that most readily evoke the specter of litigation costs run rampant.[91]

[89] In fact, the Advisory Committee Notes to Amended Rule 26 refer to the mandatory disclosure provisions "[a]s the functional equivalent of court-ordered interrogatories . . . of four types of information that have been customarily secured early in litigation through formal discovery."

[90] I leave aside a number of other criticism of mandatory disclosure, some of which may exacerbate the problems identified in this Paper. There are two basic categories of such additional problems. The first is the balkanization of procedure by having categorical rules that apply to all cases, but having a different set of rules in each local jurisdiction. While an increase in uncertainty and related costs is to be expected under any altered legal regime, the new discovery rules are likely to compound this short-term problem by allowing local jurisdictions to either bail out from the new procedures or modify them through local rulemaking. As a result, the expected processes of litigation producing more clearly defined rules of application (the informational externalities of litigation) will be frustrated by the divergent legal regimes in the various local federal courts. The information benefits of litigation for future disputants will be reduced because they apply only to specific local jurisdictions.

An additional immediate concern arises from the disruption of the attorney client relationship occasioned by the requirement that parties undertake discovery of themselves at their own initiative. *See* Bell, *supra* note 43, at 46–48 (summarizing critiques of the Bar of mandatory disclosure). The concern here is that in high stakes litigation, where the problem of excessive costs was thought to be of greatest import, the new discovery rules may create greater agency costs by complicating the attorney-client relationship. It is entirely foreseeable that placing the burden of discovery on anticipated trial counsel may lead litigants to retain additional non-trial counsel to protect against over vigilant discovery by their own attorneys.

[91] *See* Anne Y. Shields, "The Utility of Disclosure as a Reform to the Pretrial Discovery Process", 67 St. John's L. Rev. 907, 916–17 (1994) ("Since discovery would almost always be necessary in complex litigation, the general disclosure system would do nothing more than add an extra layer of expense and delay") (footnote omitted).

2.3. Procedural Rules versus Standards

To return to the original issue joined in this Paper, the adoption of mandatory disclosure legitimately raises the question of whether the litigation process should be regulated in all instances by rules rather than standards. The foreseeable problems with mandatory disclosure lead back to a fundamental question in civil procedure, that of the "trans-substantive" quality of rules. The amendment of Rule 26 is an example of addressing a specific problem while retaining a rule of general application for all cases in the federal courts. The question remains whether the allure of trans-substantive procedure is worth the anticipated problems with mandatory disclosure.[92] In other words, why choose to proceed through a categorical rule rather than a more attenuated standard that focuses on the capacity for abuse in any given case?[93]

As a general matter, both broad-gauged rules and context-specific exceptions have their benefits and their costs. As stated in the opening of this Paper, rules of general application are typically more predictable and have fewer costs associated with their case-by-case utilization.[94] But predictability exacts its own costs in terms of misapplication to nuanced situations. However, as soon as rules become highly attenuated to context, they necessarily devolve into standards which impose costs associated with the uncertainty of their application in each particular case.

No systematic effort has been made to determine what the advantages of mandatory discovery will be even in cases that were previously

---

[92] This critique of mandatory disclosure therefore echoes extensive criticisms in the scholarly literature concerning the fading allure of transsubstantive rules. *See, e.g.*, Judith Resnick, "Failing Faith: Adjudicatory Procedure in Decline", 53 U. Chi. L. Rev. 484, 547 (1986); Stephen B. Burbank, "The Costs of Complexity", 85 Mich. L. Rev. 1463, 1474 (1987). There is a further question whether the rules in practice are indeed trans-substantive in any meaningful sense. *See, e.g.*, Carl Tobias, "Public Law Litigation and the Federal Rules of Civil Procedure", 74 Cornell L. Rev. 270, 338–39 (1989); Carl Tobias, "Standing to Intervene", 1991 Wis. L. Rev. 415; Samuel Issacharoff & George Loewenstein, "Second Thoughts About Summary Judgment", 100 Yale, L.J. 73, at 89–90 (1990) (noting special reliance on summary judgment in defamation and toxic tort cases).

[93] For an overview of the trend away from trans-substantive rules and of the particular role of the judiciary through the local rulemaking process and the Manual for Complex Litigation in developing context specific application of the rules, *see* Carl Tobias, "The Transformation of Trans-Substantivity", 49 Wash. & Lee L. Rev. 1501, 1504–05 (1992).

[94] See Louis Kaplow, "Rules versus Standards: An Economic Analysis", 42 Duke, L.J. 557 (1992) (providing economic analysis of costs associated with rule promulgation versus uncertainty in case-by-case application of standards).

deemed at risk of discovery abuse.[95] Nor has there been any effort made to selectively police the discovery process through more active intervention of judges and/or magistrates. This is troubling in light of the general trend in civil procedure toward more active case management by the judiciary under decidedly looser standards. For example, the expanded power of the court to manage each case under Rules 16 and 26(f) gives courts the capacity to mold the application of the rules to the needs of the parties in any given dispute. In particular, the existence of Rule 26(f) since 1980 gives the federal courts the power to manage the discovery schedules of individual cases and to tailor discovery practices to the actual needs of the litigants.

The mandatory disclosure rule also appears to violate the experimental direction charted by the Civil Justice Reform Act of 1990,[96] which also moved federal procedure into a more case-nuanced, standards-based form of regulation. Thus, the Reform Act provided for differential management of litigation based on case-specific considerations,[97] judicially-supervised case management conferences,[98] and, where possible, voluntary discovery arrangements.[99] Perhaps the single most important feature was the tailoring of discovery to the particular case under judicial supervision,[100] which moved to an earlier stage the power for case management intervention by the federal courts under Rule 16; indeed, this prospect of judicial oversight of discovery was thought particularly promising by litigants.[101]

For example, the Eastern District of Texas has developed a system of differential case management that requires early court review of a case in order to assign it to one of six discovery tracks.[102] The various tracks range from no discovery at all to prearranged disclosure rules to

---

[95] Indeed, the early experiences with mandatory disclosure were decidedly mixed. In reviewing those data that do exist, Professor Carl Tobias concluded, "The above examination of automatic disclosure's implementation indicates that it undermined uniformity, simplicity, and trans-substantivity while increasing judicial discretion and expense and delay." Tobias, *supra* note 45, at 1615. Whether the early effects are moderated as lawyers and judges become more familiar with the new procedures remains to be seen.

[96] 28 U.S.C. §§ 471–482 (1993).   [97] 28 U.S.C. § 473(a)(1).

[98] *Id.*, § 473(a)(3).   [99] *Id.*, § 473(a)(4).   [100] *Id.*, § 473(b)(2).

[101] *See* Robert L. Haig & Warren N. Stone, "Does All This Litigation 'Reform' Really Benefit the Client?", 4 St. John's L. Rev. 843, 850–52 (1994).

[102] For an overview of phased discovery, and the specific use of "tracks" to tailor discovery to particular cases, *see* Edward F. Sherman, "A Process Model and Agenda for Civil Justice Reforms in the States", 46 Stan. L. Rev. 1553, 1566–70 (1994). In addition, the Manual for Complex Litigation recommends the use of "waves" of discovery in order to bring discipline and contain costs in large-scale litigation. *See* Manual for Complex Litigation Second § 21.421 (1985).

disclosure plus limited additional discovery to specifically tailored discovery programs for a particular case.[103]

Further, there is already an additional rule of procedure authorizing judicial management of discovery on a case-by-case basis, Rule 26(f),[104] and one governing discovery abuse, Rule 26(g), that remain virtually unused.[105] For example a review of Lexis's Genfed database identified fewer than 80 cases which involved Rule 26(g) between 1983 and 1989.[106] By contrast, Rule 11, which had fallen into disuse prior to its amendment in 1983, enjoys a vigorous life—indeed perhaps too much vitality.[107] The point is not to extol Rule 11 sanctions as much as to point out how a corresponding standard for policing discovery abuse remained untested at the time of the decision to embark upon sweeping rule-based reform.

Undoubtedly, a case-by-case examination of discovery abuse claims will result in greater demands upon the managerial competence of judges. It is perhaps because of a reluctance to engage in policing discovery practices that go largely unreviewed by either judges or magistrates that the Supreme Court so grandly opted for global reform.[108] Nonetheless,

---

[103] *See* Order Amending Civil Justice Expense and Delay Reduction Plan, General Order No. 93–13, E.D. Tex., Sept. 2, 1993. The six tracks are:
Track One: No discovery
Track Two: Disclosure Only
Track Three: Disclosure plus 15 interrogatories, 15 requests for admission, depositions of the parties, and depositions on written questions of custodians of business records for third parties.
Track Four: Disclosure plus 15 interrogatories, 15 requests for admissions, depositions of the parties, depositions on written questions of custodians of business records for third parties, and three other depositions per side (i.e., per party or per group of parties with a common interest.)
Track Five: A discovery plan tailored by the judicial officer to fit the special management needs of the case.
Track Six: Specialized treatment and program as determined by the judicial officers.

[104] *But see* Stephen C. Yeazell, "The Misunderstood Consequences of Modern Civil Process", 1994 Wis. L. Rev. 631, 651 n. 66 (1994) (discussing decision in 1993 rule amendments to remove direct judicial supervision from the initial pretrial conference).

[105] *See* Lauren Robel, "Fractured Procedure: The Civil Justice Reform Act of 1990", 46 Stan. L. Rev. 1447, 1457 (1994) (observing that judges have power under Rule 16 (discovery conferences) and Rule 26(f) to manage discovery or force parties to devise cost-effective discovery approaches to particular cases).

[106] Melissa L. Nelken, "Has the Chancellor Shot Himself in the Foot? Looking for a Middle Ground on Rule 11 Sanctions", 41 Hastings, L.J. 383, 384 n. 8 (1990).

[107] Laurens Walker, "Avoiding Surprise from Federal Civil Rule Making: The Role of Economic Analysis", 23 J. of Legal Studies 569, 570–71 (1994).

[108] This is consistent with Professor Macey's provocative claim that procedural reforms are largely inspired by the desire of the judiciary to provide increased mechanisms for getting rid of undesirable cases on non-reviewable grounds, such as settlement. Jonathan R. Macey, "Judicial Preferences, Public Choice and the Rules of Procedure", 23 J. of Legal Studies 627 (1994).

there is little reason to believe that the broad-scale rule approach of Rule 26(a) will yield either systemic efficiency or greater settlement rates.

3. CONCLUSION

Clearly, the answer to the somewhat exaggerated title of this Paper is, yes there must be rules of procedure. At a fundamental sense, there is no escaping Justice Scalia's overarching concern that, "[a] government of laws means a government of rules."[109] No complex system involving multiple actors can survive if it were to devolve into an endless set of standards. At the very least, all members of the society are entitled to repose from the prospect of legal prosecution through clearly articulated statutes of limitations. In the same way, litigants could not survive in a system that did not prescribe timely procedures for the filing of various legal pleadings. We would no more want these procedures applied on an *ad hoc* basis than we would want a system of regulation that allowed the typical construction worker to attempt "to calculate the torsional stress that a particular steel beam can bear under certain architectural and atmospheric conditions."[110]

Nonetheless, this Paper is intended to show the difficulties inherent in overly ready recourse to categorical rules, particularly when the rules necessarily respond globally to problems that emerge in a limited minority of actual cases. The choice to respond with rules rather than standards should not be reflexive. Rather we should proceed with the caution well-articulated by Professor Schauer:

[T]he choice of rule-based decision-making ordinarily entails disabling wise and sensitive decision-makers from making the best decisions in order to disable incompetent or simply wicked decision-makers from making worse decisions. Conversely, a decision procedure that avoids or diminishes the constraints of rules empowers the best decision-makers to make the best decisions, and accepts as a consequence that the same procedure also empowers less than the best decision-makers to make some number of less than the best decisions. A "best case" perspective is necessarily averse to rules, for rule-based decision-making cannot produce the best result in every case. But a "worst case" perspective is likely to embrace rules, recognizing that guarding against the worst case may in some circumstances be the best we can do.[111]

---

[109] *Morrison* v. *Olson*, 487 U.S. 654, 733 (1988) (Scalia, J., dissenting).
[110] Schauer, *supra* note 4, at 150.   [111] Schauer, *supra* note 4, at 153.

This is the dilemma confronting all regulatory regimes. The experience of American constitutional proceduralism shows the inherent difficulties in crafting broad-sweeping rules to be applied in highly nuanced fact situations. By contrast, the rush to devise a broad new rule of disclosure exposes the entire pretrial procedural regime to unanticipated stresses. The mandatory disclosure rule was adopted to address the problems presented graphically in cases where pretrial discovery costs have spiralled out of control. By contrast to constitutional procedure, the use of inflexible rules removed the critical use of judgment from the response to a problem that is not universal in litigation. Under such circumstances the inherent problem of overgeneralization in rule-based regulation returns with a vengeance.

Community Law and International Law: How Far Does Either Belong to the Other?

by Sir Franklin Berman*

The honour and pride I felt in being invited to deliver this lecture was succeeded, I have to confess, by a degree of trepidation. Not really (I must immediately say) because of the fame and repute of this great University where I felt confident of a warm and generous welcome, if only as a by-product of its close links with my own University. But trepidation certainly on reading through the list of lawyers of real distinction who have preceded me in this lecture series. And further trepidation as I began to confront the search for a topic which might do justice to an Institute of Anglo-American Law. If I have chosen one that seems to speak less loudly of Anglo-American law as such but more so of my own professional experience in a Ministry of Foreign Affairs, I did not think it any the worse for that; and I have subsequently been able to convince myself that the legal and diplomatic innovation which has in our time brought about new forms of legal regime which interpenetrate with national legal systems was indeed a theme of interest broad enough for an Institute of this kind and of this name. That my particular focus is occupied by the development of the European Communities and their law is intended to draw attention towards, not away from, the recent creation of other closed inter-State legal systems, systems which are for the most part endowed with their own judicial machinery, but which may also, as in the case of the European Communities, have a law-creating as well as a law-deciding capacity.

For seeing me through these struggles my particular gratitude goes to Professor Basil Markesinis, now happily a living embodiment of the

* This is an extended version of a lecture delivered at Leiden University's Institute of Anglo-America Law on 1 December 1995.

Oxford-Leiden link. Others, besides me, have experienced the magnetic attraction of his enthusiasm, the extraordinary range of his interests and activities, and above all, so far as I am concerned, his grasp of the connections between legal systems and the unity of law in all its various manifestations.

But please do not think that I have finished with my trepidations yet! The very coining of a title gave me difficulty. What would it betray about my approach, and about my prejudices and priorities? Did I put Community Law first, or International Law? Was "belong" a jurisprudentially defensible term? Should I speak (as I probably would were I an out-and-out Community lawyer) not of "law" but of a "legal order", and if so only for the Community or for International Law as well? In the end I ask you simply to accept my assurance that I have opted for generality, and with generality neutrality, so that nothing hoisted up my flagpost represents a vain attempt to shape the wind that blows it.

But my title is a question, and why should the question be asked at all? Indeed, I suspect that it would hardly occur to one to pose the question were it not for one or two challenging *dicta* thrown out by the European Court of Justice in its infancy, and which have since been taken as stating a crucially defining characteristic of the European Community. I am thinking of course of the 1964 judgment in *Costa* v. *ENEL*[1] when the Court said thus:

> By contrast with ordinary international treaties, the EEC Treaty has created its own legal system which, on the entry into force of the Treaty, became an integral part of the legal systems of the Member States and which their courts are bound to apply.[2]

Two years previously the Court appeared to have gone even further in the *Van Gend en Loos* case[3] when it said:

> The objective of the EEC Treaty . . . implies that this Treaty is more than an agreement which merely creates mutual obligations between the contracting states. . . . The conclusion to be drawn from this is that the Community constitutes a new legal order of international law for the benefit of which the states have limited their sovereign rights, albeit within limited fields, and the subjects of which comprise not only Member States but also their nationals.[4]

One suspects that amongst those phrases the one that has resonated most strongly since then in the minds of subsequent judges and of

---

[1] Case 6/64, [1964] ECR 585.   [2] *Ibid.*, at 593.
[3] Case 26/62, [1963] ECR 1.   [4] *Ibid.*, at 12.

commentators is "a new legal order". All this was examined in detail 13 years ago by my compatriot, Mr. Derrick Wyatt, who concluded that the "new order" was perhaps less new than had been imagined.[5] A similar conclusion has been reached by Dr. Lawrence Collins.[6] Without retracing their footsteps, let me simply single out one or two aspects of those famous judicial pronouncements which strike me, looking at them as an international lawyer.

First, there is no sign here of the Court seeking to play down the character of the EEC Treaty as a *treaty*. On the contrary, what the Court tells us on both occasions is that we are indeed in the presence of a treaty but not an *ordinary* one. Second, the Court does indeed announce the arrival of a "new legal order" but immediately describes it as a new legal order *of international law*. This is unequivocal, and we may leave aside for the present how (i.e. by what legal means) the Community legal system did become an integral part of the legal systems of the Member States on the entry into force of the Treaty, as the Court declared in *Costa* v. *ENEL* had happened.

Let me digress for one brief moment on a question of terminology which causes untoward difficulties. I am afraid you will find me wandering from "European Community" in the singular, to "Communities" in the plural, and back to the singular again in a way that may appear unpredictable and illogical, and I offer you my apologies for that. The difficulty is that, while one can in the adjectival form talk comfortably about "European Community law" as a homogeneous system, the position is not so straightforward when one refers, substantively, to the Communities themselves, as legal entities. The three Communities each have still a separate existence in law, and have not been merged into a single persona, notwithstanding the elements of amalgamation that have been introduced, such as the common institutions introduced by the Merger Treaty. But the final twist is that, by the Treaty of Maastricht, the original European *Economic* Community has been renamed the "European Community". Against this background there is, therefore, some order in my apparent disorder: I have tried on each occasion to use whichever term seems most natural in that context, without doing violence to essential legal concepts. Thus, to take one example, when I refer to the "Community treaties" I mean the founding treaties establishing or modifying each of the three Communities, and when I refer to the "Community's treaties", I mean the treaties concluded by any of

[5] "New Legal Order or Old?", 7 European Law Review (1982), 147.
[6] *European Community Law in the United Kingdom* (4th ed. 1990), 1–7.

the three Communities with other parties. I can only hope that you will accept these devices and that they will, on examination, make sense.

The questions I wish to explore in this lecture are, then: granted that the Community "legal order" is a legal order of international law, what is it that makes it special, or even unique, and what are the consequences of this for the future development of the two systems 30 years on?

The starting point must be, as the European Court of Justice reminds us (if ever we needed reminding), that the founding European Community instruments are *treaties*. The three founding instruments[7] having been cast in treaty form, it was no doubt inevitable that formal amendments to them would take the same form. It is worth remarking all the same that all major amendments,[8] modifications,[9] developments[10] or enlargements[11] of the original Communities have likewise been done in treaty form. The new Member States (my own included), now 9 in number by comparison with the 6 original founder-members, joined the

[7] Treaty establishing the European Coal and Steel Community (signed in Paris on 18 April 1951) (UKTS 2 (1973), Cmnd. 5189); Treaty establishing the European Economic Community (signed in Rome on 25 March 1957) (UKTS 1 (1973)—Pt II, Cmnd. 5179—II); Treaty establishing the European Atomic Energy Community (signed in Rome on 25 March 1957) (UKTS 1 (1973)—Pt II, Cmnd. 5179–II).

[8] Eg. Treaty amending Certain Budgetary Provisions of the Treaties establishing the European Communities and of the Treaty establishing a Single Council and a Single Commission of the European Communities (signed in Luxembourg on 22 April 1970) (1971 OJ L/2); Treaty amending Certain Financial Provisions of the Treaties establishing the European Communities and of the Treaty establishing a Single Council and a Single Commission of the European Communities (signed in Brussels on 22 July 1975) (1977 OJ L 359); Treaty amending with regard to Greenland, the Treaties establishing the European Communities (signed in Brussels on 13 March 1984) (1985 OJ L 29); Single European Act (signed at Luxembourg on 17 February 1986 and at The Hague on 28 February 1986) (1987 OJ L 169); Treaty on European Union (signed at Maastricht on 7 February 1992) (1992 OJ L 191).

[9] E.g. Treaty establishing a Single Council and a Single Commission of the European Communities (signed in Brussels on 8 April 1965) (1967 OJ No. 152).

[10] Eg. Single European Act (in **note 8 above**); Treaty on European Union (in **note 8 above**).

[11] Treaty concerning the Accession of the Kingdom of Denmark, Ireland, the Kingdom of Norway and the United Kingdom of Great Britain and Northern Ireland to the European Economic Community and to the European Atomic Energy Community, signed in Brussels on 22 January 1972 ([1972] OJ L 73/5); Treaty concerning the Accession of the Hellenic Republic to the European Economic Community and to the European Atomic Energy Community, signed in Athens on 28 May 1979 ([1979] OJ L 291/9); Treaty concerning the Accession of the Kingdom of Spain and the Portugese Republic to the European Economic Community and to the European Atomic Energy Community signed in Madrid on 12 June 1985 ([1985] OJ L 302/9); Treaty concerning the Accession of the Kingdom of Norway, the Republic of Austria, the Republic of Finland and the Kingdom of Sweden to the European Union ([1994] OJ C 241/1).

Community by way of Treaties of Accession.[12] The progressive amalgamation of the Community institutions,[13] the creation of the Court of First Instance[14] and the increase in the powers of the Parliament[15] as well as the fundamental change in the method of election of its members,[16] were brought about by treaty. The creation of the mystical "European Union" happened through a treaty in that name.[17] The deliberate introduction of inter-governmental undertakings and obligations alongside, around or parallel to "Community obligations" in the strict technical sense all came in by treaty: first the Single European Act[18] and then later the Treaty of Maastricht.[19]

Whether this represents an instinctive preference, a recognition that there is no alternative, or whether it displays a conscious choice between alternative techniques, is matter for interesting speculation. But for present purposes it is largely irrelevant, since the legal consequences are the same. It is moreover a striking fact that the form and legal style have been identical whatever the subject and object, and whether the treaty is a simple or compound one. So a treaty like the Treaty of Maastricht, which fulfils the dual object of readjusting the shape and operation of the Communities and of setting up schemes of unambiguously inter-Governmental cooperation in parallel to the Community structure, marks these vitally important distinctions only by treating different subjects in different parts or chapters with their special legal incidents,[20] but not by any difference in legal form or style. All is done within the rubric of a single and more or less homogeneous treaty instrument.

The European Community is thus an institution of international law, as is the relationship between its Member States encapsulated in the term "European Union". I shall have a little later to confront the interesting

---

[12] See **note 11 above**.

[13] Convention on Certain Institutions Common to the European Communities, signed in Rome on 25 March 1957; Treaty establishing a Single Council and a Single Commission of the European Communities signed in Brussels on 8 April 1965 (**note 8 above**).

[14] See Single European Act (**note 8 above**), Articles 4, 11 and 26.

[15] See Single European Act, Article 7; Treaty on European Union, Article G(61).

[16] Council Decision 76/787 and Act concerning the Election of the Representatives of the Assembly by Direct Universal Suffrage, 20 September 1976 ([1976] OJ L 278/5).

[17] Treaty on European Union, **note 8 above**.

[18] Single European Act, Title III.

[19] Treaty on European Union, Titles V and VI.

[20] See e.g. Title V (Articles J to J.11), containing provisions on a common foreign and security policy; and Title VI (Articles K to K.9), containing provisions on cooperation in the fields of justice and home affairs.

questions whether these last are two new and separate legal orders and what their relationship is to one another. I should like however to rest a little longer with the fact that, in order to create their Community, and to give it legal form and effect, the founding fathers relied on international law, and by their practice over the years have shown that they still do. To my mind this is a fact of a fundamental character, which one would therefore expect to have enduring consequences.

There is no doubt for example that if there is a Community legal order, entry into it is by operation of the rules of international law which regulate consent to be bound by treaties. When the Community Treaties or the Accession Treaties refer to signature or to ratification[21] there can be no room for doubt that the processes invoked are the commonly-understood processes of international law in the treaty context. Likewise, when those steps on the route to the Community legal order are themselves dependent on domestic constitutional procedures, the procedures employed in all the Member States at all stages of the Community's development have been those which apply generally to treaty commitments. A glance at the proceedings instituted in the English[22] and Scottish Courts,[23] and in the German *Bundesverfassungs-gericht*,[24] in respect of the ratification of the Maastricht Treaty by the United Kingdom and by Germany, shows the courts approaching the matter unhesitatingly as a type case of the general process by which treaty commitments are entered into for the State; nor does there appear to have been any argument raised before the courts to any different effect.

The obvious supposition must be that the Governments in question, and likewise the other constitutional organs which are competent in the law-making process, have entered into these commitments, or approved them as the case may be, on the assumption that they are commitments under international law. More, granted that these commitments are designed to produce profound legal effects within their domestic legal systems, these legal effects necessarily depend on the fact that

---

[21] E.g. Treaty establishing the ECSC, Article 99; Treaty establishing the EEC, Article 237; Treaty establishing the Eurotom Community, Article 205 (all now suspended by Treaty on European Union, Article O); Treaty on Accession of UK, Ireland, and Denmark. Article 2; Treaty on Accession of the Hellenic Republic, Article 2; Treaty on the Accession of Spain and Portugal, Article 2; Treaty on the Accession of Finland, Sweden and Austria, Article 2.

[22] *R.* v. *Secretary of State for Foreign and Commonwealth Affairs ex parte Lord Rees-Mogg* [1993] 3 CMLR 101.

[23] *Monckton* v. *Lord Advocate* 1995 SLT 1201.   [24] [1994] 1 CMLR 57.

international law gives the underlying commitments their binding legal character. The point emerges clearly enough from the Statutes by which the Parliament of my own country,[25] or that of the Republic of Ireland,[26] conferred the necessary domestic effect on Community legal obligations. But it is surely even clearer still from the actions of the six founder Member States, all of whom operate what my own discipline refers to as the "monist" system, where the approbation by the legislative bodies only sufficed under the Constitution to transmute Community obligations into domestic law *because* they were treaty obligations under international law.[27]

So far I suspect that the analysis is straightforward, perhaps even self-evident, though it may be that the depth of the international law underpinning has become obscured with the passage of time. I must now pass on though to an aspect of the analysis that may be more controversial: what effect does this have on the interpretation and application of rights and obligations under the Community treaties? Please note that I limit myself, and quite deliberately so, to rights and obligations under the treaties themselves. I reflect the apparent distinction, in other words, which basic Community texts like Article 177 of the EC Treaty make between Treaty rights and obligations, and rights and obligations that may arise from Community legislation made under the authority of the treaties.[28] Or at least I retain that distinction without pursuing where it leads. It is not a *necessary* consequence of the fact that the founding Community instruments are treaties regulated by international law, that subordinate instruments made under the treaties are also regulated by international law or that the same rules should in all circumstances govern the interpretation and application of the treaties as govern the interpretation and implementation of regulations and directives. Nor is the question concluded by the fact that some of these subordinate instruments are the result of a process of negotiation and agreement akin to the treaty process.[29] The question is one of some

[25] The European Communities Act 1972.

[26] The European Communities Act 1972, as amended by the European Communities (Amendment) Act 1973.

[27] See, e.g., Jacobs and Roberts (eds.), *The Effect of Treaties in Domestic Law* (1987), xxiv–xxvi and chapters 1, 3 and 6; and Schermers, *Judicial Protection in the European Communities* (3rd ed. 1983), 98–100.

[28] Article 177 states that: "The Court of Justice shall have jurisdiction to give preliminary rulings concerning: (a) *the interpretation of this Treaty*; (b) the validity and *interpretation of acts of the institutions of the Community* and of the ECB;" (emphasis supplied). See also Euratom Treaty, Article 150.

[29] E.g., common positions, joint actions and certain kinds of decisions of the Council.

considerable intrinsic interest and deserves to be pursued separately in
its own right.

Let me begin by exploring, however cursorily, the rules and principles of international law governing the interpretation and application of
treaties, in order to see what there is in them that we should regard as
special, and then go on to see how far international law itself prescribes
differing rules for different types of treaty. The rules on interpretation
incorporated in the 1969 Vienna Convention on the Law of Treaties[30]
represent one of the classic texts of the modern law; they had been
applied by international tribunals[31] even before the Vienna Convention
entered into force[32] and one may therefore say without any doubt that
they represent rules of customary law applicable to treaties in general
and to all treaty parties, without regard to the rather special rules which
regulate the specific application of the Vienna Convention itself.[33]

The rules of interpretation have to be seen against the background of
two cardinal principles of treaty law also reflected in the Vienna Convention, namely the principle that a treaty by definition draws its legal
force from the consent of the Parties to be bound by it and the principle
pacta sunt servanda, or as Article 26 of the Convention puts it, "Every
treaty in force is binding upon the parties to it and must be performed
by them in good faith".

The golden rule of interpretation is in the following terms:

A treaty shall be interpreted in good faith in accordance with the ordinary
meaning to be given to the terms of the treaty in their context and in the light
of its object and purpose.[34]

This rule is supported by rules defining what the "context" is (it is
specified to include the preamble and various types of instrument made
in connection with the conclusion of the treaty);[35] by rather important
rules explaining the approach to the interpretation of texts which are
equally authentic in more than one language;[36] and by rules relating to
legislative history[37] and to subsequent practice.[38] In the case of the
legislative history, it is ranked as one of two "supplementary means of

---

[30] UKTS No. 58 (1980) Cmnd. 7964, Articles 31 to 33.
[31] The European Court of Human Rights in *Golder* v. *the United Kingdom*, judgment
of 21 February 1975, 57 ILR 200 at 213–214; and the Court of Arbitration in the *Beagle
Channel Arbitration* (*Argentina* v. *Chile*), decision of 18 February 1977, 52 ILR 93 at
124.
[32] 27 January 1980.   [33] Articles 1, 3 and 4.   [34] Article 31(1).
[35] Article 31(2).   [36] Article 33.   [37] Article 32.   [38] Article 31(3).

interpretation" which may be resorted to either to *confirm* the meaning resulting from the application of the primary rule, or to *determine* the meaning when the application of the basic rule still leaves the meaning ambiguous or obscure or leads to a manifestly absurd or unreasonable result. The post-negotiating history, on the other hand, is ranked higher, as something which "shall be taken into account, together with the context", either in the form of any subsequent *agreement* between the parties regarding the interpretation of the treaty or the application of its provisions, or in the form of subsequent practice in the application of the treaty which "establishes the *agreement* of the parties regarding its interpretation". One may note traces of the operation of those rules in the instruments adopted between the first and second Danish referendums on the Treaty of Maastricht, which were expressly stated not to be modifications to the Treaty but must have been intended to colour its interpretation and application in respect of Denmark.[39]

I will go into some of the detail in a moment. But let me begin by returning to the golden rule. It may look at first sight like the mere application of educated common-sense to the interpretation of legal texts; and I would hope that it does indeed have a good deal of that in it! The formulation is however much more subtle than mere common-sense, and represents in fact the culmination of a doctrinal battle of the titans that raged amongst international lawyers for decades.[40] The final version (for which Oxford can claim credit in the person of Sir Humphrey Waldock)[41] put paid to the struggle for supremacy between the "textual" school and the "intentions" school: for the former the only thing

---

[39] European Council Decision of December 1992 concerning certain problems raised by Denmark on the Treaty on European Union; and Declarations of the Edinburgh European Council relating to Denmark, December 1992.

[40] The flavour of the controversy between H. Lauterpacht and Beckett in the 1950s and early 1960s on questions of treaty interpretation may be obtained by reading the summary of their views in Fitzmaurice and Vallat, "Sir (William) Eric Beckett, KCMG, QC", 17 ICLQ (1968), 267 at 302–313. The later controversy between McDougal and Fitzmaurice on the subject is well reflected in the latter's critique of McDougal, Lasswell and Miller, *Interpretation of Agreements and World Order* (1967). See Fitzmaurice, "Vae Victus or Woe to the Negotiators! Your Treaty or our 'Interpretation' of it?", 65 AJIL (1971), 358.

[41] As the International Law Commission's Special Rapporteur on the Law of Treaties, it was he who proposed the inclusion of draft articles on the interpretation of treaties: see Waldock's Third Report on the Law of Treaties, YBILC (1964–II), pp. 217–226. These were adopted without change in substance by the Commission and by the drafting Conference (and are now reflected in Articles 31 and 32 of the Convention): see Report of the Commission to the General Assembly (1966–II), pp. 217–226; and Official Records of the UN Conference on the Law of Treaties, Second session, thirteenth plenary session, pp. 57–59.

that mattered was the words;[42] the latter held that any evidence of what the Parties intended or expected had primary value.[43] The Vienna Convention accepted neither. Although it gave pride of place to the ordinary meaning of the words, it did so in a carefully controlled manner. And it swept away at the same time all the supposed special tenets of interpretation that had enveloped the subject like cobwebs.[44] So, for example, whatever may have been true of the old judicial and arbitral authorities, you are most unlikely today *ever* to see an international tribunal of repute deciding a disputed point of interpretation by reference to a 'teleological' doctrine of interpretation, or a 'restrictive' doctrine of interpretation, or any other supposed special doctrine thought to be specially applicable to particular types of case.

What the Vienna Convention rule does is to refer the interpreter to the text in its natural meaning, not as something sacrosanct in itself, but as the best and only reliable guide to what the Parties "must be taken to have intended . . . in relation to the circumstances with reference to which the question of interpretation has arisen".[45] But the text is *expressly* decreed not to be particular provisions taken in isolation, but read in their context and in the light of the object and purpose of the treaty as a whole. There is an interesting echo here of the form in which treaties used to be cast and are still usually cast (including the Community Treaties), a form in which the Parties, through their authorised representatives, are not stated to "agree as follows" but to "have agreed" as follows; the text is thus placed as *evidence* of an agreement already reached *aliunde*.

Without a doubt therefore the focus can fall sharply in particular cases on the "object and purpose", not of the particular provision but of the treaty as a whole, and not in its own right but as evidence of what the Parties must be understood as having undertaken through the text on which they agreed.

We have therefore a Community created by treaties which are as

---

[42] See, e.g., Fitzmaurice, "Treaty Interpretation and other Treaty Points", 33 BYIL (1957), at 204–7. This is also the view which is reflected in the 1956 resolution of the Institute of International Law (1956), in 46 Annuaire de l'Institut de droit international (1956), pp. 358–59.

[43] See, notably, H. Lauterpacht in 43 Annuaire de l'Institut de droit international (1950), pp. 377–402.

[44] See Hackworth, 5 *Digest of International Law* (1943), pp. 232–34; and McNair, *The Law of Treaties* (1961), chapters 21 and 22.

[45] *Oppenheim's International Law* (9th ed., edited by Jennings and Watts, 1992), p. 1267.

such situated within the system of international law and are to be interpreted and applied as just described. Let me come now to the question of the status of that Community itself in international law. This inquiry encompasses numerous lesser questions: what is the legal nature of the Community's external acts? what is the legal nature of the Community's relationships with non-member States? is the Community an international organisation?

It will be convenient to take the last first: should the Community—though I ought in all accuracy to say, each of the three Communities—be regarded as an international organisation? To answer this one must needs know what, in legal terms, an international organisation is. And there lies the rub. There is no general definition in international law of an international organisation. Many of the leading texts go no further than to tell us that for their particular purposes the term "international organisation" refers to an international organisation of States.[46] This is what one finds, for example, in the two Vienna Conventions on the Law of Treaties and the Law of Treaties between States and International Organisations. And leading works such as those by Schermers[47] and Bowett[48] manage (avowedly) to get by without a definition at all. Clearly the partial treaty definitions just mentioned are designed only to exclude organisations which, though inter-national, operate on a level other than the inter-State one. Nonetheless, it is possible to isolate certain features which together characterise an international organisation in the sense in which that term would normally be understood. These are reflected in the definition proposed by Bindschedler in the Max Planck Encyclopaedia[49] under which the term international organisation denotes an association of States established by and based on a treaty, which pursues common aims and which has its own special organs to fulfil particular functions within the organisation.

First of all, one would look for an entity that was capable of acting, and did in fact act, in the public international sphere and the members of which, as indicated above, were States or governments. This is not of course to say that the entity could not also act, and did not act, so as to acquire legal relationships in domestic legal systems as well; this

[46] Article 2(1)(i) of the 1969 Convention and the same provision in the 1986 Convention define the term "international organisation" as an "intergovernmental organisation".

[47] *International Institutional Law*, vols. 1–3 (rev. ed. of vols. 1 and 2, 1980; vol. 3, 1973).

[48] *The Law of International Institutions* (4th ed., 1982).

[49] Volume 5 (1981), 119 at 120.

is a commonplace of all international organisations, which at a minimum hire services, own property and purchase supplies.[50] And nowadays one would also admit (under the impulse of developments in international law which the European Communities themselves have helped to set in train) the possibility of an international organisation numbering other international organisations among its members.[51] Second, one would expect the entity to have been set up by treaty. This indicator springs naturally from the fact that one is looking for an entity with an autonomous legal status and that status can in principle only have been created, other than through a form of incorporation under the legal system of a particular State, by treaty.[52] And thirdly, the entity would be endowed with its own organs through which it acted, externally as well as internally.

Now it is clear that these somewhat loose criteria are amply fulfilled by the Communities. The Communities therefore possess *ipso facto* and *ipso jure* the capacities recognised in international organisations by international law: notably (but not exclusively) the capacity to make treaties, to become members of other organisations and to maintain international claims in their own name and on their own behalf.

Yet the proposition—or as one might say *la constatation*—that the Communities are international organisations remains a controversial one in some circles. Why? The answer is far from clear, but I think that it can be traced back to two notions which as you will see I conclude are rooted more in instinct than in legal reasoning. The first is the

---

[50] The constituent instruments of most international organisations provide either (a) that the organisation shall enjoy in the territory of its members such legal capacity as may be necessary for the exercise of its functions and the fulfilment of its purposes (e.g. the UN Charter, Article 104); or (b), more precisely, that it shall possess legal personality and have the capacity to contract, to acquire and dispose of immovable and movable property and to institute legal proceedings (e.g. the ILO, Article 9; IMF, Article 9(2); and IBRD, Article 7(2)). See, further, Schermers, *International Institutional Law* (1980), pp. 787–92.)

[51] Thus, for example, the EEC is a member of the International Wheat Council, International Wheat Agreement 1971, Article 12 and Annexes A and B, OJ 9 August 1974 No. L219, pp. 24–35; and the International Atomic Energy Agency is a member of the Middle Eastern Regional Radioisotope Centre for the Arab Countries, Seyersted, "International Personality of Intergovernmental Organisations", 4 IJIL (1964), 15, 16.

[52] The distinctive features of the Arab Monetary Fund—an organisation created by an international treaty to which the United Kingdom was not a party, but incorporated under the domestic law of a foreign State (the United Arab Emirates)—gave the English courts some pause as to whether it had the capacity to sue. In the event, however, the House of Lords held that the Fund did have the necessary legal personality for this purpose ([1990] 2 A.C. 418). For a brief account of the background and earlier cases, see Cheyne, "Status of International Organisations in English Law", 40 ICLQ (1991), 981.

feeling that somehow the international status and capacities of the Community arise autonomously out of the Community Treaties as such, and do not need to be conferred upon it by any other system of law. The second is the feeling that the Community is a legal entity of a very special, indeed unique, kind which would in some way be demeaned by lumping it in a single category with other entities of a much more modest and mundane character.

The first objection can be dismissed at once, as being obviously wrong, and yet also to some extent right, if in a rather banal sense. Wrong because the legal capacities we are talking about are capacities in international law, and it is surely trite that capacities in any legal system can only be the creation *of* that legal system.[53] In any case, there is no contradiction involved in saying that the legal capacities of a derivative organism in international law are at one and the same time the creation of international law and the creation of the instrument which gave life to the organisation in question. This is no more than another way of saying that the particular powers of the organisation, and the limits on them, although recognised and given effect within the system of international law, are laid down by the organisation's own constituent instrument. Or the proposition could equally validly be put the other way round, by saying that States, in establishing an organisation with powers to operate on the international plane, are taking advantage of a facility offered them by international law.

The second objection is altogether more serious. It requires us to examine whether the Community is indeed an organism of a unique kind, and if so whether its uniqueness prevents it from being classified with international organisations of a more traditional kind.

The claim of uniqueness (in this context) can rest on two possible foundations: the institutional structure of the Community, with the particular law-making and judicial powers of Community institutions; or the theory that the autonomous powers exercised by the Community on the international plane are powers irrevocably *transferred* by the Member States, so that the Community is acting in the exercise of sovereign powers of a State-like character not in the exercise of derivative powers of the kind that a traditional international organisation may possess.

As for the claim to uniqueness on the basis of the Community's institutional structure and powers, there is little doubting that the

---

[53] See, e.g., O'Connell, *International Law* (2nd edn. 1970), vol. I, 80–81.

Community is unique, as far and away the most advanced and developed economic union yet devised and put into practice. And the jurisprudence of the European Court of Justice is certainly beyond compare amongst international tribunals for its richness and depth.[54] And yet, and yet . . . , these characteristics, marked as they are to observe, do not of themselves dispose of the question whether they represent differences of quality, as opposed to depth, by comparison with other treaty-based institutions and arrangements. Other organisations have complex institutional structures: the International Labour Organisation.[55] Other organisations control large sums of capital with vital economic effects: the World Bank and International Monetary Fund.[56] Other organisations are equipped with organs having the power of binding decision: the United Nations, where the 15-member Security Council not only has these functions in the sovereign area of war and peace, but operates under so powerful a form of qualified majority voting[57] that the like would never be dreamed of for the Council of Ministers in Brussels. And the North Atlantic Council has the world's most powerful collection of armed forces under its integrated command. Other organisations have Parliamentary Assemblies with significant consultative and recommendatory functions that fall short of legislative decision: the Council of Europe.[58] Other organisations have courts with binding powers of judicial decision capable of entering deep into the fabric of national society: the European[59] and Inter-American Human Rights[60] systems.

So as an internationalist one is somewhat sceptical in face of the

---

[54] The Court has decided 300–400 cases a year for the last few years. [NB: have omitted ref. to Crt of 1st Instance, since its jurisprudence doesn't meet the qualitative description.]

[55] Constitution of 1919, as amended (Peaslee, *International Governmental Organizations: Constitutional Documents* (rev. 3rd edn. 1974), vol. II, p. 994).

[56] Respectively, Articles of Agreement of 27 December 1945, as amended 17 December 1965 (Peaslee, *International Governmental Organizations: Constitutional Documents* (rev. 3rd edn. 1974), vol. II, p. 883); and Articles of Agreement of 27 December 1945, as amended 28 July 1969 (*ibid.*, p. 1014).

[57] Decisions on matters other than "procedural matters" require an affirmative vote of nine members, "including the concurring votes of the (five) permanent members" (Article 27(3) of the UN Charter). As a result, any permanent member may prevent, by its sole vote (or veto), the taking of a decision which has the support of a majority of the Council, i.e. of nine members.

[58] The Statute of the Council of Europe, signed at London 5 May 1949, 1 European Yrbk (1955), 275, Articles 10(ii) and 22–35.

[59] The European Convention on Human Rights, signed at Rome on 4 November 1950, 213 UNTS 221, Article 19(2).

[60] The American Convention on Human Rights, signed at San Jose on 22 November 1969, 1144 UNTS 124, Article 33(b).

suggestion that putting a number of these elements together has the effect of creating something which—in a legal sense—is different in *kind* from what has gone before.

The decisive answer is however slightly different. It goes, surely, as follows. The European Community, even if unique, is unique in fact, not in principle. It is open to any other group of States to create by treaty an organisation with exactly analogous functions and powers, or even identical ones. It is theoretically possible, in other words, for there to exist a whole series of organisations of the same type as the European Community. If that were so, the international legal system would by definition continue to function much as it does now. Nor is there great reason to suppose that it would be found necessary to adopt at that stage a different taxonomy, any more than at present it has been found necessary (from a legal point of view) to abandon the category "international organisation" in order to cope with organisations of vastly differing functions, powers and membership. In truth the category has always been amply flexible to cater for a wide variety of individual cases.

The other ground for a claim of uniqueness is the exercise of transferred sovereign powers. That brings me directly to the treaty-making activity of the Community, to which I will now turn.

The EC[61] and Euratom[62] Treaties expressly confer on these Communities power to enter into international agreements both with States and other international bodies, powers which have been much used. The ECSC is not given such a power in express words, but is endowed with the "legal capacity it requires to perform its functions and attain its objectives"[63] and in practice it, too, has concluded many agreements. The exercise of these powers has produced a lengthy and colourful list of agreements. At one end of the spectrum are the massive "association agreements" concluded with third States by some or all of the Communities jointly with the Member States.[64] These include the Agreement on a European Economic Area,[65] the Lome Convention[66] and the

---

[61] Articles 109(3), 113, 130m, 130r, 130y and 238 EC. The procedure for conclusion of agreements by the European Community is in Article 228.

[62] Articles 29, 46, 52 and 206 Euratom. The procedure for conclusion of agreements is in Article 101 Euratom.

[63] Article 6 ECSC.

[64] The power to conclude association agreements is in Articles 238 EC and 206 Euratom.

[65] [1994] OJ L 1/1.

[66] Fourth ACP-EEC Convention signed at Lomé on 15 December 1989 ([1991] OJ L 229/1).

Europe Agreements,[67] the contents of which range across every area of Community activity, and which create institutional mechanisms of their own. At the other end of the scale are agreements on imports of cheese,[68] or new potatoes.[69] And in between lie agreements on trade and economic co-operation with countries in Latin America,[70] Asia,[71] and the Mediterranean;[72] agreements on protection of the environment;[73] on transport;[74] on research and development;[75] on co-operation in the field of thermo-nuclear fusion;[76] on electronic data interchange systems;[77] on fisheries conservation and management;[78] on access to fishing grounds;[79] on international commodities trading;[80] and on the application of competition law and policies.[81]

---

[67] See, e.g., the Europe Agreements with Hungary ([1993] OJ L 347/1); Poland ([1993] OJ L 348/1); Romania ([1994] OJ L 357/1); Bulgaria ([1994] OJ L 358/1); the Slovak Republic ([1994] OJ L 359/1); and the Czech Republic ([1994] OJ L 360/1).

[68] E.g. Agreement in the form of an exchange of letters amending the Agreement of 14 July 1986 adjusting the Agreement between the EEC and Norway concerning mutual trade in cheese. ([1987] OJ L 196/78).

[69] Exchange of letters between the EEC and the Republic of Cyprus as regards imports into the community of new potatoes originating in Cyprus ([1987] OJ L 393/31).

[70] E.g. with Argentina ([1990] OJ L 295/66); Chile ([1991] OJ L 79/1); Paraguay ([1992] OJ L 313/72).

[71] E.g. with India ([1994] OJ L 223/23); Sri Lanka ([1995] OJ L 85/32).

[72] E.g. with Israel ([1975] OJ L 136/1); Egypt ([1978] OJ L 266/1); Jordan ([1978] OJ L 268/1); Syria ([1978] OJ L 269/1).

[73] Eg. Convention on the Prevention of Marine Pollution from land-based sources (Paris Convention) ([1975] OJ L 194/5); Convention on the conservation of migratory species of wild animals ([1982] OJ L 210/11); Vienna Convention for the protection of the ozone layer ([1988] OJ L 297/10); United Nations framework Convention on Climate Change ([1994] OJ L 33/13).

[74] E.g. Agreement between the EEC, the Kingdom of Norway and the Kingdom of Sweden on civil Aviation ([1992] OJ L 200/21; Agreement on International Carriage of Passengers by Road by means of Occasional Coach and Bus Services ([1982] OJ L 230/39); Agreement with Hungary on Land Transit ([1992] OJ L 407/48).

[75] E.g. Framework Agreements for scientific and technological cooperation with Iceland ([1990] OJ L 14/18) and Australia ([1994] OJ L 188/17).

[76] E.g. Agreements with Switzerland ([1978] OJ L 242/1) and Japan ([1989] OJ L 57/62).

[77] E.g. Agreements with Iceland ([1989] OJ L 400/11) and Norway ([1989] OJ L 400/16).

[78] E.g. Convention on Future Multilateral Cooperation in Fisheries in the North West Atlantic ([1978] OJ L 378/1); Conservation of Antarctic Marine Living Resources ([1981] OJ L 252/26).

[79] These are numerous. There are agreements with, e.g., Norway ([1980] OJ L 226/47); the Faeroes ([1980] OJ L 226/12); Angola ([1987] OJ L 341/1); Mauritius ([1989] OJ L 159/1); Senegal ([1980] OJ L 226/17); and Argentina ([1993] OJ L 318/1).

[80] E.g. Agreement establishing the Common Fund for Commodities ([1990] OJ L 182/1); International Sugar Agreement ([1992] OJ L 379/15); International Natural Rubber Agreement ([1992] OJ L 219/56); International Copper Study Group ([1991] OJ L 89/39).

[81] E.g. Agreement between the European Communities and the US regarding the application of their competition laws ([1995] OJ L 95/45).

Without a doubt all those agreements in their various kinds are governed by international law as indeed they were intended to be. There seems nothing there to question. And yet a trace of a question does remain, as to the basis on which the Communities contract treaty relations in international law and as to what the legal consequences are. The answer must surely be—there is no other—that the Communities contract treaty obligations in international law as international organisations recognised as having the capacity to do so. How far the extent of their treaty-making capacities has been accepted without question or contested I will come to in a moment.

The position becomes even clearer if one breaks down Community treaties into kinds according to a different set of criteria. Thus, there are treaties between a Community and one of its Member States;[82] treaties between a Community and a third State;[83] treaties between a Community, jointly with some or all of its Member States, and one or more third States;[84] and general multilateral treaties entered into by a Community on its own or jointly with the Member States.[85] It is obvious that in only one of these instances (the treaty between the Community and a Member State) is there room even for a question as to whether the legal relations set up by the treaty may be governed by a special system of law. In all of the remaining instances the only available possibility is that the treaty is governed by public international law. The most striking case of all may be that of the "mixed competence" treaty, where the Community and the Member States are both treaty parties, each so far as its own rights and competences are concerned. In such a case, the legal relationships between the Member States and third States party to the treaty must necessarily be regulated by public international law, so it would be very odd indeed if the legal relationships under the treaty between those third States and the *Community* were regulated by anything other than the same system of law. There may of course also be legal relationships in respect of the treaty as between the Community as party to the treaty and its Member States as parties to the treaty, but it is by no means so evident whether those relationships are also regulated by the treaty and thus by international law, or are special relationships *inter se* governed exclusively by the internal law

---

[82] E.g. Agreements on fisheries with Denmark in respect of the Faeroes ([1991] OJ L 371/1) and Greenland ([1990] OJ L 252/14).

[83] See, e.g., the examples in **notes 68, 69, 70, 71, 72, 74, 75, 76, 77, 79 and 81 above**.

[84] E.g. the Agreements referred to in **notes 65 and 67 above**.

[85] E.g. the Agreements referred to in **notes 73, 78 and 80 above**.

of the Community. This question has been little explored in the literature, although it is beginning to rear its head in practice.

An interesting special case is the European Economic Area Agreement of 1992.[86] Its purpose was to create a homogeneous economic area between the EC and EFTA and the parties to it are two of the Communities and their Member States and certain Member States of EFTA. It was not an agreement for membership of the European Community. Thus there is no room for the possibility mentioned above that the relations created by it are regulated by anything other than international law. Yet the Agreement was conceived as a half-way house between membership and non-membership, so that questions inevitably remain as to the rules that were intended to govern the application within the EEA of Community rules. The Agreement is virtually unique amongst treaties, and certainly amongst Community treaties, in containing explicit provisions as to its own interpretation at least so far as prior (and possibly subsequent) "relevant rulings" of the European Court of Justice were concerned;[87] the intricate "Homogeneity"[88] and settlement of disputes procedures[89] in Part VII of the Agreement suggest, however, that this was not thought likely to be enough to remove all problems of future interpretation and application. In its well-known first Opinion on the draft EEA Agreement[90] the European Court treated it as a treaty subject in the normal way to international law. It specifically invoked, for example, the Vienna Convention rules on treaty interpretation, while indicating that *these very rules of public international law* did not, in its view, produce the same result for the interpretation of the European Community Treaties as in the case of the EEA Agreement.[91] This differential effect is traced from the different objectives of the two treaties, and goes back in turn to the Court's characterisation of the nature of the Communities and thus of the treaties which constituted them, which I remarked at the outset of this lecture. What is of especial interest, however, is the Court's conviction that the appropriate results in the case of *both* treaty regimes, including in other words the European Communities themselves, are reached through the application of the orthodox rules of international law, which are recognised as coping naturally with unorthodox situations. If the starting point is that the *Community Treaties* are governed by international law, there should

---

[86] **Note 65 above.**   [87] EEA Agreement, Article 6.
[88] *Ibid.*, Articles 105 to 107.   [89] *Ibid.*, Article 111.
[90] Opinion 1/91, the EEA Agreement, [1991] ECR 6079.
[91] *Ibid.*, paragraphs 14 to 29.

be no difficulty in assimilating the conclusion that the *Community's* treaties are governed by international law.

This last suggestion is reinforced rather strongly by the notion that in their areas of exclusive external competence the Communities claim to exercise powers irrevocably transferred to them by the Member States. If the Community is thus claiming, *vis-a-vis* the outside world, to exercise powers of a State-like character, it must necessarily be part of this claim that acts undertaken in exercise of these powers are subjected to international law, as they would have been if undertaken by a State.

It has been a thesis of this lecture so far that the European Communities are not merely institutions created by means of international law and situated within the system of international law, but that more and more they are acting, as they were intended to act, externally in ways that engage the mechanisms of international law and depend upon international law. It follows intuitively from this that it would be awkward and unsatisfactory to find that Community activity and Community institutions were subject to sharply different legal principles in these and in other phases of their activity.

I must now return however to deal briefly with an item set aside earlier, namely the legal nature of the Community's relations with non-Member States, and then say something about the Common Foreign and Security Policy (CFSP).

If the Community negotiates and concludes treaties, if it participates in international organisations and conferences, if in short it maintains a network of relationships with non-Member States, does it conduct diplomatic relations and if so on what legal basis?

This question can be looked at from two angles: the so-called "active right of legation" (the capacity to send diplomatic representatives) and the "passive right of legation" (the capacity to receive diplomatic representatives of third States). The capacity to receive diplomatic representatives is clear from the Community treaties themselves: Article 17 of the Protocol on the Privileges and Immunities of the Community provides that "(t)he Member State in whose territory the Communities have their seat shall accord the customary diplomatic immunities and privileges to missions of third countries accredited to the Communities". From which it follows at the same time that the legal basis on which the status of these third country missions is regulated is for all practical purposes the international law governing diplomatic missions— so far as relevant. The practice is equally clear: over one hundred and fifty States have missions in Brussels accredited to the Communities, a larger *corps diplomatique* than in many national capitals.

Whether the Communities themselves have an active right of legation is more difficult to determine. The Community treaties are silent about a right on the part of the Community as such to send diplomatic missions to third countries. Nor has any corresponding practice built up. The numerous overseas delegations sometimes referred to (though misleadingly) as "Community embassies", are Commission delegations. They receive instructions from the Commission, report to it, and act in its name. Their legal basis seems to reside in the Commission's power to organise its own resources. But they nevertheless play a part in the wider picture of the external relations of the Community, insofar as the Commission itself possesses powers and functions in this field, and their reception and treatment by third countries is a consequence of the Community's network of external relations.

The CFSP by contrast is something expressly provided for *eo nomine* in Title V[92] of the Treaty of Maastricht. It has been said that the CFSP is nonetheless largely a codification of previously existing practice to which it gave an additional impetus and which it provided with new forms of action.[93] Given that the CFSP as such is still in its infancy, I would like to make only three points about it. The first is that it is inter-Governmental in nature: although a single institutional structure is employed, and although Title V and practice under it both use the terminology of "the Union and its Member States", the Union itself is not an entity with international legal personality,[94] so that actions undertaken and engagements entered into are those of the Member States. First faltering steps around the idea that in some circumstances the

---

[92] Treaty on European Union, Articles J to J.11 (**note 8 above**).

[93] Eaton, "Common Foreign and Security Policy", in O'Keeffe and Twomey (eds.), *Legal Issues of the Maastricht Treaty* (1994), chapter 14 at 215–16.

[94] No provision of the Treaty on European Union confers legal personality on the Union, and subsequent practice makes clear that there was no intention to confer such personality. Thus, in changing its name from "Council of the European Communities" to "Council of the European Union", the Council declared that this change in no way affected the current legal position that the European Union does not enjoy legal personality: Agence Europe, 9 November 1993. A Commission Note Verbale in August 1994 noted that a number of third States' missions had decided to adopt the title "Mission to the European Union". The Commission reminded missions that under Community law, legal personality was expressly conferred only on the European Communities. Changes to the titles of missions should thus not in any way affect references to the European Communities in legal acts. For the position of the UK Government, see Hansard, HL Debs vol. 546, cols. 710–11, 8 June 1993; HL Debs, vol. 549, WA2, 11 October 1993. For the position in German law, see the judgement of the Federal Constitutional Court of 12 October 1993 [1994] 1 CMLR 57.

Presidency might enter into treaty-like instruments *on behalf of the Member States* have shown just how delicate the legal as well as the political problems would be. So the second point to note is that, as external activity by the Member States, CFSP is by definition intended to operate within the system of public international law that regulates their international relations more generally.

The final point to note is the stress that the Treaty of Maastricht itself lays on *consistency*. The term is used no less than three times[95] in Title I, which contains Common Provisions to apply to all three "pillars". While the reference in Article A may have no clear relationship to CFSP, the same is hardly true of Article C. This provision requires not only "consistency and continuity" of the Union's activities in general but also, in the specific context of external activities, a consistency which the Council and Commission are charged with "ensuring". What does "consistency" mean? It cannot be looking towards any form of merger between external activity by the Community under the founding treaties and external activity by the Member States under the CFSP; the negotiators of the Treaty of Maastricht evidently wished to maintain a clear separation between them. The reference to "consistency" therefore certainly has an impact on the substantive policy underlying external activity; it would obviously be detrimental if the policy objectives pursued by the Community in exercise of its external competences were inconsistent with the policy objectives pursued by the Member States under CFSP and *vice versa*. But I would suggest that there may be a hint of a signpost on the legal pathway as well: both sets of activity, different as their legal bases are, should nevertheless be consistent in their practice and approach towards international law.

So much for the CFSP and the light it sheds on the external relations of the Community as such. I would now like to say a little more about what is entailed in the proposition that the Community's external activities are governed by international law and to do so by reference to the Community's treaties which constitute so important a part of its external activity. Clearly to say that the Community's treaties are "governed by" international law means more than simply that they are to be interpreted and applied in accordance with the rules of international law. It must also mean that the rules regulating consent to be bound by them and their essential validity are those of international law.[96] And it

---

[95] See Article A, paragraph 3; Article C, paragraphs 1 and 2.

[96] Vienna Convention on the Law of Treaties between States and International Organisations or between International Organisations 1986, Articles 11–15; and Article 42.

must also mean that, insofar as any question arises of capacity to enter
into any particular treaty, that too is to be decided by international law.

Is this a problem for the Community? I think not. It would be a
problem only if there were some limitative doctrine in international law
that stood in the way of the full development of the Community's
functions and activities. In fact, the second Vienna Convention,[97] that
which regulates the treaty-making of international organisations, (but to
which the Community has not become a party: more of that in a moment) contains an entirely flexible rule well adapted to the needs of the
Community in particular. The rule in question was arrived at following
a lengthy negotiating process in which the Community played a major
part in its own right. It provides that the treaty-making capacity of an
international organisation is governed by the rules of that organisation,[98] and the "rules" themselves are defined to mean "in particular"
the constituent instruments, decisions and resolutions adopted in accordance with them, and established practice of the organisation.[99] The
crucial element is therefore that the rule does not limit treaty-making to
what may have been provided for in express words in the constituent
instrument, and moreover contains a dynamic element to allow for the
development of the external functions of an organisation. While these
provisions, to be sure, stand in contrast to the inherent treaty-making
capacity of States, there is nothing particularly surprising about that.
The point of importance is how far the formula corresponds now and
corresponded then to the actual practice of the Community, and whether
it allows scope for future development. On neither score is it easy to
discern any difficulty. What counts for the Community, in other words,
within the context of an all-embracing formula that elegantly caters
for the enormous variety of international organisations, is the way in
which the formula *operates* in relation to the Community's usual
activities.

One might perhaps go on to enquire how the Convention dealt, from
that point on, with the quality of the participation of an international
organisation in a treaty. In fact it says nothing explicit on the subject.
Several leading States took the position of principle during the negotiations that, once it was admitted that an international organisation
duly became party to a treaty, its legal position thereafter ought to be

---

[97] The Vienna Convention on the Law of Treaties between States and International
Organisations or between International Organisations, signed at Vienna on 21 March
1986. Not yet in force.
[98] Article 6.   [99] Article 2(1)(j).

identical to that of any other party.[100] It would seem that this is what
the Convention achieves. The number of points on which the terms of
the Convention deviate at all from the terms of the first Vienna Convention is small, and the points themselves of no practical significance.[101]
One may suspect that they were conceded more as an ideological sop
to the rigid orthodoxy of the Communist *bloc* than out of any expectation (on either side of the ideological divide) that they would make
the least practical difference. Moreover, the Convention's provisions
would seem to cope, without strain, both with the straightforward case
in which an organisation contracts within the scope of its own special
purposes, and with the case that may well be special to the European
Community alone, in which the Community exercises unique external
competence by transfer from the Member States (and to the exclusion
of any continuing competence on the part of the Member States).

The only point of apparent importance not included in the final text
is the notorious Article 36 *bis*. This draft Article provided a mechanism
by which obligations and rights could arise directly for the States
members of an international organisation from treaties concluded by
the organisation. It had been included by the Special Rapporteur of the
International Law Commission specifically in order to meet the case of
the EC Member States in respect of rights and obligations arising out
of treaties concluded by the Community[102] and proved very controversial within the International Law Commission, as indeed it did at the
Vienna Conference itself.[103] As the debate proceeded, however, it became
clear for the first time that the draft clause may have been based on a
false analogy between the Member States of an integrated organisation

[100] See, e.g., the comments of the Governments of the United Kingdom, the Federal
Republic of Germany and France (by implication) on the draft articles on the subject
adopted by the ILC between its 26th and 31st sessions, Annex II to the Report of the
Commission on its 33rd Session, YBILC (1981–II): respectively, p. 190, para. 4; p. 185,
para. 2; and p. 184, para. 4.
[101] But see Gaja (a delegate of the Italian Government at the drafting Conference), "A
'New' Vienna Convention on Treaties between States and International Organizations or
between International Organizations: a Critical Commentary", 58 BYIL (1987) 253 at
258.
[102] See the Special Rapporteur's initial proposal, *Yearbook of the ILC* (1977–II), Pt I,
pp. 128–33.
[103] For the discussions in the Commission, see, e.g., YBILC (1977–I), 134–143; and
YBILC (1978–I), 193–202, leading to the adoption of draft article 38 *bis* in square
brackets, and YBILC (1982–I), 36–59, 119–120. For the discussion at the Vienna Conference, see the summary records of the 19th, 20th, 25th and 28th meetings of the
Committee of the Whole (A/CONF. 129/16 (vol. I), pp. 140–45, 145–52, 172–78 and
194–95).

and Third States in the true sense of the term. To put the matter con-
cisely, the treaties duly concluded by an organisation are not *res inter
alios acta* to its members. This being so, it became clear that the clause
was not only unnecessary but might indeed turn out a hindrance; the
matter was best left to be regulated by the internal rules of the Community itself.[104]

The Community has not however become a Party to the Vienna
Convention, although the way was expressly open to it to do so as of
right as one of the international organisations invited to participate in
the Conference which concluded it.[105] This is at first sight curious: not
only would one have expected the Community to take advantage of this
opportunity after its active participation in the Conference, but one
would also have reckoned with a strong desire on the part of the Community to stake its claim to a role in the development of international
law in this important area by establishing itself as an equal partner in
this codification instrument. Why the opportunity has not so far been
taken up is far from clear. In a purely formal sense the reason is that
the Commission has not put a proposal to the Council to that effect.
The substantive reasons why have never been fully explained so one
can but speculate, drawing as evidence on an article published in 1987
by Professor Manin[106] who attended the Vienna Conference as adviser
to the Community's delegation. While concluding that accession to the
Convention would not affect the Community's operating rules and
practices, Professor Manin criticises the Convention's dispute settlement procedure in its application to international organisations[107] and
says (in somewhat opaque terms) that the Convention has "implications" that run counter to some of the Community's "demands" and that
it is "likely to correspond less and less closely to the basic character of
the Community as the latter evolves".[108] It must be said that the purport
of these objections is far from clear. It looks rather, in the light of the
more detailed content of the article, to be a claim that, while the Community is indeed an international intergovernmental organisation, it is
not like other organisations. It looks also like a root-and-branch objection to a formulation of the rules of international law in such a way as

---

[104] See the Preamble and Article 74(3) of the 1986 Vienna Convention.

[105] Article 82(c).

[106] "The European Communities and the Vienna Convention on the Law of Treaties
between States and International Organizations or between International Organizations",
24 CMLR (1987) 457.

[107] *Ibid.*, 471–73.   [108] *Ibid.*, 481.

to mark any category difference, even of a purely verbal character, between States and the Community.

These objections seem in turn excessively ideological. They are hard to sustain either at the factual level or at the level of practical consequences. To imagine that the United Nations might have established a codifying instrument which gave special treatment to the Community on its own, differentiating it from other organisations and assimilating it to States, is wholly unrealistic. It is also unjustified as a matter of law. It is to be hoped therefore that the Commission will find an opportunity to reconsider the position. In doing so the sound approach would be to cast aside residual impressions of the political circumstances of an international negotiation which ended a decade ago and consider instead in an objective fashion the interest of the Community in playing its due part in the codification and development of international law.

Let me now look briefly at the Community's treaty-making activity in the exercise of what have been referred to as the "sovereign powers" transferred to it. Its main interest for present purposes lies in the fact that this is a field of activity designed as it were expressly to operate within the framework which international law provides for the conduct of international relations. Without the international law framework to give this activity a legal structure and legal effect externally to the Community proper, it would be essentially meaningless. For example, Community engagements contracted towards Third States could only become a source of rights and obligations for the Member States and within their national legal systems, as "Community law", on the footing that they were to begin with legal engagements giving rise to binding rights and obligations in international law.

There is by now a sizeable body of practice in this area. The Community has become party, within the area of its exclusive competence, to multilateral treaties of a general character and has participated in a similar fashion in the work of general international organisations. The European Community is for example a party in its own right to important environmental treaties such as the Vienna Convention for the Protection of the Ozone Layer and to the UN Convention on Narcotic Drugs, and it will become a party to the Third UN Law of the Sea Convention. The EC is a separate member of several international organisations, including the Food & Agriculture Organisation of the UN and a number of regional fisheries organisations and most recently of the World Trade Organisation. In other international organisations, such as the ILO, the WHO and UNESCO, the EC has observer status (and is not as such party to the constituent treaty). It also has observer status at the United Nations itself.

The difficulty of working out this participation in practical terms has been twofold: first to secure the recognition by third States that the Community is indeed "competent" in the full sense of the term for the activity in question and second to sort out the incidents of Community participation in cases of "shared competence" where both the Community and the Member States may have powers to act in the area in question. The first problem, that of establishing the Community's competence, has frequently been overcome through the device of a formal "Declaration of Competence" by the Community specifying the extent of its powers. Although initially unpopular with the Commission, the practice is not at all unreasonable if one puts oneself in the position of the other Parties seeking some form of guarantee that the Community is genuinely endowed with the capacity to make good its undertakings in place of the Member States. At the theoretical level it is a reflection of the fact that these competences of the Community, being derivative, must to be effective under international law receive some form of recognition from other international actors in regard to whom the capacities in question are being exercised.

The question of how the Community should be treated as a member of such organisations is not without its fascination either. A particularly intriguing problem is that of voting rights: should the Community be allowed to exercise one vote (as one member) or should it have as many votes as its Member States? And should this question be dealt with in the same way when the Community is a member on its own as when it is a member alongside its own Member States (each acting within the scope of its own competence)? At the level of principle the matter could be argued either way, and at the practical diplomatic level the politics of power and influence naturally enter into it. So the pattern has varied, sometimes the one, sometimes the other; there is even one case (admittedly a special one) where the Community's voting and speaking rights are additional to those of its Member States.

The conclusion is that the Community's transferred external competence, while undoubtedly a defining characteristic of the internal structure of Community law as it has developed, has not proved to be self-executing on the international plane. A degree of pragmatic problem-solving has been required, with solutions fitted to the circumstances of particular cases. It would seem however as if the general system of international law has proved itself perfectly capable of finding appropriate solutions as required.

Against this growing pattern of external activity anchored by its very nature within the system of international law, it is time to revisit the question of treaty interpretation as it affects the Community, its powers in the external field and its external activities. How do the rules operating internally as between the Member States relate to those operating externally in their dealings and the Community's dealings with Third States?

The European Court has repeatedly said that the essential reason why the Community Treaties give rise to a "new legal order" is that they are not treaties which "merely" create rights and obligations as between the Contracting Parties but provide for a transfer of sovereign rights to the inter-governmental institutions which they set up.[109] Now the interesting feature of the *Treaty of Maastricht* is that, except in those areas where it modifies or extends existing Community rules, it does, without a doubt, operate by creating rights and obligations as between the Member States, as the Parties to it, and it does not contemplate any transfer of sovereign powers to inter-governmental institutions, new or old. So it would seem that on this reasoning the Treaty is a most unusual hybrid, containing within itself sets of provisions of an essentially different, perhaps even fundamentally different, character and that these differences have a direct impact on its interpretation and application. But this conclusion would have to be read into the treaty by implication, since there is no sign of such an intention in the treaty text, nor any explicit rule of interpretation as in the EEA Agreement. Some might perhaps take it as a clue that the Chapters of the Maastricht Treaty which constitute the Foreign & Security Policy and the Justice & Home Affairs pillars are not made justiciable before the European Court of Justice.[110] But that cannot be a complete and satisfactory explanation: in the first place, there are many other possible reasons why the Member States might have wished not to make these international undertakings justiciable in principle at all;[111] in the second place, they are not in any case excluded *ex hypothesi* from the Court's purview if the Member States choose in particular cases to give jurisdiction to the Court[112] in the Justice and Home Affairs field; and in the third place the Court had itself already indicated (as just noted) that treaty provisions of an inter-governmental character might have to be interpreted through

---

[109] See, for example, Case 26/62, **notes 3 and 4 above**.

[110] Article L, Treaty on European Union.

[111] As, for instance, the political sensitivity of many of the matters considered within the framework of Titles V and VI.

[112] See Article K.3(2)(c) T.E.U.

a qualitatively different approach.[113] The matter is perplexing. More-over the perplexity is not lessened if one looks at the founding treaties themselves. When they say (as in Article 164 of the EC Treaty) that the function of the Court of Justice is to ensure that in the interpretation and application of the Treaty "the law" is observed, they offer no spe-cific indication of what that "law" consists in. Similarly, Article 177 of the Treaty (already mentioned above) seems to view the interpretation of the Treaty as a class of legal operation different from other heads of the Court's jurisdiction. And further tantalising indications are to be found in the infraction provisions, Articles 169 and 170. Both talk about the failure of a Member State to fulfil obligations under the Treaty in terms which do not really sustain a thesis that the special features of the Community Treaties, at the *inter-State* level, are any-thing more than, or different from, treaty obligations owed by one Party to the others. And very much the same notion is implicit in Article 219, where the undertaking by the Member States not to invoke extraneous settlement procedures is stated as applying to "disputes concerning the interpretation and application of the Treaty". It is by no means self-evident how the fact that the Community regimes have as an additional characteristic their direct effect on natural and legal persons would in or of itself change the obligations which the Member States contracted towards one another under the terms of the Community Treaties. The matter is indeed perplexing. One does however wonder quite hard whether the supposed dichotomy of interpretation, under which the Community obligations require different "approaches, methods and concepts" from those under "ordinary treaties" was seen in quite the same way by the Member States at the time.

Let us return then to the question of treaty interpretation in general, to try to discover whether the differences are ones of rhetoric or reality. Commentators distinguish in the European Court's style of treaty inter-pretation four methods or "approaches": the literal, the historical, the contextual and the purposive (or teleological).[114] Although the Court itself has been remarkably reticent in analysing or describing its own approach, in more than one significant *dictum* the Court has said that it must consider the "spirit, the general scheme and the wording" of the provisions under consideration.[115] Some have wondered whether

[113] See the discussion in **note 91 above**.
[114] Brown and Kennedy, *The Court of Justice of the European Communities* (4th ed. 1994), 301–321.
[115] Case 26/62, *Van Gend en Loos* [1963] ECR 1 at 12.

particular significance should be attributed to the fact that, in this trilogy, the wording of the provision comes last.[116] The truth however is that, like many other tribunals, the European Court has shied away from tying itself down to the intricacies of a complex or hierarchical system of interpretative norms. It prefers instead to keep its hands free to find the proper interpretative approach for the circumstances of the individual legal problem before it. It seems often to be applying several different interpretative methods at once in varied mixtures.[117] In this approach the European Court seems remarkably similar to the International Court of Justice. There is an interesting question as to whether this undogmatic and free-wheeling approach is equally suited to the work of a tribunal which (as the European Court frequently and rightly reminds us) is laying down law direct for private citizens and private interests, and in this respect is unique amongst international tribunals. It is perhaps a curious paradox that the common-law systems, with their great pride in their pragmatism and empiricism, are the ones which have in the past developed the most rigid doctrines of interpretation.[118] Again, there may be material for worthwhile further study of the concept of *legal certainty*, to which both Community law and the national laws of Member States are firmly attached, but which may be susceptible of differing subjective assessments.

Let us take the examination further: is there anything in the four approaches identified which does in fact mark out the European Court of Justice as bringing a fundamentally different technique to bear on the task of treaty interpretation? The answer must be no. All of the four "approaches" will be instantly familiar to international lawyers, even though they may sometimes know them by different nicknames. Text, context, purpose and history all appear amongst the primary or supplementary means of interpretation in the Vienna Convention which I mentioned earlier.[119] The European Court was, as indicated, entirely comfortable in citing the Vienna Convention rules in its Opinion on the draft EEA Agreement.[120] Moreover, as also indicated, "schools" or "canons" of interpretation are out of fashion in international law, in favour of the composite rules laid down at Vienna.

---

[116] See Brown and Kennedy (**above note 114**) at 304.

[117] See Brown and Kennedy (**above note 114**) at 301–321.

[118] See, for instance, Cross, *Statutory Interpretation* (1976), chapter 3, for a statement of the "basic rules", and p. 157, for the position in countries with codified systems.

[119] See discussion at **pp. [9–10] above**.

[120] Opinion 1/91 (**above note 90**) at paragraph 14.

Where an international lawyer would notice differences, at least of emphasis, would be in the following:

—the place given to the terms of the treaty: for an international tribunal the words, as the common element on which the negotiating parties have agreed, would be the central pole around which the reasoning of the interpretative process would turn[121]—not of course the words in a mechanistic sense, but in the broad and balanced context set out in Article 31 of the Vienna Convention, the essential aim being to uncover the proper meaning of the terms of the treaty.

—the underlying agreement between the parties: an international tribunal would be acutely conscious, throughout the process of interpretation and adjudication, of the fact that the underlying legal basis both for the treaty obligation as such and for the jurisdiction of the tribunal itself was the agreement of the parties.

—the place given to "effectiveness": in fact the "effect utile" is a perfectly familiar concept to international lawyers, often conjured up in the Latin maxim *ut res magis valeat quam pereat*, under which an international tribunal will always start from the presumption that the parties intended each provision and phrase in their treaty to have a meaning, from which it follows that the task of the interpreter is to uncover the meaning and give sensible effect to it in the context of the treaty as a whole;[122] but the tribunal is most unlikely to elevate any method or technique of interpretation to a central position in which it appears to be given precedence over other means of ascertaining the true interpretation.

Against that background, I would like before offering some conclusions to return to what meaning we can reasonably extract from the European Court's pronouncement that the European Community treaties are not "ordinary treaties". To recapitulate, what the Court declared (most recently in the context of the EEA Agreement) was that an ordinary treaty "essentially, merely creates rights and obligations as between the Contracting Parties and provides for no transfer of sovereign rights to the inter-governmental institutions which it sets up".[123] The EEC Treaty, in contrast, albeit concluded "in the form of" an international agreement, "none the less constitutes the constitutional charter of

---

[121] See, e.g., Fitzmaurice, "Treaty Interpretation and certain other Treaty Points, 1947–1951", 28 BYIL (1951), 1 at 7 and 9; and *id.*, "Treaty Interpretation and other Treaty Points, 1951–1954", 33 BYIL (1957), 203 at 252.

[122] *Ibid.*, 28 BYIL (1951) 1 at 8–9; and 33 BYIL (1957) 203 at 220–223.

[123] Opinion 1/91, [1991] ECR 8079, at paragraph 14.

a Community based on the rule of law. . . . [T]he Community treaties established a new legal order for the benefit of which the States have limited their sovereign rights, in ever wider fields, and the subjects of which comprise not only Member States but also their nationals".[124] The Court goes on to describe the essential characteristics of this legal order as being in particular its primacy over the law of the Member States and the doctrine of direct effect.[125] In a subsequent significant passage the Court seems to move further up through the gears when it describes itself as having the task to secure observance of this legal order "and to foster its development".[126] And as the final culmination of this process of reasoning the Court fends off any challenge to its own central position under the treaties by pointing out that the relevant article of the EEC Treaty provided no legal basis for doing so and indeed that the incompatibility could not be cured by amendment of the treaty article in question.[127] To be fair, this last proposition is qualified by reference to a particular question that had been put before the Court by the European Commission. If the proposition had intended to go beyond this, it would clearly have been too far. This cannot indeed have been the intention of the European Court since it would otherwise have been suggesting that the Community Treaties had ceased to be the property of the Parties to them and had entered into a special arena which, if the reasoning were taken to its ultimate conclusion, put them beyond the reach of any law-giving body whatsoever. So it is no doubt best to leave the matter on the basis that the Member States could indeed have amended the EEC Treaty so as to allow the creation of an EEA Court of the kind envisaged, only they could not do so by changing Article 238; quite why this should be so is however again the source of some perplexity, which the absence of any legal reasoning in the Opinion on the point does nothing to resolve. One may simply remark that we seem to have gone beyond the realms of treaty interpretation as such into the discourse of struggle between constitutional organs, an area into which, with your leave, I do not propose to follow.

It may perhaps be thought from the above that I have been reproaching the European Court for ignoring international law altogether. Such a suggestion would however be far from the truth whether applied to the Court or to the Commission. There is a remarkably large number of references to international law in legal argument put before the Court

---

[124] *Ibid.* at paragraph 21.   [125] *Ibid.*
[126] *Ibid.* at paragraph 50.   [127] *Ibid.* at paragraphs 69 to 72.

or in its judgements. A high proportion of these references, to be sure, are descriptive only. The number of instances in which the Court has cited, or analysed, a rule of international law is much smaller. Yet there are signs that this is changing. Let me cite some striking recent examples.

In its judgement of 1992 on the Regulation permitting the use of beam trawls in certain coastal areas, the Court made it plain precisely that the competences of the Community must be exercised within the framework of international law. So the Court decided that the Regulation in question was to be interpreted, and its field of application limited, in the light of the rules of the international law of the sea, which it discovered by a detailed analysis of the 1958 UN Conventions, the Third UN Convention of 1982 on the Law of the Sea and three cases decided by the International Court of Justice. In 1992, in a preliminary ruling given at the request of the English High Court, the European Court considered the legal effect of the non-recognition of the authorities in Northern Cyprus in the light of an Advisory Opinion of the International Court of Justice concerning Namibia, and justified its interpretation of the Cyprus Association Agreement expressly in terms of Article 31 of the Vienna Convention on the Law of Treaties. Finally, in 1994, in rejecting at the request of three Member States the competence of the Commission to enter into an "Agreement" with the US authorities on the application of competition law, the Court, in order to determine whether it was in the presence of an international agreement breach of which would engage the international responsibility of the Community as such, expressly invoked the provisions of the Vienna Convention on the Law of Treaties between States and International Organisations.

May I now offer some tentative conclusions? Let me list them in a series of 11 points:-

1. The Communities clearly are creations of international law and the constitutive Community Treaties clearly are international treaties governed in all relevant senses by international law. About that there is neither doubt nor dispute. All parties are in agreement over this, even if the European Court of Justice sometimes phrases its utterances in elliptic terms.

2. Where doubt and difference may creep in is over the proposition that the Community Treaties are not "ordinary" international treaties. In one form or another the proposition of a "specialness" of the Communities originating in their Treaties would probably be

accepted by all. Quite what is meant by it remains however slightly obscure. It does not seem to be part of a fully worked-out doctrine, and no *international law* precedents or authorities are cited for it. At times it may seem little more than a reservation of the right to apply different legal rules in the case of the Communities.

3. What this approach has led to is a form of mystification of Community law. Community law seems often to have thrown up a defensive barrier around itself. At the public or political level this is capable of contributing to a widespread unease or even suspicion about the Communities and their doings. At the professional legal level it is certainly a barrier to mutual understanding, and it may even have prevented the Community from making its full contribution to the development of international law.

4. The "specialness" of the European Community has been described by the European Court as consisting, variously, in the following characteristics: that Community law has supremacy over national law;[128] that Community rules (thus including Community decisions) take effect directly in national legal systems;[129] and that the Community is endowed with autonomous organs each having its own functions and also its individual *purposes*.[130] By contrast an "ordinary" international treaty is one that only creates rights and obligations as between the parties.[131]

5. These postulates are however more impressive at a distance than on close examination. For example, it is a common feature of all treaties that the obligations to which they give rise cannot be displaced by inconsistent national law. This is not merely a common feature but a necessary feature; without it there would be no true treaty obligation since a party could at any time evade it by procuring a change in its national law. As the Vienna Convention on the Law of Treaties puts it, a party to a treaty may not invoke the provisions of its internal law as a justification for its failure to perform the treaty.[132] Much the same is true for direct effect: it is *open* to any State to provide through its constitutional system for rights and obligations under any treaty, or under treaties in general, to enter directly into national law, or to prevail over other sources of law, and many States do.[133] The distinguishing feature in the

[128] Case 6/64, *Costa* v. *ENEL* [1964] ECR 585.
[129] Case 26/62, *Van Gend en Loos* [1963] ECSC 1.   [130] See the EEA Opinion.
[131] Case 6/64, **note 128 above**.   [132] Article 27.
[133] E.g. Belgium, France, the Netherlands and the United States.

case of the European Community is no doubt that the founding Treaties (as subsequently interpreted) *require* all the Parties to do so,[134] and one of the results is that Community decisions (including decisions of the European Court of Justice) may be directly available to a litigant in the national courts as the final arbiter of his rights and obligations. None of this serves however to solve the age-old conundrum with which international lawyers are very familiar: what if the national legislature does enact rules which are inconsistent with treaty obligations? what if the national courts do decline to recognise what are asserted to be treaty obligations? To an international lawyer the answer is equally familiar: the national law would be what it is, the treaty obligation under international law would remain intact and any conflict between the two would engage the international responsibility of the defaulting State towards the other treaty Parties.[135] The fact that the Community legal structure and the rules of recognition applied under it by national courts make this state of affairs less likely to arise does not alter the basic legal situation.

6. Likewise, it is also commonplace for modern treaties to create treaty organs, which may be given legal personality and status in domestic law, each organ being endowed with its own functions and powers. Again, far from being special, this seems rather to be self-evident, and it seldom gives rise to serious legal problems within national legal systems. As for the notion that individual treaty organs have autonomous "purposes", it is obviously of limited application only, even in the case of the European Community, since it is easy to see why the same notion would sound strange, to the point even of absurdity, if it were to be applied to the European Parliament or to the Council. But plainly other international organs are endowed with "purposes" of their own, the UN Security Council being a good example,[136] and the "purposes" are usually seen as a distillation of the common purposes of the Member States.

7. The agreement on which treaties—all treaties—are based is what gives them their legal force as well as their political legitimacy.[137]

---

[134] Article 228(7) EC and Case 26/62, **note 129 above**.

[135] See, e.g., *Oppenheim's International Law* (9th ed., 1992), vol. I, 84–86. See also the ILC's Draft Articles on State Responsibility, Article 4: YBILC (1973–II), p. 184.

[136] UN Charter, Article 24.

[137] See, e.g. Fitzmaurice, "Treaty Interpretation and other Treaty Points, 1951–1954", 33 BYIL (1957), 203 at 252.

The importance of this element becomes if anything greater still where for any given State the process of becoming bound by the treaty is subjected to parliamentary approval; in such a case the compact between the international contracting partners is sealed by a further form of compact between the national executive and legislative powers, and the more delicately poised that constitutional balance the more sensitive the national compact may be.

8. This is the background against which the task of the interpreter has to be performed—without great difference whether the interpreter is the government of a State Party, a national court or an international tribunal. "Rules" or "methods" of interpretation may help, so far as they foster consistency and predictability, and are an aid to explaining and understanding the decisions reached, but ultimately the task of the interpreter remains to look at the words in which the parties expressed what they were agreeing on and to decide, in context, what meaning and what consequences the parties must reasonably have intended their agreement to have. This reflects amongst other things the fact that even the powers and functions conferred on treaty organs are part of the international rights and obligations between the treaty Parties.[138] This is as true of the European Community Treaties as of any other treaty system. Before the International Court of Justice the principle is recognised in the provision which permits intervention as of right by other treaty Parties whenever a multilateral treaty is up for interpretation by the Court in contentious proceedings[139] and in the provision giving every Member State the right to take part before the Court in advisory proceedings.[140] The same principle is recognised, in very much the same way, before the European Court of Justice by permitting intervention by Member States in proceedings of all kinds: direct actions, advisory proceedings and Article 177 references.[141]

9. There are good grounds therefore for thinking that the asserted "specialness" of the European Community system could equally well be regarded from a legal point of view as within the normal margin of tolerance within the wider system of international law.

10. Does it serve the interests of either the Community system or the

---

[138] See, for instance, Schermers, *International Institutional Law* (1980), 202–203.
[139] Statute of the International Court of Justice, Article 63.
[140] *Ibid.*, Article 66.
[141] Article 228(7) EC and Case 26/62, **note 129 above**. And generally, Usher, *European Court Practice* (1983), chapter 11.

international system to play up the differences or to minimise them? The answer to that question seems to lie in two parts. For the first part, let me stand within the Community system and look outwards. Here, as I hope to have demonstrated, a substantial and growing part of what I might call, loosely and imprecisely, "Community activity" is designed specifically to operate within, and therefore to be regulated by, the general system of international law. This activity embraces the Community's agreements with other States and groups of States, agreements of mixed competence to which the Community and its Member States are both parties, the Community's participation in its own right in international or regional organisations and latterly the congruent activity of the Member States under the Common Foreign and Security Policy. Can it possibly be beneficial for the Community, or for the smooth development of these areas of activity, to open up any kind of gulf between internal activity, regulated by some kind of "pure" Community law and doctrine, and mixed or Member State activity, regulated by the normal rules and practices of public international law? My personal answer is a clear No: it can neither be good for the Community itself nor for international law. The more the Community claims to be "special", the less its influence and practice will be seen as of general relevance.

11. For the second part of the answer, let me situate myself within the mainstream of public international law and turn towards the Community in all its rich and varied manifestations, including its powerful and influential judicial arm. There is a lively debate on the go in international law circles, at two levels. At the broader level, the debate is about fragmentation versus unity, and covers everything from legal education to professional specialisation to the cross-fertilisation between the general law and specialised treaty systems and the universal relevance of the general principles of international law. At the more specific level, the debate is about the advisability of creating standing judicial bodies of a specialised character with jurisdiction to deal with disputes arising under particular treaties. Within recent months, four Judges of the International Court of Justice have delivered lectures, one bewailing the creation of the International Tribunal on the Law of the Sea,[142] one

---

[142] Judge Shigeru Oda, "Dispute Settlement Prospects in the Law of the Sea", 44 ICLQ (1995), 863, based on a lecture given in July 1993 to the Hague Academy of International Law.

touching on this theme as an aspect of the unity of international law more generally,[143] one expressing surprise at the "disturbing insistence" of the European Court of Human Rights on the separateness of its system[144] and one expressing anxiety at what she called "the fragmentation of authoritative decision-making".[145] None of them expressly brought the European Community into the reckoning, but why not indeed? For my part I stand firmly within the unity school, because it makes for good law and better decisions; and I look forward to the day when the barriers of mutual misunderstanding between Community lawyers and public international lawyers are finally swept away, when the practice of Community institutions is greeted with respect by international lawyers for its sheer legal value, and most of all when the European Court of Justice and the International Court of Justice are to be seen freely citing and analysing one another's judgments to the mutual benefit of them both and of us all.

[143] Judge Gilbert Guillaume, "The Future of International Institutions", 44 ICLQ (1995), 848, based on the 3rd Wilberforce Lecture given on 11 May 1995 in the Great Hall, Lincoln's Inn.

[144] Judge Sir Robert Jennings, "The Judiciary—International and National—and the Development of International Law", lecture delivered at the London School of Economics and Political Science on 5 October 1995 on the occasion of the publication of the 100th volume of the International Law Reports.

[145] Judge Rosalyn Higgins, "The Reformation in International Law", lecture delivered at the London School of Economics and Political Science on 20 November 1995 as part of the LSE Centenary Lectures in Law and Society.